FRENZIED FINANCE

BY

THOMAS WILLIAM LAWSON

FRENZIED FINANCE

CHAPTER I

THE TORTUOUS COURSE OF AMALGAMATED

Amalgamated Copper was begotten in 1898, born in 1899, and in the first five years of its existence plundered the public to the extent of over one hundred millions of dollars.

It was a creature of that incubator of trust and corporation frauds, the State of New Jersey, and was organized ostensibly to mine, manufacture, buy, sell, and deal in copper, one of the staples, the necessities, of civilization.

It is a corporation with $155,000,000 capital, 1,550,000 shares of the par value of $100 each.

Its entire stock was sold to the public at an average of $115 per share ($100 to $130), and in 1903 the price had declined to $33 per share.

From its inception it was known as a "Standard Oil" creature, because its birthplace was the National City Bank of New York (the "Standard Oil" bank), and its parents the leading "Standard Oil" lights, Henry H. Rogers, William Rockefeller, and James Stillman.

It has from its birth to present writing been responsible for more hell than any other trust or financial thing since the world began. Because of it the people have sustained incalculable losses and have suffered untold miseries.

But for the existence of the National City Bank of New York, the tremendous losses and necessarily corresponding profits could not have been made.

I laid out the plans upon which Amalgamated was constructed, and, had they been followed, there would have been reared a great financial edifice, immensely profitable, permanently prosperous, one of the world's big institutions.

The conditions of which Amalgamated was the consequence had their birth in Bay State Gas. To explain them I must go back a few years.

In 1894 J. Edward Addicks, of Delaware, Everywhere, and Nowhere, the Boston Gas King, invaded the gas preserves of the "Standard Oil" in

Brooklyn, N. Y., and the "Standard Oil," to compel him to withdraw, moved on his pre-empted gas domains in Boston, Mass.

Late in 1894 a fierce battle was raging in Boston between Gas King Addicks and Gas King Rogers; the very air was filled with denunciation and defiance—bribery and municipal corruption; and King Addicks was defeated all along the line and in full retreat, with his ammunition down to the last few rounds.

Early in 1895 I took command of the Addicks forces against "Standard Oil."

By the middle of 1895 the Addicks troopers had the "Standard Oil" invaders "on the run."

In August, 1895, Henry H. Rogers and myself came together for the first time, at his house in New York, and we practically settled the Boston gas war.

Early in 1896 we actually settled the gas war, and "Standard Oil" transferred all its Boston gas properties ($6,000,000) to the Addicks crowd.

In October, 1896, the whole Bay State Gas outfit passed from the control of Addicks and his cohorts into the hands of a receiver, and as a result of this receivership, with its accumulated complications, "Standard Oil," in November, 1896, regained all its old Boston companies, and in addition all the Addicks companies, with the exception of the Bay State Gas Company of Delaware.

In 1896 I perfected and formulated the plans for "Coppers," a broad and comprehensive project, having for its basis the buying and consolidating of all the best-producing copper properties in Europe and America, and the educating of the world up to their great merits as safe and profitable investments.

In 1897 I laid these plans before "Standard Oil."

In 1898 "Standard Oil" was so far educated up to my plans on "Coppers" as to accept them.

In 1899 Amalgamated, intended to be the second or third section of "Coppers," was suddenly shifted by "Standard Oil" into the first section, and with a full head of steam ran out of the "City Bank" station, carrying the largest and best train-load of passengers ever sent to destruction on any financial trunk-line.

In 1899, after the allotment of the Amalgamated public subscription, the public for the first time, in a dazed and benumbed way, realized it had been "taken in" on this subscription, and a shiver went down America's financial spinal column.

In 1900, after the price of Amalgamated had slumped to 75 instead of advancing to 150, to 200, as had been promised, the "Standard Oil"-Amalgamated-City Bank fraternity called Wall Street's king of manipulators, James R. Keene, to the rescue, and under his adroit handling of the stock in the market Amalgamated was sent soaring over its flotation price of 100.

In 1901 Boston & Montana and Butte & Boston, after long delay, drew out of the "Standard Oil" station as the second section of Amalgamated, carrying an immense load of investors and speculators to what was at that time confidently believed would be Dollar Utopia; and the price of the enlarged Amalgamated fairly flew to 130. These were the stocks which I had originally advertised would be part of the first section of the consolidated "Coppers," and which, after Amalgamated had been run in ahead of them, I advertised would follow in due course.

In the latter part of 1901 President McKinley was assassinated, and the great panic which might have ensued was averted by the marvellous power of J. Pierpont Morgan.

Then the Amalgamated dividend, without warning and in open defiance of the absolute pledges of its creators, was cut, and the public, including even James R. Keene, found itself on that wild toboggan whirl which landed it battered and sore, at the foot of a financial precipice.

This, briefly, is the tortuous course of Amalgamated, and it is along this twisting, winding, up-alley-and-down-lane way I must ask my readers to travel if they would know the story as it is.

CHAPTER II

THE "SYSTEM'S" METHOD OF FINANCE AND MANAGEMENT

At the lower end of the greatest thoroughfare in the greatest city of the New World is a huge structure of plain gray-stone. Solid as a prison, towering as a steeple, its cold and forbidding façade seems to rebuke the heedless levity of the passing crowd, and frown on the frivolity of the stray sunbeams which in the late afternoon play around its impassive cornices. Men point to its stern portals, glance quickly up at the rows of unwinking windows, nudge each other, and hurry onward, as the Spaniards used to do when going by the offices of the Inquisition. The building is No. 26 Broadway.

26 Broadway, New York City, is the home of the Standard Oil. Its countless miles of railroads may zigzag in and out of every State and city in America, and its never-ending twistings of snaky pipe-lines burrow into all parts of the North American continent which are lubricated by nature; its mines may be in the West, its manufactories in the East, its colleges in the South, and its churches in the North; its head-quarters may be in the centre of the universe and its branches on every shore washed by the ocean; its untold millions may levy tribute wherever the voice of man is heard, but its home is the tall stone building in old New York, which under the name "26 Broadway" has become almost as well known wherever dollars are juggled as is "Standard Oil."

Wall Street and the financial world know that there are two "Standard Oils," but to the public there is no clear distinction between Standard Oil, the corporation which deals in oil and things which pertain to the manufacture and transportation of oil, and "Standard Oil," the giant, indefinite system which sometimes embraces all the "Standard Oil" group of individuals and corporations, and sometimes only certain of the individuals.

This giant creature, "Standard Oil," can best be described so that the average man may understand it as a group of money-owners—some individuals and some corporations—who have a right to use the name "Standard Oil" in any business undertakings they engage in. The right to use the name is of priceless value, for it carries with it "assured success."

Standard Oil, the seller of oil to the people, transacts its business as does any other corporation. It plays no part in my story and I shall not hereafter touch upon its affairs, but confine my meaning, wherever I use the name "Standard Oil," to the larger and many times more important "System."

There are only three men who can lend the name "Standard Oil," even in the most remote way to any project, for there is no more heinous crime against the "Standard Oil" decalogue than using the name "Standard Oil" unauthorizedly. The three men are Henry H. Rogers, William Rockefeller, and John D. Rockefeller. Sometimes John D. Rockefeller uses the name alone in projects in which Henry H. Rogers and William Rockefeller have no interests. Henry H. Rogers or William Rockefeller seldom, if ever, uses the name in projects with which neither of the other two is associated. Sometimes, but not often, John D. and William Rockefeller use the name in connection with projects of their own in which Henry H. Rogers has no interest. Henry H. Rogers and John D. Rockefeller, I believe, never are associated in projects in which William Rockefeller has no interest. Henry H. Rogers and William Rockefeller frequently bring to bear the influence of the magic-working syllables in connection with joint affairs in which John D. Rockefeller has no interest—in fact, during the past ten years the name "Standard Oil" has been used more in their combined undertakings than in all others put together.

There are eight distinct groups of individuals and corporations which go to make up the big "Standard Oil":

1st. The Standard Oil, seller of oil to the people, which is made up of many sub-corporations either by actual ownership or by ownership of their stock or bonds. Probably no person other than Henry H. Rogers, William Rockefeller, and John D. Rockefeller knows exactly what the assets of the Standard Oil corporation are, although John D. Rockefeller, Jr., son of John D. Rockefeller, and William G. Rockefeller, that able and excellent business man, son of William Rockefeller and the probable future head of "Standard Oil," are being rapidly educated in this great secret. In this first institution all "Standard Oil" individuals and estates are direct owners.

2d. Henry H. Rogers, William Rockefeller, and John D. Rockefeller, active heads, and included with them their sons.

3d. A large group of active captains and first lieutenants, men who conduct the affairs of the different corporations or sections of corporations in which some or all of the "Standard Oil" are interested. Many of these are the sons or the second generation of men who held like positions in Standard Oil's earlier days. Of these Daniel O'Day and Charles Pratt are fair examples.

4th. A large group of captains retired from active service in the Standard Oil army, who participate only in a general way in the management of its affairs, and whose principal business is looking after their own investments. These men are each worth from $5,000,000 or $10,000,000 to $50,000,000 or $75,000,000. The Paynes and the Flaglers are fair illustrations of this group.

5th. The estates of deceased members of this wonderful "Standard Oil" family, which are still largely controlled by some or all of the prominent "Standard Oil" men.

6th. "Standard Oil" banks and banking institutions, and the system of national banks, trust companies, and insurance companies, of which "Standard Oil" has, by ownership and otherwise, practically absolute control. The head of this group is James Stillman, and it is when these institutions are called into play in connection with "Standard Oil" business that he is one of the "Standard Oil" leaders, second to neither of the Rockefellers nor to Mr. Rogers.

7th. The "Standard Oil" army of followers, capitalists, and workers in all parts of the world, men who require nothing more than the order, "Go ahead," "Pull off," "Buy," "Sell," or "Stand Pat," to render as absolute obedience and enthusiastic cooperation as though they knew, to the smallest detail, the purposes which lay behind the giving of the order.

8th. The countless hordes of politicians, statesmen, law-makers and enforcers, who, at home or as representatives of the nation abroad, go to make up our political structure, and judges and lawyers.

To the world at large, which looks on and sees this giant institution move through the ranks of business without noise or dissension and with the ease and smoothness of a creature one-millionth its size, it would seem that there must be some wonderful and complicated code of rules to guide and control the thousands of lieutenants and privates who conduct its affairs. This is partially true, partially false. "Standard Oil's" governing rules are as rigid as the laws of the Medes and Persians, yet so simple as to be easily understood by any one.

First, there is a fundamental law, from which no one—neither the great nor the small—is exempt. In substance it is: "Every 'Standard Oil' man must wear the 'Standard Oil' collar."

This collar is riveted on to each one as he is taken into "the band," and can only be removed with the head of the wearer.

Here is the code. The penalty for infringing the following rules is instant "removal."

1. Keep your mouth closed, as silence is gold, and gold is what we exist for.

2. Collect our debts to-day. Pay the other fellow's debts to-morrow. To-day is always here, to-morrow may never come.

3. Conduct all our business so that the buyer and the seller must come to us. Keep the seller waiting; the longer he waits the less he'll take. Hurry the buyer, as his money brings us interest.

4. Make all profitable bargains in the name of "Standard Oil," chancy ones in the names of dummies. "Standard Oil" never goes back on a bargain.

5. Never put "Standard Oil" trades in writing, as your memory and the other fellow's forgetfulness will always be re-enforced with our organization. Never forget our Legal Department is paid by the year, and our land is full of courts and judges.

6. As competition is the life of trade—our trade, and monopoly the death of trade—our competitor's trade, employ both judiciously.

7. Never enter into a "butting" contest with the Government. Our Government is by the people and for the people, and we are the people, and those people who are not us can be hired by us.

8. Always do "right." Right makes might, might makes dollars, dollars make right, and we have the dollars.

All business of the gigantic "Standard Oil" system is dealt with through two great departments. Mr. Rogers is head of the executive, and William Rockefeller the head of the financial department. All new schemes, whether suggested by outsiders or initiated within the institution, go to Mr. Rogers. Regardless of their nature or character, he first takes them under advisement. If a scheme prove good enough to run the gantlet of Mr. Rogers' tremendously high standard, the promoter, after he has set forth his plans and estimates, hears with astonishment these words:

"Wait while I go upstairs. I'll say Yes or No upon my return."

And upon his return it is almost always "Yes." If the project, however, does not come up to his exacting requirements, it is turned down without further ado or consultation with any of his associates.

Those intimate with affairs at 26 Broadway have grown curiously familiar with this expression, "I am going upstairs." "Upstairs" means two distinct and separate things. When a matter in Mr. Rogers' department is awaiting his return from "upstairs," it means he has gone to place the scheme before William Rockefeller, on the thirteenth floor, and laying a thing before William Rockefeller by Mr. Rogers consists of a brief, vigorous statement of Mr. Rogers' own conclusions and a request for his associate's judgment of it. William Rockefeller's strong quality is his ability to estimate quickly the practical value of a given scheme. His approval means he will finance it, and William Rockefeller's "say-so" is as absolute in the financing of things as is Mr. Rogers' in passing upon their feasibility. It does not matter whether it is an undertaking calling for the employment of $50,000 capital or $50,000,000 or $500,000,000, Mr. Rockefeller's "Yes" or "No" is all there is to it. He having passed on it, Mr. Rogers supervises its execution.

The other "upstairs" is one that is heard every week-day of the year except summer Saturdays. At 26 Broadway, just before eleven o'clock each morning, there is a flutter in the offices of all the leading heads of departments from Henry H. Rogers down, for going "upstairs" to the eleven o'clock meeting is in the mind of each "Standard Oil" man the one all-important event of every working day.

In the big room, on the fifteenth floor, at 26 Broadway, there gather each day, between the hour of eleven and twelve o'clock, all the active men whose efforts make "Standard Oil" what "Standard Oil" is; here also come to meet and mingle with the active heads the retired captains when "they are in town." Around a large table they sit. Reports are presented, views exchanged, policies talked over, republics and empires made and unmade. If the Recorders in the next world have kept complete minutes of what has happened "upstairs" at 26 Broadway they must have tremendously large fire-proof safes. It is at the meeting "upstairs" that the "melons are cut," and if one of the retired captains were asked why he was in such a rush to be on hand each day when in town, and if he were in a talkative mood—which he would not be—he would answer: "They may be cutting a new melon, and there's nothing like being on hand when the juice runs out."

If a new melon has been cut—an Amalgamated Copper, for instance—it is at one of these meetings that the different "Standard Oil" men are informed for the first time that the scheme, about which they may have read or heard much outside, is far enough along for them to participate in it. Each is told what sized slice he may have if he cares for any. It is a very exceptional thing for any one to ask for more than he has been apportioned, and an unheard-of thing for any one to refuse to take his slice, although there is absolutely no compulsion in the connection.

And here, perhaps, may not come amiss an incident which illustrates what may happen in a few minutes "upstairs."

Before Amalgamated was launched, in bringing together the different properties of which it was composed I negotiated for the acquisition of the Parrott mine, the majority of whose stock was held by certain old and wealthy brass manufacturers in Connecticut. They had never seen any of the Rockefellers nor Henry H. Rogers, but we were several months getting the deal into shape before it was finally arranged, and they became familiar with the great "Standard Oil" institution. So much so that the chief of the owners—to whom was delegated the duty of turning over the securities to my principals—looked forward with much eagerness to the time when he must necessarily meet the mysterious and important personages who guided 26 Broadway's destinies. Finally the day came, and at precisely a quarter of eleven I let him into one of the numerous private offices which are a part of Mr. Rogers' suite. He had under his arm a bundle of papers representing the stocks which he was to exchange for the purchase money, amounting to $4,086,000, and I think he fully expected that in their examination, in the receipting for so large an amount of money, and in the general talkings over, which he thought must of course be a necessary part of the delivery, the greater part of the day would be taken up. It took me some six or seven minutes to get him located, and it was close on to five minutes of eleven when Mr. Rogers stepped into the room. I was well into the introduction, when out came Mr. Rogers' watch, and with what must have appeared to the visitor as astonished consternation.

"I do hope you will excuse me," he exclaimed in the middle of a handshake, "but, my gracious, I am overdue upstairs," and he bolted.

His place was taken fifty seconds after by Mr. Rogers' secretary, who in less than five minutes had exchanged a check of $4,086,000, made out to herself and indorsed in blank, for the bundle of stocks, and in another minute I was ushering the old gentleman into the elevator.

When he came to on the sidewalk he got his breath sufficiently to say: "Phew! I thought my trade was a big one, but that friend of yours, Rogers, must have had some other fellow upstairs who was going to turn in $40,000,000 of stuff, because he did appear dreadfully excited!"

The success of "Standard Oil" is largely due to two things—to the loyalty of its members to each other and to "Standard Oil," and to the punishment of its enemies. Each member before initiation knows its religion to be reward for friends and extermination for foes. Once within the magic circle, a man realizes he is getting all that any one else on earth can afford to pay him for like services, and still more thrown in for full measure. Moreover, while a "Standard Oil" man's reward is always ample and satisfactory, he is constantly reminded in a thousand and one ways that punishment for disloyalty is sure and terrible, and that in no corner of the earth can he escape it, nor can any power on earth protect him from it.

"Standard Oil" is never loud in its rewards nor its punishments. It does not care for the public's praise nor for its condemnation, but endeavors to avoid both by keeping its "business" to itself. As an instance, in connection with certain gas settlements I made with "Standard Oil," it voluntarily paid one of its agents for a few days' work $250,000. He had expected at the outside $25,000. When I published the fact, as I had a right to, "Standard Oil" was mad as hornets—as upset, indeed, as though it had been detected in cheating the man out of two-thirds of his just due, instead of having paid him ten times what was coming to him.

CHAPTER III

THE MEN IN POWER BEHIND THE "SYSTEM"

In the great Thing known to the world as "Standard Oil," the most perfect embodiment of a "system" which I will endeavor to get before my readers in later chapters, there are three heads, Henry H. Rogers, William Rockefeller, and John D. Rockefeller. All the other members are distinctively lieutenants, or subordinate workers, unless possibly I except James Stillman, who, from his peculiar connection with "Standard Oil" and his individually independent position, should perhaps be placed in the category of heads.

Some one has said: "If you would know who is the head of a family, slip into the home." The world, the big, arbitrary, hit-or-miss, too-much-in-a-hurry-to-correct-its-mistakes world, has decided that the master of "Standard Oil" is John D. Rockefeller, and John D. Rockefeller it is to all but those who have a pass-key to the "Standard Oil" home. To those the head of "Standard Oil"—the "Standard Oil" the world knows as it knows St. Paul, Shakespeare, or Jack the Giant-killer, or any of the things it knows well but not at all—is Henry H. Rogers. John D. Rockefeller may have more money, more actual dollars, than Henry H. Rogers, or all other members of the "Standard Oil" family, and in the early days of "Standard Oil" may have been looked up to as the big gun by his partners, and allowed to take the hugest hunks of the profits, and may have so handled and judiciously invested these as to be at the beginning of the twentieth century the richest man on earth, but none of these things alters the fact that the big brain, the big body, the head of "Standard Oil," is Henry H. Rogers.

Take station at the entrance of 26 Broadway and watch the different members of the "Standard Oil" family as they enter the building: you will exclaim once and only once: "There goes the Master!" And the man who calls forth the cry will be Henry H. Rogers.

The big, jovial detective who stands all day long with one foot resting on the sidewalk and one on the first stone step of the home of "Standard Oil" will make oath he shows no different sign to Henry H. Rogers than to a Rockefeller, a Payne, a Flagler, a Pratt, or an O'Day; yet watch him when Mr. Rogers passes up the steps—an unconscious deference marks his salutation—the tribute of the soldier to the commanding general.

Follow through the door bearing the sign, "Henry H. Rogers, President of the National Transit Co.," on the eleventh floor, and pass from the outer office into the beautiful, spacious mahogany apartment beyond, with its decorations of bronze bulls and bears and yacht-models, its walls covered with neatly framed autograph letters from Lincoln, Grant, "Tom" Reed, Mark Twain, and other real, big men, and it will come over you like a flash that here, unmistakably, is the sanctum sanctorum of the mightiest business institution of modern times. If a single doubt lingers, read what the men in the frames have said to Henry H. Rogers, and you will have proof positive that these judges of human nature knew this man, not only as the master of "Standard Oil," but also as a sturdy and resolute friend whose jovial humanity they had recognized and enjoyed.

Did my readers ever hear of the National Transit Company? Very few have—yet the presidency of it is the modest title of Henry H. Rogers. When the world is ladling out honors to the "Standard Oil" kings, and spouting of their wondrous riches, how often is Henry H. Rogers mentioned? Not often, for he is never where the public can get a glimpse of him—he is too busy pulling the wires and playing the buttons in the shadows just behind the throne. Had it not been that that divinity which disposes of men's purposes compelled this man, as he neared the end of his remarkable career, to come into the open on Amalgamated, he might never have been known as the real master of "Standard Oil." But if he is missing when the public is hurrahing, he is sufficiently in evidence when clouds lower or when the danger-signal is run to the masthead at 26 Broadway. He who reads "Standard Oil" history will note that, from its first deal until this day, whenever bricks, cabbages, or aged eggs were being presented to "Standard Oil," always were Henry H. Rogers' towering form and defiant eye to be seen in the foreground where the missiles flew thickest.

During the past twenty years, whenever the great political parties have lined-up for their regular once-in-four-years' tussle, there would be found Henry H. Rogers, calm as a race-track gambler, "sizing-up" the entries, their weights and handicaps. Every twist and turn in the pedigrees and records of Republicans and Democrats are as familiar to him as the "dope-sheets" are to the gambler, for is he not at the receiving end of the greatest information bureau in the world?

A Standard Oil agent is in every hamlet in the country, and who better than these trained and intelligent observers to interpret the varying trends of feelings in their communities? Tabulated and analyzed, these reports enable Rogers, the sagacious politician, to diagnose the drift of the country far ahead of the most astute of campaign managers. He is never in doubt about who will win the election. Before the contest is under way he has picked his winner and is beside him with generous offers of war expenses.

When labor would howl its anathemas at Standard Oil, and the Rockefellers and other stout-hearted generals and captains of this band of merry money-makers would fall to discussing conciliation and retreat, it was always Henry H. Rogers who fired at his associates his now famous panacea for all Standard Oil opposition: "We'll see Standard Oil in hell before we will allow any body of men on earth to dictate how we shall conduct our business!" And the fact that "Standard Oil" still does its business in the Elysian fields of success, where is neither sulphur nor the fumes of sulphur, is additional evidence of whose will it is that sways its destinies.

An impression of the despotic character of the man and of his manner of despatching the infinite details of the multitudinous business he must deal with daily may be gained by a glimpse of Henry H. Rogers at one of the meetings of the long list of giant corporations which number him among their directors. Surrounded though he be by the élite of all financialdom, the very flower of the business brains of America, you will surely hear his sharp, incisive, steel-clicking: "Gentlemen, are we ready for the vote, for I regret to say, I have another important and unavoidable meeting at ?" You look at your watch. The time he mentions is twelve, or, at the most, fifteen minutes away. There is no chance for further discussion. Cut-and-dried resolutions are promptly put to the vote, and off goes the master to his other engagement which will be disposed of in the same peremptory fashion.

At a meeting of the directors of "financed" Steel, during the brief reign of its late "vacuumized" president, Charlie Schwab, an episode occurred which exhibited the danger of interfering with Mr. Rogers' iron-bound plans. The fact that the steel throne was many sizes too large for Schwab had, about this time, become publicly notorious, but Carnegie and Morgan on the surface, and "Standard Oil" beneath, were so busy preparing their alibis against the crash which even then was overdue that they had neither time nor desire to adjust themselves on the seat.

In advance Mr. Rogers made his invariable plea for quick action on a matter before the board when Schwab, with a tact generated by the wabbling of a misfit Wall Street crown chafing a generous pair of ears, blurted out: "Mr. Rogers will vote on this question after we have talked on it."

In a voice that those who heard it say sounded like a rattlesnake's hiss in a refrigerator, Rogers replied: "All meetings where I sit as director vote first and talk after I am gone."

It is said, and from my knowledge of these and after-events I believe with truth, that this occurrence was the spark that started the terrific explosion in United States Steel, for not long afterward some unknown and mysterious power began that formidable attack on Steel stock which left Wall Street full of the unattached ears, eyes, noses, breastbones, and scalps of hordes of financial potentates and their flambeau carriers. Whether or not Mr. Rogers was the instigator of this movement no man, of course, can positively state, but I can vouch for the fact that about this time he displayed, when talking "Steel" affairs with intimates, a most contemptuous bitterness against "King Charlie" and certain of his associates.

At sixty-five Henry H. Rogers is probably one of the most distinguished-looking men of the time; tall and straight, and as well-proportioned and supple as one of the beautiful American elms which line the streets of his native town. He was born in Fairhaven, a fishing village just over the bridge from the great whaling port, New Bedford. He comes of stalwart New England stock; his father was a sea-captain, and his lot, like that of most of the sons of old New England seaport towns, was cast along those hard, brain-and-body-developing lines which, beginning in the red village school-house, the white meeting-house, and the yellowish-grayish country store, end in unexpected places, often, as in this instance, upon the golden throne of business royalty.

Mr. Rogers' part in the very early days of Standard Oil was that of clerk and bookkeeper. He makes no secret that when he had risen to the height of $8 a week wages he felt as proud and confident as ever in after-life when for the same number of days' labor it was no uncommon occurrence to find himself credited with a hundred thousand times that amount.

All able men have some of God's indelible imprints of greatness. This man's every feature bespeaks strength and distinction. When he walks, the active swing of his figure expresses power—realized, confident power. When at rest or in action his square jaw tells of fighting power, bull-dog, hold-on, never-let-go fighting power, and his high, full forehead of intellectual, mightily intellectual power; and they are re-enforced with cheek-bones and nose which suggest that this fighting power has in it something of the grim ruthlessness of the North American Indian. The eyes, however, are the crowning characteristic of the man's physical make-up.

One must see Mr. Rogers' eyes in action and in repose to half appreciate their wonders. I can only say they are red, blue, and black, brown, gray, and green; nor do I want my readers to think I put in colors that are not there, for there must be many others than those I have mentioned. I have seen them when they were so restfully blue that I would think they never could be anything but a part of those skies that come with the August and September afternoons when the bees' hum and the locusts' drone blend with the smell of the new-mown hay to help spell the word "Rest."

I have seen them so green that within their depths I was almost sure the fish were lazily resting in the shadows of those sea-plants which grow only on the ocean's bottom; and I have seen them as black as that thunder-cloud which makes us wonder: "Is He angry?" And then again I have watched them when they were of that fiery red and that glinting yellow which one sees only when at night the doors of a great, roaring furnace are opened.

There is such a kindly good-will in these eyes when they are at rest that the man does not live who would not consider himself favored to be allowed to turn over to Henry H. Rogers his pocket-book without receiving a receipt. They are the eyes of the man you would name in your will to care for your wife's and children's welfare. When their animation is friendly one would rather watch their merry twinkle as they keep time to their owner's inimitable stories and non-duplicatable anecdotes, trying to interpret the rapid and incessant telegraphy of their glances, than sit in a theatre or read an interesting book; but it is when they are active in war that the one privileged to observe them gets his real treat, always provided he can dodge the rain of blazing sparks and the withering hail of wrath that pours out on the offender. To watch them then requires real nerve, for it is only a nimble, stout-hearted, mail-covered individual that can sustain the encounter.

I have seen many forms of human wrath, many men transformed to terrible things by anger, but I have never seen any that were other than jumping-jack imitations of a jungle tiger compared with Henry H. Rogers when he "lets 'er go"—when the instant comes that he realizes some one is balking the accomplishment of his will.

Above all things Henry H. Rogers is a great actor. Had his lot been cast upon the stage, he might easily have eclipsed the fame of Booth or Salvini. He knows the human animal from the soles of his feet to the part in his hair and from his shoulder-blade to his breastbone, and like all great actors is not above getting down to every part he plays. He is likely also so to lose himself in a rôle that he gives it his own force and identity, and then things happen quite at variance with the lines. The original Booth would come upon the stage the cool, calculating, polished actor, but when well into his part was so lost in it that it was often with difficulty he could be brought back to himself when the curtain fell. Once while playing Richard III. at the old Boston Museum, Richmond, by whom he was to be slain, made, at the ordained moment, the thrust which should have laid him low, but instead, Booth in high frenzy parried it, and with the fiendishness of the original Richard, step by step drove Richmond off the stage and through the wings, and it was not until the police seized the great tragedian, two blocks away, that the terrified duke, who had dropped his sword and was running for dear life, was sure he would ever act again.

When in the midst of his important plays, it is doubtful whether Henry H. Rogers realizes until the guardians of the peace appear where the acting begins and the reality should end. His intimate associates can recall many times when his determination to make a hit in his part has caused other actors cast with him to throw aside their dummy swords and run for their lives.

The entire history of "Standard Oil" is strewn with court-scenes, civil and criminal, and in all the important ones Henry H. Rogers, the actor, will be found doing marvellous "stunts." Standard Oil historians are fond of dwelling on the extraordinary testifying abilities of John D. Rockefeller and other members of the band, but the acrobatic feats of ground and lofty tumbling in the way of truth which they have given when before the blinking footlights of the temples of justice are as Punch-and-Judy shows to a Barnum three-ring circus compared to Henry H. Rogers' exhibitions.

His "I will tell the truth, the whole truth, and nothing but the truth, so help me God," sounds absolutely sincere and honest, but as it rings out in the tone of the third solemnest bell in the chime, this is how it is taken down in the unerring short-hand notes of the recording angel and sent by special wireless to the typewriter for His Majesty of the Sulphur Trust: "What I tell shall be the truth and the whole truth, and there shall be no truth but that I tell, and God help the man or woman who tells truth different from my truth." The recording angel never missed catching Henry H. Rogers' court-oaths in this way, and never missed sending them along to the typewriter at Sulphurville, with this postscript: "Keep your wire open, for there'll be things doing now!"

At the recent but now famous sensational Boston "Gas Trial," Henry H. Rogers in the rôle of defendant was the principal witness. I was in court five hours and a half each sitting as day after day he testified. I watched, as the brightest lawyers in the land laid their traps for him in direct and cross-examination, to detect a single sign of fiction replacing truth, or going joint-account with her, or where truth parted company with fiction; and I was compelled, when he stepped from the witness-stand, to admit I had not found what I had watched for. This, too, when I was equipped with actual knowledge and black-and-white proofs of the facts. Weeks before the trial began Attorney Sherman L. Whipple, one of the great cross-examiners of the time, had made his boast that he would break through the "Standard Oil" magnate's heretofore impenetrable bulwarks, and when H. H. Rogers entered the court-room for the first time and let his eagle eye sweep the lawyers, the laymen, and the judge until it finally rested on Whipple, the glance was as absolute a challenge and a defiance as ever knights of old exchanged.

I followed Mr. Rogers on the witness-stand and was compelled to give testimony directly opposite to that which he had given, and at one time, as I glanced at the row of lawyers who were in "Standard Oil's" hire, I felt a cold perspiration start at every pore at the thought of what would happen if I even in a slight detail got mixed in my facts. Then I fully realized the magnificence of Mr. Rogers' acting, for not once in all the hours I had sat and watched him had I detected a single evidence of cold, hot, or lukewarm perspiration coming from his pores.

Yet away from the intoxicating spell of dollar-making this remarkable man is one of the most charming and lovable beings I have ever encountered, a man whom any man or woman would be proud to have for a brother; a man whom any mother or father would give thanks for as a son; a man whom any woman would be happy to know as her husband, and a man whom any boy or girl would rejoice to call father. Once he passes under the baleful influence of "The Machine," however, he becomes a relentless, ravenous creature, pitiless as a shark, knowing no law of God or man in the execution of his purpose. Between him and coveted dollars may come no kindly, humane influences—all are thrust aside, their claims disregarded, in ministering to this strange, cannibalistic money-hunger, which, in truth, grows by what it feeds on.

In describing one head of "Standard Oil," I have necessarily used many words because nature cast him in a most uncommon and chameleon-like mould. The other two require less of my space, for neither is unusual nor remarkable.

John D. Rockefeller, however great his ability or worldly success, can be fully described as a man made in the image of an ideal money-maker and an ideal money-maker made in the image of a man. A foot-note should call attention to the fact that an ideal money-maker is a machine the details of which are diagrammed in the asbestos blue-prints which paper the walls of Hell.

With William Rockefeller it is different. When I read in my Bible that God made man in His own image and likeness, I find myself picturing a certain type of individual—a solid, substantial, sturdy gentleman with the broad shoulders and strong frame of an Englishman, and a cautious, kindly expression of face. And that is the most fitting description I can give of William Rockefeller. A man of few, very few words and most excellent judgment—rather brotherly than friendly, clean of mind and body; and if I have not given you the impression of a good, wholesome man made in the image of his God, I have done William Rockefeller a greater wrong than an honest man can afford to do another.

CHAPTER IV

MY OWN RESPONSIBILITY

As to my personal responsibility for the crime of Amalgamated, right here, before proceeding further, I shall briefly explain the transaction, state my share in the deal, and point out how completely I was hoodwinked by the "System."

The great Anaconda mine and affiliated properties, previous to the creation of the Amalgamated, were owned by J. B. Haggin, Lloyd Tevis, and Marcus Daly. The control of the properties and their operations were absolutely vested in Marcus Daly, and he alone knew where the lean veins ended and the fat ones began. For many years he had kept a close guard over the very fat ones, never letting his right eye know what the left one saw when he was examining them. For deep down in his mind Marcus Daly cherished a dream—a dream of immense riches, and it was to be realized in a simple enough way. He would get together the millions to buy out his partners on the basis of a valuation of the "ore in sight," then in supreme ownership himself reap untold profits out of the milling of the plethoric veins he had been so careful to leave unworked. The immense natural endowments of the Anaconda rendered this easy enough, for even the lean veins "in sight" contained a vast store of copper and gold and silver.

Just about the time the world awaited the first section of "Coppers" which I had advertised should consist of the rich Boston & Montana, and Butte & Boston properties, it "happened" that Mr. Rogers "met" Marcus Daly. The result of the conjunction of the two personalities—the whole-souled, trusting miner and the fascinating and persuasive master of Standard Oil—was decisive; the miner confided his dreams and his aspirations to the magnate, who at once magnificently undertook to realize them. The trade was almost instantly made. Mr. Rogers would buy the properties of Daly, Haggin, and Tevis, at "in-sight" prices, and Daly would be his partner, but the partnership must remain secret until the purchase was consummated.

The ownership of the Anaconda Company at the time consisted of 1,200,000 shares, and the purchase of a few shares over the majority at the "in-sight" lean-vein valuation of $24,000,000 would carry the turnover of the management and the control. It took but a very brief time to get together the other properties which were finally included in the first section of Amalgamated. They consisted of the Colorado, Washoe, and Parrott Mining companies and timber, coal, and other lands, and mercantile and like properties situated in the State of Montana, for which Mr. Rogers paid in round figures $15,000,000, a total of $39,000,000 for what within a few days after purchase was capitalized at $75,000,000 in the Amalgamated Company.

No one but Henry H. Rogers, William Rockefeller, myself, and one lawyer knew the actual figures of the cost, although a number of the members of the different groups, including Marcus Daly, the silent partner, were sure they were in the secret.

As soon as the properties were secured, they were capitalized for $75,000,000 as the Amalgamated Copper Company and were immediately offered for sale to the public. It will thus be seen that the profit on this section alone was $36,000,000, probably the largest actual profit ever made by one body of men in a single corporation deal, yet so nicely does "Standard Oil" discriminate in dispensing its generosity that in this case those who received the $36,000,000 profit refused to deduct from it $77,000 of expenses connected with the formation of the company, thereby compelling it to start $77,000 in debt. This was something Marcus Daly never forgave and to the day of his death he repeatedly referred to the act as the personification of corporation meanness.

In the organization of the Amalgamated Corporation certain individuals and institutions, for various considerations, were entitled to some share in the profits of the deal. First there was Marcus Daly who knew what the major portion of the property had cost and was a silent partner in the winnings as he knew them. The Amalgamated Company was organized in and floated on the public from the National City Bank, and so James Stillman, its president and head, who is also one of the inner circle of "Standard Oil" chiefs, should participate. Something was due also to J. Pierpont Morgan & Co., and to Frederick Olcott, president of the Central Trust Company of New York, who were on the board of directors. On the board of directors, too, was Governor Flower, of the banking and brokerage house of Flower & Co., who had acted as fiscal agents for the corporation at its formation. Nor must I forget the Lewisohn Brothers, who had been compelled to turn in all their copper business at a fraction of its worth—or at just the aggregate of its cost and raw material—to be incorporated in the United Metals Selling Company, a part of the Amalgamated scheme, but not included in the corporation. Every one of these men had elaborate assurances that he was in on the cellar floor.

This is what actually occurred. Before Mr. Rogers and William Rockefeller let any one at all in, they built a superbly designed water-, air-, and light-proof structure (particularly light-proof), consisting of five floors, each one being the exact duplicate of the $39,000,000 one upon which they, and they only, stood. Marcus Daly alone was ushered in on the first floor, elevated just a few million dollars above their own. James Stillman and Leonard Lewisohn, of Lewisohn Brothers, were admitted to the next one, the $50,000,000 floor. In other words, Mr. Stillman and Mr. Lewisohn were given an unnamed percentage, the percentage to be arranged later by Mr. Rogers, in all profits above actual cost, and such actual cost was called $50,000,000 and was arrived at by adding the $11,000,000 of secret profits to the actual $39,000,000 cost. Then J. P. Morgan & Co., Frederick Olcott, Governor Flower, and one or two of the dearest friends and closest associates, were let in on the $60,000,000 floor—were given an unnamed percentage, the percentage to be arranged by Mr. Rogers, in all profits above actual cost, and such actual cost was called $60,000,000, and was arrived at by adding $21,000,000 of secret profits to the actual $39,000,000 cost. Then selected ones from the eight different groups of "Standard Oil" were allowed to move in to the fifth, or underwriters' floor, which was affirmed to be $70,000,000 cost; and then, as a solid phalanx, all the different floor-dwellers marched upon the dear public to the tune of $75,000,000, in the front ranks of which were those of the eight groups of the Standard Oil army who had not already been admitted to any of the secret floors.

Right here the crime of Amalgamated was born, not so much the legal crime but the great moral crime. In the ethics of Wall Street the heinousness of the transaction lies not in the fact that the public was compelled to pay $36,000,000 profit to a few men who had invested but $39,000,000—and, as I shall show when I approach this part of my story, the $39,000,000 did not even belong to them—but in the fact that Mr. Rogers and Mr. Rockefeller had given to their associates what, in the vernacular of "the Street," is termed "the double cross."

The every-day people, the millions who do not know Wall Street, realm of the royal American dollar; Wall Street, its sidewalks inlaid with gold coin and paved from curb to curb with solid gold bricks; Wall Street, lined with huge money-mills where hearts and souls are ground into gold-dust, whose gutters run full to overflowing with strangled, mangled, sand-bagged wrecks of human hopes, to be poured, in a never-ending stream, into the brimming waters of the river at its foot, for deposit at the poor-houses, insane asylums, States' prisons, and suicides' graves, washed daily by that grim flood's ebb and flow—the every-day people, I am sure, will not take in the blackness of this transaction at this stage of my story, but before it is ended I will lay this and many more of an equally hellish nature before them in such A B C simplicity that all can read the portent as clearly as the Prophet Daniel read the writing on the wall in the banquet-hall of Belshazzar.

When I consented to allow property which had cost only $39,000,000 to be sold to the public for $75,000,000, it was under a pressure which it was practically impossible for me to withstand. I do not think I use too strong a word when I say "pressure." For three years I had been advertising to the world the great merits of "Coppers," and for over a year I had announced that when the public was given an opportunity to participate in the consolidated "Coppers" it would be upon a basis most carefully worked out: that the properties included in the first section would surely be worth more than the price at which they would be offered to the public, and that all the power, capital, and ability of "Standard Oil" were behind the promises I made. I did this advertising openly and in the frankest possible way, and in all of my announcements, whether printed, oral, or otherwise, used the names of Henry H. Rogers, William Rockefeller, James Stillman, the National City Bank of New York, and "Standard Oil" as freely as I did my own, and in many ways led the public to believe that the very rich Boston & Montana and Butte & Boston companies were to be included in this section of "Coppers."

At that time my alliance with "Standard Oil" was close. A business connection had developed into a strong personal relation between Mr. Rogers and myself. We were engaged, together with William Rockefeller, on a great financial deal which was based on certain conclusions I had worked out in regard to the copper industry. These men were to me the embodiment of success, success won in the fiercest commercial conflict of the age. Their position at the helm of the greatest financial institution in the world gave weight and importance to their judgment and opinions. Nor had aught occurred between us to suggest they would dare perpetrate the crimes they did. Besides all this, indeed an integral part of it, my personal resources were completely involved in the transaction, for the most part pledged with Mr. Rogers and William Rockefeller in stocks of the Butte & Boston and Boston & Montana corporations.

This was, then, the nature of our connection when Mr. Rogers, suddenly and without previous intimation of his schemes, notified me of his purchase of the Daly-Haggin-Tevis properties, and practically ordered me to put them upon the tray which I was preparing and take them to the eagerly waiting public, who by this time were fairly howling for the good things we had been promising them.

In support of this extraordinary change of plan Mr. Rogers urged the secret wealth of the Anaconda and the great value of the other properties which I myself had helped purchase, but I bitterly opposed the new proposition until there was nothing before me but these alternatives—to accept the change Mr. Rogers insisted on or break with "Standard Oil." The latter would mean that I must announce to the public that it was in danger of being tricked, and it was by no means certain that my warning would carry weight against the denials and assurances of "Standard Oil." However much influence I had obtained through my long years of dealings with the public, independent of "Standard Oil," I realized that "Standard Oil's" influence and prestige were much greater, for it must be remembered that at this time the public had not had the evidence since acquired of the "System's" cold-blooded trickery. If I took this course it would mean not only my own ruin financially, for Mr. Rogers and William Rockefeller could call my loans and wipe me out completely, but also the ruin of my friends and allies, who, under my direction, had invested their own millions in the properties concerned. On the other hand, I had the most earnest assurances from Mr. Rogers and William Rockefeller that the new properties were worth much more than the $75,000,000 at which it was proposed to capitalize them. They took me to task for my distrust of them, and went far to demonstrate to me the accuracy of their estimates. They not only gave me Marcus Daly's minute estimates of the values and legitimate possibilities of Anaconda, but consented to have these verified by outside experts in whom I had implicit confidence, and whose personal examination more than bore out Daly's appraisal. I have never yet had reason to doubt the correctness of the figures then shown me, although since I began this story "Standard Oil," in an endeavor to get me to abandon my efforts to secure justice for the thousands I assisted in duping, have stated for the first time that Marcus Daly deceived them and really, to use the words of their chief counsel, sold them a "gold brick."

After this examination I felt convinced that the properties "Standard Oil" insisted on substituting for those originally intended for the first section of Amalgamated were such that the public, if honestly dealt with, could not possibly meet with loss in purchasing. But even then I only consented to go ahead with the flotation under a definite agreement which seemed to me completely to guard against all contingencies of jugglery or deception. This agreement stipulated that all the profits from the transaction should be taken by those to whom they were due in the stock of the Amalgamated Company, and no part of them in cash—that the public should be sold, at the flotation, only $5,000,000 of the $75,000,000, and that "Standard Oil" and all associated with "Standard Oil" in the profits should retain the remaining $70,000,000 until such time as it had been absolutely demonstrated to the public that the property behind the $75,000,000 of stock was worth more than the amount it had been capitalized for. Furthermore, I was also promised that the $5,000,000 cash to be taken from the public should be kept intact, and in my handling of the market it should always be available for the repurchase from the investors of what had been sold to them, at the price which they had paid for it.

This was the basis on which I went on with Amalgamated. I would not have my readers understand me as asserting it would have been possible for me to have stopped the flotation had I attempted it. But, on the other hand, I would not have them think that I desire to be absolved from the disastrous results of the great mistake I made at this time in not at any cost doing that which after-happenings have shown would have been the most honest course for me to have pursued. Nor would I have them think I desire to be absolved from the consequences of many other mistakes which this one led me into—mistakes in temporizing with the situation and postponing action which I should have boldly and fearlessly forced, regardless of all consequences to the public, my friends, and myself.

The subsequent proceedings, the manner in which Amalgamated was actually sold to the public, the flagrant disregard of the conditions of my agreement with Mr. Rogers and William Rockefeller, will, when fully told in their proper place in my story, show that the "System," by whose methods the public is as ruthlessly plundered as though the fruits of its labors were taken away from it by highwaymen, admits also of its own votaries being tricked and despoiled by their associates. The men who participated in the transaction I have just described are among the most astute financiers in the country and presumably possessed of invincible capacity to protect their own interests. But with all their knowledge of the "System's" tricks they were, in this instance, as shrewdly duped as the veriest tyro in the Wall Street game.

My own experience with the "System" in this deal was different in degree but not in principle from that of these others, and it must be remembered that I was better equipped to protect my interests than any of them. I knew that the actual cost of the properties comprising the first Amalgamated was $39,000,000, and that when sold to the public at $75,000,000 there must be a profit of $36,000,000. I had every right to think I knew all the other details connected with the transaction, for as organizer and executant of the deal my share in the profits was to be equal to that of Henry H. Rogers and William Rockefeller respectively. We were each to have twenty-five per cent., the remaining twenty-five per cent. going to others. This was no gentleman's "leave-it-to-me-and-I'll-see-you-get-what's-coming-to-you" arrangement either, but a hard, cold, mutually satisfactory and settled-in-advance agreement. But when it came to the final accounting, the "System" had so regulated things that the participants on the various floors, except, of course, Mr. Rogers and William Rockefeller, must each accept without question the share finally handed over to him. Having no means of knowing how large the other interests were, or what the "extraordinary expenses" had been, they were in no position to question the payments made them, which represented sums below what they would have had if the business had been conducted as they thought it had been. When my final account was presented to me I was startled. Notwithstanding the "cleverness" of the "System," the deception was so obvious, so audacious, that the instant Mr. Rogers submitted it to me I exploded and denounced the transaction with such vehemence and conviction that within a few minutes there was forthcoming a second statement, revising the account, by which I was given just double the amount first tendered, and the figures in both accounts ran into millions; yet the amount in the second account upon which I settled was only one-half the share received by my equal partners, Henry H. Rogers and William Rockefeller, as I afterward learned.

This is a fair statement of my own share in the first Amalgamated transaction. I have no desire to evade the issues suggested and raised by these revelations. My frankness should be absolute proof of that. As I promised, I shall hew to the exact line of fact, letting the chips of responsibility, legal and moral, fall where they may, though many of them stick to my own clothes. My own burden of error I am ready and willing to shoulder, but I decline any longer to take and carry responsibilities which belong absolutely to others. There should be a time-limit on martyrdom, and mine anyhow is up.

CHAPTER V

THE POWER OF DOLLARS

At no time in the history of the United States has the power of dollars been as great as now. Freedom and equity are controlled by dollars. The laws which should preserve and enforce all rights are made and enforced by dollars. It is possible to-day, with dollars, to "steer" the selection of the candidates of both the great parties for the highest office in our republic, that of President of the United States. It is possible to repeat the operation in the selection of candidates for the executive and legislative conduct and control of every State and municipality in the United States, and with a sufficient number of dollars to "steer" the doings of the law-makers and law-enforcers of the national, State, and municipal governments of the people, and to "steer" a sufficient proportion of the court decisions to make absolute any power created by such direction. It is all, broadly speaking, a matter of dollars practically to accomplish these things. I must not be misunderstood as even insinuating that there are not absolutely honest law-makers and law-enforcers, nor that there are not as many of them in proportion to the whole body as there were at the creation of our republic. I believe there is at the present time as large a percentage of honesty among Americans as ever there has been, but it is plainly evident to any student of the times that at no other period in the history of the United States has honesty been so completely "steered" by dishonesty as at this, the beginning of the twentieth century.

I shall go further and say that there to-day exists uncontrolled in the hands of a set of men a power to make dollars from nothing. That function of dollar-making which thepeople believe is vested in their Government alone and only exercised under the law for their benefit, is actually being secretly exercised on an enormous scale by a few private individuals for their own personal benefit. This, I am well aware, is a startling statement, but not more so than the facts which support it. Throughout the country we have all grown accustomed to the spectacle of men who, poor yesterday, to-day display more dollars than the kings and queens of olden times controlled. In flaunting this money these men proudly boast: "We made all this yesternight, and are going to multiply it five-or fifty-fold to-morrow night."

The fact that there must be in this country some secret method of gaining vast fortunes gradually dawned on the minds of the people. This method, they argued, must be outside the laws of the land which they themselves had made, and they were confronted with the fact that the possessors of these fabulous fortunes were creating a power not recognized by their Government and which practically placed the Government in the hands of the fortune-owners. They realized that in some way the magic of this fortune-making was connected with, or seemed to be compounded in, institutions called corporations and trusts, and that among these the head and centre was a great affair called "Standard Oil." Wherever this "Standard Oil" was, all knew that strange wonders were worked. Within the sphere of its influence dirt changed to gold, liquids to solids, and what was, was not, and what was not, was. Whoever became a part of this mysterious "Standard Oil," at the same time was rendered "powerful"; as though touched by a fairy's wand, he changed from pauper to millionaire. But what was "Standard Oil"? The people knew that at the beginning it was only an aggregation of men, private individuals, who had accumulated much money by securing a monopoly of selling oil, and that these men were "Rockefellers," and that Standard Oil and "Rockefellers" had been cute and cunning in the conduct of their oil-selling to a degree greater than had been rival sellers of oil or of other necessities. And as time wore on much more was heard of the cleverness of Standard Oil and "Rockefellers," as the victims of the cuteness and the cunning "hollered" in public places, and the newspapers and writers of books exclaimed against their practices and exactions. But many other things were happening simultaneously, and to the great bulk of the people it was interesting rather than portentous that there existed in the country a giant oil-thing whose owners were reputed the richest men in the world.

It was not until the beginning of the twentieth century that the monster "Standard Oil" loomed up before the people as the giant of all corporate things and that its ominous shadow seemed to dwarf all other institutions, public or private. In multitudinous forms it was before the people.

In awed whispers men talked of its mysterious doings and canvassed its extraordinary powers as though "Standard Oil" were a living, breathing entity rather than a mere business institution created by men and existing only by virtue of the laws of the land.

About the time that the world had begun mistily to take in the tremendous forces which radiated from "Standard Oil," there occurred a financial crash, and the people saw their savings, invested in what they supposed were the legal and absolute titles of ownership in the material things of their country, suddenly decline in value and contract to prices representing a loss to them of billions of dollars. Throughout the misery and suffering this terrible collapse occasioned, "Standard Oil" remained undisturbed as before and amid all the confusion kept sternly on its dollar-"making" way. Indeed, it seemed to gain in bulk as other institutions diminished or disappeared. Then it was that the people first began to demand, what they are still to-day fiercely demanding, "What is this 'Standard Oil'?" "What is its secret?" "Whence came it?" and, "Can our republic endure if it, too, endures?"

To-day "Standard Oil," the "Private Thing," is the greatest power in the land—more powerful than the people individually or as a whole, and its secret is the knowledge of the trick of finance by which dollars are "made" from nothing in unlimited quantities subject to no laws of man nor nature. The dollars that "Standard Oil" makes are of the same value as the dollars of the people as made by the Government, which dollars we know can be coined and put into circulation only in accordance with law and for the benefit of all the people.

For the better understanding of those readers not versed in the technical phrases of finance and economics I shall in my narrative make use of certain terms of my own which will convey meanings readily grasped when the sense in which they are used is once comprehended. In speaking of "Standard Oil," for instance, I will speak of it as a "Private Thing." By that term I desire to typify the active, private identity of a corporation which comprehends, but exists independently of, its legalized functions. Some corporations have a real personality in addition to that which their name and the corporation laws prescribe for them, an inherent power, or individuality, which exists above and apart from their physical functions as sellers of oil, of coal, or of ice. This may be an incarnation of the power developed in the transaction of their legalized occupations, but the "Private Thing" is uncontrolled by any of the restrictions by which the law defines and curbs the corporation whose name it bears. Already I have distinguished between "Standard Oil" which wields all the powers of its subsidiary companies, and Standard Oil, the seller of oil. In the same way we have "American Sugar Refineries" and "United States Steel," the "Private Things" which are not one whit better than nor different from "Standard Oil," the "Private Thing." Though this narrative will deal only with the "Private Things," Bay State Gas and Amalgamated Copper, I have no hesitancy in saying that the methods employed and the results, good or bad, which accrued in the case of any of the other "Private Things" with which the public have had to do, differ only in details from those with which I shall deal in my story.

In speaking of dollars brought into existence by the trick of finance I have referred to I shall call them henceforth "made dollars," to distinguish them from dollars coined by the Government and legitimately acquired by the individual or corporation. These "made dollars," it must be remembered, are really "made" for all purposes of use as surely as if they had the Government's stamp, yet they are not made in the sense of the known volume of the people's money being added to. So, however many of these "made dollars" are brought into existence by this trick of finance, only the men who "made" them can know and profit by their existence. The people are no wiser nor can they adjust themselves to the change of conditions brought about by the creation of all this new money; yet if "unmade" or lost, the entire volume of the nation's wealth would be contracted.

I can set before my readers better by an illustration than by any process of definition, the trick of finance by which "made dollars" are brought into existence. Let us suppose that the United States Government at Washington, the only power legally entitled to issue money for circulation among the people, puts forth a particular $10,000. All the conditions prescribed by law have been followed, and all the people in the country are benefited by the issue and circulation of this particular $10,000, each in the proportion the laws prescribe.

"B," a Western farmer, tills his soil and receives, by the sale of his wheat, the particular $10,000, which he then deposits in The Bank. The Bank, being a part of the Government machinery, only receives, holds, and uses the $10,000 under safeguards provided for by the laws of the land, so hereafter "B's" material life is conducted on the basis that he is the full and actual possessor of $10,000. He knows, further, that his $10,000 cannot be expanded nor contracted, nor its relation to any of the other money of the people which is in circulation altered without his knowledge, because he knows such changes cannot come about except through the Government. I say he knows this—he has every right to believe he knows it—but, in fact, it is not so, because of the working of the secret financial device of the Private Thing. At this stage enters "C," the Private Thing.

"C" purchases with $3,300 ("B's" money) which he borrows from The Bank, a copper-mine, depositing the title which he receives from the seller with The Bank as collateral for the $3,300. After purchasing he arbitrarily calls the copper-mine worth $10,000—arbitrarily because his act is not controlled nor regulated by any of the laws of the land—arbitrarily because the actual cost, $3,300, is his secret and his alone. Then, arbitrarily, "C" organizes his $3,300 of copper property into the Arbitrary Copper Company, and issues to himself a piece of paper, which he arbitrarily stamps "10,000 stock dollars." This he takes to The Bank, and by loan or other device exchanges it for the remaining $6,700 belonging to "B," and thereafter "C" conducts his affairs on the basis that he is the possessor of $6,700, his "made dollars" in the transaction. At this stage there is actually in use among the people $16,700 where "B," the legitimate factor, and his kind, the people, suppose there is but $10,000—$10,000 which is recorded, known and legal, being used by the legitimate factors, "B" and The Bank, and $6,700 which is unrecorded and unknown to any but "C" and The Bank, being used by the illegitimate Private Thing "C."

Right here is the secret device, the financial trick, by which the greatest power in the land has been created, and by which the people can be absolutely plundered of their savings for the benefit of the few.

At this stage the two-thirds of "B's" $10,000, of which he later is to be plundered, has not been actually taken away, so he cannot possibly have any evidence yet of the process of pillage which has been begun, or that the volume of money which he supposes is all that exists has been tremendously expanded. The next step is where "C" sells his $3,300, stamped "10,000 stock dollars" (which, as already shown, he has exchanged with The Bank for the $10,000 deposited by "B"), to "B" for $10,000, which $10,000 "B" withdraws from The Bank by simply making out a check in favor of "C." ("B's" inducement to exchange his dollars for the stock dollars of "C" is the high rate of interest that they will return in the form of dividends, which rate is much larger than The Bank can afford to pay.) "C" deposits "B's" check with The Bank and hereby liquidates his $10,000 indebtedness to The Bank.

At this stage "B" is still the possessor of $10,000, but it is "10,000 stock dollars." "C" is the possessor of $6,700, and "D," from whom the copper-mine was purchased, is the possessor of $3,300; but the two latter amounts make up the 10,000 real dollars, and The Bank remains where it was at the beginning of the transaction. The people, however, are no wiser; but they know, because they have been most carefully educated to such knowledge by "C's" agents, Wall Street, and the press, that their country is tremendously prosperous—that its great prosperity is evidenced by the $6,700 added wealth in the form of 6,700 new stock dollars. At the next stage the financial trick accomplished by the secret device is complete. "B," the farmer, who has contracted for new machinery and other necessities and luxuries to be paid for "next season," attempts next season to turn his 10,000 stock dollars into real dollars, and "C," the Private Thing, knowing their real value to be but $3,300, refuses to make the exchange, but instead, by proclaiming their real value, compels "B," who must have real dollars to meet his debts, to sell them for what "C," the Private Thing, is willing to pay. "C," the Private Thing, is willing to pay their worth, which he alone knows is $3,300; he repurchases them at that price from "B," that he may repeat the operation at the return of the next "wave of the country's prosperity."

By this operation "B," the farmer, has lost, as absolutely as though they had been taken away from him by a Government decree, $6,700 of his own making, and "C," the Private Thing, has "made," as absolutely as though the Government had allowed him to coin them for his own benefit, 6,700 real dollars, and The Bank, created, regulated, and controlled by law, and existing because of the people's deposits of money, has been the instrument by which "C," the Private Thing, has deprived "B," the farmer, of his savings, because "C," the Private Thing, is at one and the same time during the operation I have outlined, himself and The Bank.

A careful study of this illustration, by even laymen unacquainted with financial or corporation affairs, will clearly show that the foundation of this transaction was The Bank's putting in jeopardy $3,300 of "B's" deposited $10,000, and that if the $3,300, after being put in jeopardy, had been lost, "B" would have been the loser, which, in turn, means that the compensation for the jeopardy in which the $3,300 was placed was the possibility of $6,700 profit; and that, therefore, the $6,700 profit when made should have gone to the owner of the $3,300, "B," instead of to "C," the user of it.

It is therefore in this sense that I shall use the term "made dollars"—wherever they are "made" or "unmade" through one set of men using the dollars of another set of men without that other set knowing that their dollars are being so used; and wherever the result of such use is that when dollars are "made," they are "made" by the ones who use others' money, and where dollars are "unmade," they are lost by the ones who own the dollars which they don't know are being used.

CHAPTER VI

CONSTRUCTION OF "STANDARD OIL'S" "DOLLAR-MAKING" MILL

I believe "Standard Oil" was the first to utilize this secret device for circumventing the safeguards which the law has erected to protect the savings of the people. It was the first practically to apprehend that, a large proportion of all the moneys in circulation, which belong to the people or the Government, being in the custody of the national and savings-banks and trust and insurance companies, it would only be necessary for a set of men to obtain control of sufficient of the principal national and savings-banks and trust and insurance companies to control practically unlimited amounts of such funds. Once in control of these funds dollars could be absolutely "made" at will by the three following steps: 1st. Using the money in these institutions to acquire properties. 2d. Consolidating such properties on an inflated basis, and selling them to the people (who, in fact, already owned them; because they owned the funds with which they had been purchased); and, 3d, by stock-market trickery scaring their owners into re-selling them at an enormous shrinkage from the price they had paid. To understand a situation with "Standard Oil" is to act, and twenty years ago it began to weave a net to secure control of the four classes of institutions I have named.

Its first move was to establish a great corporation, the Standard Oil Company, and make its stock, 1,000,000 shares, sell at from $650 to $800 per share, or $650,000,000 to $800,000,000. It kept its affairs mysteriously secret, it paid enormous dividends, and from time to time it caused to be published broadcast throughout the world the statement thatit was held in such value by its creators, the Rockefellers, Rogers, etc, that they continued to own all but a few shares of the entire capital. To prove that there could be no doubt of such continued ownership, the public's attention was repeatedly called to the fact that the Standard Oil Company was the only great corporation which did not allow its shares to be traded in upon any of the stock-exchanges. As a matter of fact, though they are not traded in on the regular stock-exchanges, they are actively bought and sold daily on the New York "Curb."

At the height of the recent financial storm word went round that the crafts of three over-night-made multimillionaires, men foremost in the seventh group of "Standard Oil" votaries, were in the trough of the financial sea and headed for the breakers, which were already strewn with the wrecks of the people's savings. Following closely on the heels of these stories came the astounding one that each of these enormously rich men had, in his endeavors to raise large amounts of cash, disclosed among his assets blocks of "Standard Oil" stock ranging from 5,000 to 20,000 shares each. Hardly had the public heard this before all financialdom knew that the storm-tossed crafts had received succor, and that the crisis had passed. For one brief day the financial press of the country printed the item: "Standard Oil came to the rescue by buying for cash large blocks of Standard Oil stock which had long been held by this or that interest for investment," and no more was thought of the incident. Even the most alert financiers never suspected that the most important stock secret of the age had been on the verge of becoming public property.

Planted deep in the minds of the public that watches the comings and goings of the Street is the conviction that Standard Oil is the holy of holies among stocks. The world has been taught to believe that the owners of Standard Oil regard the shares of the great oil corporation as their most precious, most sacred possessions. Yet while "Standard Oil" has been so scientifically spreading abroad the impression that the public would never be permitted to own Standard Oil stock, secretly it has been engaged in exchanging that stock for the securities of the people in the form of banks and trust companies, railroads, and other assets of definite value. So completely has "Standard Oil" pulled the wool over the eyes of the votaries of finance that there cannot be found in or out of Wall Street a single great financier who would not laugh to scorn the suggestion that "Standard Oil" is engaged in a campaign for the distribution of its Standard Oil stock to the public. Yet pin your great financier down to the facts, and he'll admit that he himself has quite a block of the stock, and that institutions of which he is a director include among their assets in one form or another good-sized parcels of the inestimable security. But so completely are these very wise men held by the spells woven over them when for this or that special reason they were allowed as a favor to acquire their holdings, and so impressively have they been shown that their ownership in Standard Oil stock must be kept secret, that no suspicion has ever entered their minds that they were playing the part of lambs in its purchase.

Nor was the episode I have described above allowed to disturb their serenity. It soon became known to the innermost circle of Wall Street that the stock the three men had resold to "Standard Oil" represented the share of each in some of the gigantic deals to which he had been a party during the last ten years, and that with its acquirement had gone a pledge that it would always be kept in the purchaser's "tin box," and whenever inspected by "Standard Oil" would be free from "pinholes." And so, adroitly, dangerous deductions were prevented.

For the uninstructed I may say that a capitalist's "tin box" is the receptacle for the stocks and bonds that largely represent his fortune, and pinholes in a stock certificate are in Wall Street conclusive evidence that such certificate has, at some period, temporarily passed into other's hands as collateral for loans, for there has been pinned to it a memorandum or note stating the details of the transaction in which its owner parted with it. Pinholed securities are looked upon by the upper crust of big financiers with much the same horror as that with which members of the American social upper crust look upon their No. 10 boots and gloves—reminders of their peasant ancestry.

But to return to "Standard Oil's" financial weavings: Their next move was to use Standard Oil stock as the basis for loans, that is, as collateral for money borrowed from the banks, trust and insurance companies, and treasuries of other great corporations and estates. The money thus acquired was paid out to purchase the control of banks and trust and insurance companies in all parts of the United States, the Standard Oil ownership being represented by dummy directors and officers.

The next move represents another of the dazzling devices of finance in which "Standard Oil" is adept, and brings the process of artificial expansion still further along. Control of a certain number of these savings and national banks and trust and insurance companies having been acquired, the funds of each were so manipulated by depositing those of one institution with another, and the latter's in turn with the first, as to swell the deposits of all and create in all of them an apparently legitimate basis for increases of capitalization. At the same time there was shown an apparently legitimate necessity for the establishment of additional banking and trust companies, which were duly organized and their assets juggled around by the same process. The result of all this manipulation defies description. Throughout the series of correlated institutions loans and deposits are multiplied in such an intricacy of duplication that only a few able experts, employed by the "System" because of their mathematical genius, are able to unravel the tangle to the extent of approximating the proportion the legitimate funds bear to those which have been created by the financial jugglery I have indicated.

When "Standard Oil" had gathered into its net sufficient of the important private institutions of finance there still remained the federal Government, the largest handler of money in the country. It was not hard for "Standard Oil" to introduce its expert votaries into the United States Treasury and thus to steer the millions of the nation into the banks subject to the

"System's" control. This accomplished, the structure was complete and the process of "making" dollars proceeded on a magnificent scale.

That there may be no possible doubt in the minds of those of my readers who are unacquainted with such matters that I am citing every-day, actual happenings, I will tell just how the Daly-Haggin-Tevis-Anaconda-Amalgamated transaction was worked out, showing that but for the existence of the National City Bank of New York, or a like institution of the people, it could not have been brought about.

When Mr. Rogers and William Rockefeller "traded" with Messrs. Daly, Haggin, and Tevis for the Anaconda stock, and with others for like stock or other properties which I have already named, the price agreed upon was $24,000,000 to Daly, Haggin, and Tevis, and $15,000,000 to the others, or $39,000,000 in all. This was to be paid by "Standard Oil" and received by Daly, Haggin, and Tevis, and the others, but one of the stipulations in the "trade" was that instead of the money's being paid to Daly, Haggin, and Tevis, and others direct, it was to be credited to them on the books of the National City Bank of New York and was to be, by agreement, not withdrawn from the bank before a given time, the bank agreeing that the new owners of this money should receive interest at a low rate upon it while it so remained deposited. At the same time the bank agreed to loan Mr. Rogers and William Rockefeller the $39,000,000 at the same rate of interest upon the collateral which the $39,000,000 was used in purchasing. Therefore the first part of the transaction was as follows:

The bank, having $39,000,000 on hand belonging to the public in the form of savings deposited, or having a fictitious $39,000,000 in the form of book-keeping accounts made possible by the deposits of the public and the manipulation of the funds in other banks and trust and insurance companies belonging to the public or the Government, caused an entry to be made in its books showing that this $39,000,000 had been loaned to Mr. Rogers and William Rockefeller, and that they, having transferred it to Daly, Haggin, Tevis, and others, were, upon the books of the bank, the real owners.

The second part was the summoning into the City Bank of certain "Standard Oil" lawyers, office-boys, and clerks, and the organization by them of the Amalgamated Copper Company. The lawyers drew up the papers and the office-boys and clerks signed them. First, the papers certified that "whereas we (the office-boys and clerks) are desirous of taking advantage of the corporation laws of the State of New Jersey, we (the said office-boys and clerks) do so take advantage of the said laws and form ourselves into the Amalgamated Copper Company, which will have a capital of $75,000,000, and which will be allowed by said laws to own copper-mines and other things, to mine copper and other things, to manufacture, buy, sell, and trade in copper and other things, and to do numerous and variegated other things; and that whereas we (the said office-boys and clerks) have now become the Amalgamated Copper Company, one of our number will purchase the entire capital stock of the said Amalgamated Copper Company for $75,000,000 cash, which $75,000,000 cash we herewith certify to have been paid in the form of a check for $75,000,000, herewith delivered to the treasurer, one of our number, by the clerk who drew it; and the treasurer, herewith certifying that he has received the $75,000,000, herewith delivers unto said clerk the $75,000,000 capital stock of the Amalgamated Copper Company, and we (the said office-boys and clerks) herewith certify that there is within the treasury of the Amalgamated Copper Company $75,000,000, and we (the said office-boys and clerks) vote that it, the said $75,000,000, shall be used in the purchase of certain stocks and properties, and said certain stocks and properties shall be the same stocks and properties previously purchased by Mr. Rogers and William Rockefeller, and now owned by them, and we (the said office-boys and clerks) herewith certify that we have paid from the treasury $75,000,000, that said $75,000,000 is in the form of a check, and said check is the one previously received, or its equivalent, by our treasurer, from one of our number, to wit, the clerk referred to earlier in these papers, and said $75,000,000 has been paid to Henry H. Rogers for his and William Rockefeller's use." Henry H. Rogers, now having $75,000,000, where formerly he had stocks and properties which had cost him $39,000,000, and being desirous of investing it, purchased from the clerk the $75,000,000 of Amalgamated stock which he, the clerk, had previously purchased from the treasury of the Amalgamated Company, Mr. Rogers promptly paying for said purchase with the $75,000,000 check or its equivalent, which has already done such yeoman service.

The organization of the Amalgamated Copper Company of New Jersey now being complete, and the company being in possession of all the property which had formerly belonged to Mr. Rogers and William Rockefeller, and which had cost them $39,000,000, and the clerk having again come into possession of his $75,000,000 check, and Mr. Rogers and William Rockefeller being the sole owners of the $75,000,000 of Amalgamated stock, the second part of this transaction was completed. The third began by the office-boys and clerks resigning from their positions as directors and officers of the Amalgamated Copper Company of New Jersey in favor of the more responsible and better known "Standard Oil" votaries. Mr. Rogers and William Rockefeller then had the National City Bank of New York offer for sale to the public the $75,000,000 of stock in such a way that, although it was then the private property of Mr. Rogers and William Rockefeller, the public were led to believe it was the property of the Amalgamated Copper Company. Simultaneously, the National City Bank of New York offered to loan the public its deposits at the rate of ninety cents on the dollar, on any amount of the Amalgamated stock it, the public, purchased; whereupon the public, taking advantage of this offer, agreed to purchase from the National City Bank of New York the $75,000,000 of stock for $75,000,000, thereby enabling it to certify upon its books that the $39,000,000 it had loaned to Messrs. Rogers and Rockefeller had been repaid, and enabling Mr. Rogers and William Rockefeller, after paying said debts to the National City Bank of New York, to become the absolute owners of $36,000,000 of money, none of which they had owned before, and which they had "made" as absolutely as though they had coined it by permit from the Government of the people who had parted with it.

The fourth part of the transaction began when months afterward the public, who had borrowed their money from the National City Bank of New York and other banks and trust and insurance companies to buy Amalgamated stock at 100 cents on the dollar, were compelled to repay it, and to do so were obliged to sell the Amalgamated stock which they had purchased at $100 per share for the best price they could get, which was $33 per share; and if we suppose for a moment that the "Standard Oil," after repurchasing it at $33 per share, at a later day repeated the operation of selling it for $100 per share, it will be seen that "Standard Oil," the "Private Thing," would thereby "make" an additional $50,000,000, as absolutely as though they had been allowed by the Government to coin it.

This explanation is not the creation of an extravagant fancy. It is not romance, but reality. The thing described was a supreme manifestation of the "System," of the perfect working of that tremendous financial machine which reaps, grinds, and harvests for its own benefit, the earned savings of the American people.

In showing how these thirty-six millions were made in the brief space of this creature's (Amalgamated Copper's) life, I deal with reality and not romance; but let my readers for a moment give their imaginations play and picture to themselves one scene in this stupendous drama. A great room in the greatest banking house in America, if not in the world—silent, solemn—an atmosphere of impregnable rectitude—the solid furniture, the heavy carpets, the chill high walls, the massive desks, the impressive chairs, the great majestic table portentously suggestive of power. Presto! the dim calm is broken; the air vibrates as when an ancient church is invaded by a swarm of vampire-bats. Into the great room enter a group of men and a flock of youths, who settle in the impressive chairs round the majestic table. You wonder what is the motive of the assemblage. These grave lawyers, whose names are weighty in the nation's councils, and these gray-haired, dignified financiers might well be gathered to arbitrate a dispute involving empires; but why these office-boys and clerks, with their restless, surprised eyes and uneasy gestures? The flourishing of papers, the murmuring of voices in a confusion of "seventy-five million," "we buy," "we sell," "we are," "we will"—words, nothing but words; then silence as one reads from a stiff parchment certain resolutions which the suave gentleman with incisive steel-clicking manners, at the head of the table, puts to a vote. Then these youths, whose souls are afire with the hope of a director's $5 gold fee, timidly sign the record, trembling the while lest a blot call down on them a scolding; a head clerk, whose fondest dream is a raise of salary as the result of coming under the Master's eye in a seventy-five-million-dollar deal, affixes a seal, and there is an exchanging of thin slips of paper—checks—dollars—magically "made dollars." Exit office-boys and lawyers.

The door closes—silence again. Then the air vibrates with the sound of a hearty hand-slap and the genial, whole-souled greeting of the "Master" to his partner. "William, I feel as though I had done an honest day's labor! Thirty-six million dollars 'made' and no hitch, no delay!" Then follows the partner's mild answer: "Yes, Harry, but don't forget James' and the others' shares will shrink it up quite a bit."

Thirty-six million dollars for one honest day's labor! Thirty-six million dollars—and Alaska cost us but seven millions and Spain relinquished to us her claims on the Philippines for only twenty millions. Thirty-six million dollars!—more than a hundred times as much as George Washington, Thomas Jefferson, and "Abe" Lincoln together secured for the patriotic labors of their lifetimes. And this vast sum was taken from the people to enrich men whose coffers were already, as the results of similar operations, so full of dollars that neither they nor their children, nor their children's children could count them—as the people count their savings, a dollar at a time—as thoughtlessly taken as are the apples that the school-boy steals after he has eaten so many that he can eat no more.

A thousand times have I tried to figure out in my mind what worlds of misery such a sum of millions might allay if issued by a government and intelligently distributed among a people—and do my readers know that never in the world's recorded history has any nation felt itself rich enough to devote thirty-six millions to the cause of charity—even in the midst of the most awful calamities of fire, flood, war, or pestilence? On the other hand, I have had to know about the horrors, the misfortunes, the earthly hell, which were the awful consequences of the appropriation of this vast amount. I have had to know about the convicts, the suicides, the broken hearts, the starvation and wretchedness, the ruined bodies and lost souls which strewed the fields of the "System's" harvest.

Pondering all these things, I have ceased to wonder at the deep murmurs of discontent that are rising, rising to my ears from all parts of the continent.

Can it be that a just God suffers the sons and daughters of some of us to eke out a bare existence as the best reward of earnest effort and sterling worth, and at the same time rewards these other men with $36,000,000 for one day's labor? Is this the freedom which our fathers and our sons died on many a bloody, hard-fought field to preserve? I am conscious of a haunting fear that these men and women may not always be patient, may not always be put off with skilled evasion or slippery subterfuge, and for one brief moment I see visions of a marching people, bearing aloft grisly heads on gory poles, and hear above the low, bestial murmur of the mob the cry for bread and for revenge.

And then I remember that this is America, not France; that our laws are strong—if but the people are aroused to see them obeyed; that our prisons are ample, even though they be for the present filled with petty rascals who can do but little harm though turned loose to make room for the real scoundrels who are undermining the foundations of our Republic.

CHAPTER VII

JUGGLING WITH MILLIONS OF THE PEOPLE'S MONEY

For the purposes of the transaction I have just described the machinery of a great bank or trust company was essential. The vast profit gained here was absolutely "made" through the instrumentality of the National City Bank of New York, but some other tractable institution would have been equally efficient. In order that my readers may focus such great financial concerns as this National City Bank, I give right here brief résumés of its career and resources and of those of two of its affiliated institutions:

The "City Bank" was chartered by the New York Legislature in 1812, and reorganized as a National Bank July 17, 1865. The capital paid in was $1,000,000. Moses Taylor held the office of president for thirty-four years, and died in 1892, when Percy R. Pyne, son-in-law of Moses Taylor, was elected president and held office until the election of James Stillman, of Woodward & Stillman, cotton merchants, when the capital stock of the bank was increased to $10,000,000, and again increased to $25,000,000. The sworn report of the officers and directors filed with the Controller of the Currency shows that the condition of the bank, January, 1904, was:

RESOURCES

The company was incorporated by special act of the New York Legislature in 1841. It is the third largest insurance company in the United States. The assets of the company January 1, 1892, were $125,947,290, and income $31,854,194. In 1904 the assets were $352,652,048; income, $88,269,531.

THE NATIONAL SHAWMUT BANK, OF BOSTON

This institution was incorporated in 1898 with a paid-in capital of $3,000,000. In 1904 its total resources, also liabilities, were $63,471,639, of the same general character as those of the National City Bank of New York.

A calm examination of these figures, illuminated by the explanation of the "System's" methods I have previously given, will awaken the American people to a comprehension of what use "high finance" makes of the savings of the public intrusted to it for legitimate investment.

Nor must it be supposed for one minute that the insurance company and the Boston bank which I have used for illustrations differ in any way from scores and scores of their kind which are as absolutely "steered" in their operations by the National City Bank of New York as the National City Bank of New York is absolutely "steered" by its president, James Stillman, or as James Stillman is absolutely "steered" by "Standard Oil," the Private Thing, or as "Standard Oil," the Private Thing, is absolutely "steered" by its supreme heads, Henry H. Rogers, William Rockefeller, and John D. Rockefeller. And if any doubt remains in the minds of my readers of the absolute power of "Standard Oil," the Private Thing, to "make" dollars at will, or of the dead-sure working of their "heads-I-win-and-tails-you-lose" gambling game, I ask them carefully to analyze the above statements in connection with the facts in the Amalgamated transaction which just precede them.

Fourteen years ago the National City Bank passed out of the legitimate management of old-fashioned business men of the Moses Taylor stamp and into the hands of the "System," the Private Thing. Then its capital was $1,000,000; it is to-day $25,000,000, and after having paid out millions in dividends and other profits it has, in addition, a surplus of $16,000,000, and it has the absolute power to juggle with a total of $235,000,000, $36,000,000 of which belong to other national banks, $6,000,000 to State banks and bankers, $29,000,000 to trust companies and savings-banks, $82,000,000 to individual depositors, $10,000,000 to the holders of certified checks, $7,000,000 to the holders of cashiers' checks, $13,000,000 to the Government directly, and $4,000,000 in Government bonds, to say nothing of scores of hundreds of millions more through its affiliated institutions. And all this juggling is done in such a fearless manner that we find it in the Amalgamated deal loaning in one transaction an amount so great that if it had been lost, the bank's entire capital would have been more than completely wiped out. That my readers may not base their conclusions upon this one transaction of this mighty engine of the "System," vicious as it shows on the surface and destructive as it really was to the thousands who were parties to it, I will later in this story show the National City Bank in another section of the Amalgamated deal, doing things which in intention and in result were so much bolder and grosser that this transaction will by comparison appear pure and legitimate.

During the past thirty years the American people have become so used to enormous figures in connection with corporations and trusts that they have not stopped to discriminate between different classes of fortunes nor to figure out that fortunes of certain kinds are absolute self-evidence that they were acquired by illegal methods, and that if allowed to multiply the people will surely be enslaved and the republic destroyed. For instance, there are in New York City alone dozens of national and savings-banks and insurance and trust companies which control money enough to make them practically omnipotent in whatever direction their controllers exert their power. I will name but seven, showing what enormous amounts their managers control; and let it be borne in mind that all such institutions are linked together by the "System" as firmly and surely as any human things can be linked. The Equitable, Mutual, and New York Life Insurance companies have a combined capital of $1,200,000,000 of assets, a yearly income of $230,000,000, and $4,500,000,000 of insurance in force; the National City Bank, United States Trust, Mercantile Trust, and Union Trust companies $30,000,000 capital, and $45,000,000 surplus, and they have the vast sum of $450,000,000 of the people's money to juggle with.

CHAPTER VIII

"STANDARD OIL" INVESTS "MADE DOLLARS" IN GAS

And now I shall have to go back a bit in my story. After "Standard Oil" had firmly established, through the agency of the curb, the value of the 1,000,000 shares of Standard Oil, the corporation seller of oil, at between $600,000,000 and $800,000,000, and had used it as collateral in securing control of the four classes of money institutions I have named—the national and savings-banks and trust and insurance companies—it proceeded to use the funds thus controlled to manipulate the stocks of great public corporations for its own profit, forming them into trusts with capitals far beyond their values, represented by new stocks and bonds, which it sold to the public at prices aggregating a hundred to five hundred per cent. over the old capitalization. It then engaged in a wonderfully clever campaign to work off on the people—directly, the very rich people, but indirectly, the people as a whole—through institutions which exist because of the people's savings—the $600,000,000 to $800,000,000 of Standard Oil stock which had at this stage served the principal use for which it had been created. It must be borne in mind that while "Standard Oil" is grinding out "made dollars," its owners never for an instant lose sight of that dim, distant day of reckoning when the people will awaken to their losses. The "Rogerses" and the "Rockefellers" know well that the public cannot always be kept in ignorance of the methods of the "System" by which it has been plundered, and that once it is in possession of the secret of how the savings of the many have become the property of the few, there may be reprisals of such a nature as will compel the "System" to yield up its gains. They know that when that day comes it will not be best for them to have their enormous fortunes in such get-at-able property as real estate, in which so many of the legitimately acquired American fortunes are invested. In a quiet way, therefore, they have put the bulk of their "made dollars" into unrecorded forms, such as Government bonds; bonds and preferred stocks of what they consider non-duplicatable franchise corporations such as railroads, which require rights of way; into municipal public service enterprises, such as gas companies, the existence of which depends upon rights of way for pipes; and into the stocks of banks and trust and insurance companies, which they believe the people will never dare attack because their savings are largely deposited in them.

I would not have my readers think that the principal motive actuating "Standard Oil" in parting with its Standard Oil stock is doubt of its present intrinsic worth, for such is not the case. The masters of "Standard Oil" are very able, far-seeing men, and they know that so thoroughly have the

American people been educated to the crimes which created Standard Oil, the crimes by which it has existed and does exist, that no passage of time or "pious-ing" of latter-day methods, will ever blind them to its iniquities, and that when reprisal day comes, as come it surely will, the first thing the people in their frenzy will look for will be Standard Oil. This is the reason which, more than any other, influences them in selling to others an enterprise which has up to the present time not only enjoyed tremendous prosperity, but which has as yet met with no obstacle or hindrance.

Of all forms of tangible investment "Standard Oil" has looked most favorably upon gas stocks, and its secret devices have been worked overtime in consolidating gas companies throughout the United States. In a general way, as manufacturers of illuminating oil, "Standard Oil" had early become familiar with the problems of supplying large communities—cities—with gas light; and with the advent of water-gas, as sellers of petroleum they controlled an important factor in the production of that volatile commodity. All the talent of the "System," trained in "handling" municipal authorities, came into play in this big new business of lighting cities—a business which perforce became a monopoly as soon as the powerful tentacles grasping it were recognized as "Standard Oil."

At the time my story opens (1894) "Standard Oil" had already captured the gas-lighting corporations of certain of the great cities of the United States, including the immensely rich ones of New York (directly), Philadelphia and Chicago (indirectly); and for two years previously had been besieging the several independent Brooklyn companies for the purpose of consolidating them into a single gigantic corporation. This project it has since accomplished. Its intention is to weld this corporation with the great one that already holds the monopoly of Manhattan.

The task of diagramming a territory for invasion is one after Henry H. Rogers' own heart. His campaigns are planned with Napoleonic power and foresight. When the capture of Brooklyn was decided on, the several corporations to be subdued were "sized up" as to their revenues and liabilities; the resources of their stockholders were studied out, and a plan of action organized to separate each one from his shares at "hard-pan" prices. In the "Standard Oil" armory there are many instruments of "persuasion," and he is indeed a hardy fellow who can resist the various "trying-out" processes to which mutineers are subjected. This obstinate capitalist will be summarily knocked on the head; that other inveigled into a dark corner by a strong-arm man; another group owe money to one of the "System's" banks and a brief spell on the financial rack will weaken their grip. Sooner or later all succumb. While such details as these were being attended to, lines were being strung here and there to bring about the passage by the city of Brooklyn and the Legislature of New York State of ordinances and laws which should allow this and compel that to be done, and so rivet the various links of the great venture.

While in the midst of this campaign, to which Henry H. Rogers' genius, matured in many a hard-fought business battle, foresaw an early and easy triumphal termination, there came athwart his victorious path a financial guerilla, "balloony," mysterious, yet as sticky as a jelly-fish, who was destined to exert a most maleficent influence on his after-life. Fate hangs no red lights at the cross-roads of a man's career. No "pricking of his thumbs," no strange portents warned the Master of "Standard Oil" that the impudent Philadelphia swashbuckler who dared interfere with the execution of his plan to fetter the "System's" yoke to the necks of the citizens of Brooklyn was the factor that destiny had chosen to shape the ends that he had rough-hewn.

The financial guerilla was J. Edward O'Sullivan Addicks, votary of rotten finance, perpetual candidate for the United States Senate, wholesale debaucher of American citizenship and all-round corrupter of men—J. Edward O'Sullivan Addicks, a corporation political trickster, who has done more to hold up American laws, American elective franchises, and American corporations to the scorn of the civilized world than any other man of this or any previous age.

CHAPTER IX

A VOTARY OF THE "SYSTEM"

The "System" has all sorts of votaries. About J. Edward O'Sullivan Addicks there is nothing that remotely suggests coworkers of the types of Mr. Rogers and William Rockefeller. A description that left him in any part a duplicate of either would do him and them a grievous wrong. Henry H. Rogers and William Rockefeller have two sides, their social side and their business side. Socially, they are good men; in business they work evil. J. Edward O'Sullivan Addicks is a bad man, socially, in business, in every way. The term "bad man" is used advisedly. My idea of a "bad man" is that like a bad dollar he is a counterfeit. A counterfeit has all the appearances of reality, and is yet devoid of its properties and virtues. So with Addicks. It is easy to find men who will declare by all that is sacred that Henry H. Rogers is one of the best fellows in the world, though as many more will as earnestly proclaim him the fiend incarnate. About Addicks, among those who know the man, there is but one opinion. I have yet to meet the man, woman, or child who would say aught of Addicks, after a month's acquaintance, other than, "Don't mention him! He is the limit." And it will be said with the calm of dispassionate conviction, as one might speak of a stuffed tiger in a dime-museum jungle.

Here we have a man without a heart, without a soul, and, I believe, absolutely without conscience—the type of man who even his associates feel is likely to bring in after their deaths queer bills against their estates as an offset for what he owes them; the type of man whose promise is just as good as his bond, and whose bond is so near his promise as to make it absolutely immaterial to him which you take.

Exhibited in the side show of one of the great circuses some years ago was a strange creature which, for lack of a better name, its owner and the public dubbed, "A What Is It?" This freak had the semblance of humanity, and yet was not human. All its functions and feelings reversed the normal. Tickle it and it would cry bitterly; pinch or torture it and it would grin rapturously; when starved it repelled food, and when overfed it was ravenous for more. It had heart-beats but no heart. The public gave it up. The public would long ago have given up J. Edward O'Sullivan Addicks if he would have let them.

Illustration is better than explanation, and perhaps I can more graphically set J. Edward O'Sullivan Addicks before my readers by a few incidents which show his contradictory characteristics in action than by verbal diagrams, however laborious.

Once upon a time Addicks, entering Delmonico's for dinner, stumbled on a couple of newsboys at the entrance. One, broken-hearted, was being consoled by the other. Addicks, observing the deep sobs, asked: "What's the matter with you, bub?" The consoler explained that his chum had lost $2, his day's earnings and capital, and "His mudder—his fadder's dead—an' de baby'll git trun outter de tenement." Addicks, without more ado, slipped the suffering young news-merchant a bill which his friends supposed was $2 to replace the lost funds. As they were taking off their coats in the hall, however, the little newsboy pushed his way in with: "Say, boss, did yer mean ter guv me de twenty?" Addicks nodded a good-natured assent, and his friends registered silently a white mark to his score, and felt that, after all, somewhere beneath the surface he was more of the right sort than they had given him credit for being. After dinner, as they left, the newsboy again approached. "'Scuse me, boss, but me chum 'd like ter t'ank yer too. I'm goin' ter give him a V outter it." Addicks looked at the boy in his mildly cold way and said: "Let me have that bill. I will change it for you." The boy gave it up, and Addicks, after methodically placing it in his purse, handed him back a $2 bill with: "That's what you lost, isn't it? And you" (to the second little fellow, who by this time had mapped out visions of new duds for the kids and a warm seat in the gallery of a Bowery theatre), "you didn't lose anything, did you? Well, both of you run along now!"

His friends looked at each other, and from their slates wiped away the white mark and replaced it with a deep, broad, black one. And yet Addicks had made good the loss—done a good deed, but in an—Addicks way. I should perhaps remark that J. Edward O'Sullivan Addicks has never smoked, nor used a swear-word, nor taken liquor in any form.

During the Addicks gas campaign in Boston one of his lieutenants demanded as his share of the deal a large amount of money, which he claimed Addicks was withholding from him. Addicks refused to pay. Friends and associates urged him to settle. While yet refusing, he agreed to meet this man at one of the leading hotels in the presence of counsel and lieutenants. The interview was a hot one. Addicks surprised all by his absolute fearlessness in the face of a savage attack, which culminated in the production of a document signed by certain Massachusetts legislators, wherein they receipted for the bribe money Addicks had paid for their votes. The man who claimed he was being cheated threatened this would be laid before the Grand Jury the following day. All the witnesses were dumfounded at the situation and in concert begged Addicks to hush the matter up by paying what was claimed. "Gentlemen," said this great financier, "my honor, my business and my personal honor, has been assailed, and rather than submit to this outrage I would die! I now ask you all to bear witness that under no circumstances will I pay to this man a single dollar!" And he indignantly left the meeting.

While his counsel and associates were appalled at what might be the outcome, they admired Addicks' manly pluck, and asked themselves if they had not, after all, been mistaken in their estimates of his courage and principle. In the middle of the same night, the man with the document was surprised by a telegram reading: "Meet me in Jersey City to-morrow sure with paper; keep absolutely secret." Next day in Jersey they met, and Addicks simply said: "There is the full amount. Give me the paper. You don't suppose I would compound a felony in the State in which it was committed, and before witnesses, do you?"

In the national election of 1896 J. Edward O'Sullivan Addicks was a candidate for the United States Senate in Delaware, and for a variety of reasons was anxious to secure a Republican victory. Within the State, however, the real contest was not over national issues, but to obtain control of the Legislature which in the following January had to elect a United States Senator. There were three factions, the Democrats and two wings of the Republicans, the Addicks and anti-Addicks parties, the latter calling themselves "regulars." On Election Day Addicks used an even $100,000 buying votes, and that evening Delaware was safe for McKinley—both the "regulars" and the men whom Addicks' money bought having voted for a Republican President. But it was early bruited around that if the vote of Sussex County (there are three counties in Delaware—Newcastle, Kent, and Sussex) were allowed to stand as received, all Addicks' efforts to control the Legislature would have been fruitless and his "made dollars" expended for nothing. The ex-flour dealer of Philadelphia was not satisfied to accept the people's sacred verdict. He quickly called his lieutenants together, mapped out a campaign of almost reckless audacity and daring, and assigned his best men to its execution.

The ballot-boxes with their contents were in the sheriff's charge and stored under lock and key in the court-house. The sheriff was an Addicks tool. At midnight he turned over his charge to one of the would-be statesman's trustiest lieutenants, who, with the aid of a lantern and a slip of paper containing the directions, sorted over the legal ballots, threw some out, and put in new ones. When another sun arose the dastardly outrage upon the American elective franchise had been completed, and Addicks was busily scheming to carry out the remainder of the plot. On the declaration which he or one of his associates would make, that there had been fraud in Sussex County, the Government at Washington must send on an investigating committee to whom it would be asserted that the voting lists had been doctored by the Democrats. To prove it the boxes would be opened, the ballots counted, and lo! the villany of the Democrats would be, beyond contradiction, demonstrated.

But the scheme was an Addicks scheme. Had it been the plot of any other man with the brains, the nerve, and the lack of principle to concoct it and set it in motion, inevitably it would have been carried through to the designed conclusion. As it was, this is what happened: The lieutenant who had charge of the actual commission of the crime thoughtlessly chuckled over the details of it with another, and this other "in the presence of witnesses" laughingly congratulated Addicks on his plan's success. What was the astonishment of the group to hear the candidate for the Senate say: "Gentlemen, I could not countenance such a transaction. This is the first I have heard of it, and it is so outrageously criminal that I refuse to allow it to proceed further. There will be no investigation, and if it is a fact that those ballots have been changed in the box, the ones who changed them shall receive no benefit from their nefarious work. I have spoken."

Mind you, every member of the group was a party to the scheme and had been carefully rehearsed in the part assigned him by Addicks himself, but alone, that is, without witnesses; nevertheless so earnest and apparently honest was the man in his protest that for an instant they doubted their senses—until they remembered it was Addicks.

The investigation was never held, and to this day Addicks' lieutenants, especially he who did the midnight work and who still lives in the peaceful State of Delaware, turn with disgust when Addicks' daring is mentioned.

It should be explained here that, whenever Addicks plans an illegal transaction—one for which he might be made civilly or criminally liable—he invariably coaches each of his accomplices alone, "without witnesses." And when it becomes necessary in developing the plot to have a confab, at which the several parties to the proceeding must meet, Addicks is most careful to preserve a legal semblance of ignorance of incriminating details. At intervals, when a danger-place in the discussion is approaching, he will get up from his seat and, moving to the door, will say: "Gentlemen, halt right there, until I step out of the room; tap at the door when you are over that bad spot, and I will return."

Addicks' "Wait until I step out of the room" is as familiar among his coworkers as the "I am going upstairs" is among the "Standard Oil" family.

Try to conjure before your mind's eye a picture of the anomalous character these instances suggest. I'll warrant your mental image as little resembles the original Addicks as Mr. Hyde did Dr. Jekyll in the story. He does not look the part assigned him here, nor any other part for that matter. I saw him coming toward me on State Street one summer day some years ago, a tall, wiry man, in a white-flannel suit, perfect in fit and spotless as snow, wearing a fine Panama hat. This was in the period before Panamas were commonly worn. He was to the life the elegant and luxurious Southern planter of ante-bellum days. Six months afterward in about the same place I saw approaching me a splendid person in rich sable outer garments who looked for all the world like an exiled Russian grand duke. It was Addicks in winter. You will not surprise his secret from that pleasant, rather ambiguous, but square-jawed face, nor from the mouth hidden under a long, drooping, gray, military mustache. His is a good-sized, well-shaped head, you might say, and the gray, shallow eyes that look out at you are almost merry in their glances. But they are inscrutable eyes which seem to have a challenge in their gaze, a sort of "look-me-over-as-long-as-you-like-and-you'll-never-guess-what's-under-the-surface" expression that is baffling and provocative. Yet this sybarite, this daring coward, this stingy prodigal, this sincere hypocrite, this extraordinary blending of contradictory qualities, is the man who from 1887 to 1892 made Boston look like the proverbial country gawk at circus-time.

Power the man certainly has, and of a distinct quality, yet his intimates cannot explain the reason of their obedience to him. After a brief acquaintance he is revealed as the very soul of insincerity—he "works" his friends, he pays toll to his enemies, he frankly shows himself without the sense of moral obligation. I believe his talent resides in his capacity to select the proper type of man to "make rich" in the illicit schemes his abnormal mind conceives. These coworkers of his are of different grades; some have a super-abundance of cash; others a desire to get it—in common are their lack of principle and dearth of brains. Addicks cannot do business long with men of real ability, nor does he understand them, whereas he can read the minds of his ordained victims as if they were an open book. The big men who have encountered or been associated with Addicks are prone to characterize him as a mountebank, a joker, or a chump.

CHAPTER X

ADDICKS COMES TO BOSTON

J. Edward O'Sullivan Addicks was born in Philadelphia in 1841, and was in the eighties plodding along the ordinary, uneventful path of a seller of flour to the people of that city which since the death of William Penn holds the record for the highest and densest percentage of sleep per capita of any English-speaking community.

In the eighties two things happened that changed the whole course of J. Edward O'Sullivan Addicks' life. Some one invented water-gas and "let in" Addicks on the invention; and the Philadelphia branch of the "Standard Oil," represented by Widener, Elkins, and Dolan, "trustified" the gas companies of the city of Chicago, which enabled Addicks to "hold up" the "trustification" until Dolan and Dolan's associates paid him the sum of $300,000 for the instrument with which he had done the holding up, $10,000 worth of the stock of one of the necessary Chicago companies.

The law of compensation, which gets in its deadly work on all the prettiest plans of man, but decreed that what goes up must come down when it ceases going up. It has a shrewd trick of grafting sorrows on our joys, and of handicapping success with discomfiting conditions. The favorite of fortune whose feet have fallen in pleasant places sooner or later stubs his toe.

Addicks' first "made dollars" certainly came easy—so easy, indeed, that those who watched his early career marvelled at his success; but nowhere on God's footstool is there to-day a more terrible illustration of the inevitable workings of the law of compensation than the present standing of J. Edward O'Sullivan Addicks affords.

The thief whose first excursion into a wayfarer's pocket is rewarded with the equivalent of days and nights of honest labor will surely be convinced thereafter of the superiority of theft over toil as a means of money-getting. Invariably the manufacturer of "made dollars," after his first coup, forsakes forever after the cold arithmetic of commerce for the rule of guess, dream, hope, and "I will," which constitutes the mathematics of high finance. Addicks' first "made dollars" came with such magical ease that there awoke in his slumbering substitute for a soul a disgust for those prosaic pursuits at which one could never, try how one might, make more than four by the addition of two and two. He probably argued to himself: "Why should I work in the flour business when I know a way of getting overnight more than I can make out of flour in a lifetime? If people are so simple in guarding their savings that I can by a trick take away from them enormous wealth without the slightest danger to my own safety or my profit, even if detected, why should I not devote my life to such healthful and profitable occupation?" The logic of the proposition was convincing. Accepting its conclusions, J. Edward O'Sullivan Addicks, of Philadelphia, embarked on his career. Soon afterward he discovered gas in Boston.

This was in 1887. Equipped with his "made dollars" for capital, his impressive name, sublime effrontery, and a pedigree free from anything suggestive of his new purpose in life, the ex-flour merchant "lit" into our everything-figured-out-ahead-and-every-promise-made-taken-at-par town of Boston. To appreciate the lights and shadows of this event, one should know Boston and, at the same time, Addicks. Every country boy will remember Tom Hood's poem beginning:

I remember, I remember the house where I was born,With the little lattice window where the sun came peeping in at morn,

and can recall milking-time in July or August when, sitting on the rail-fence surrounding the barn-yard, he watched the pigeons snipping up grain, the old hen scratching up worms for the chicks, the ducks and the drakes and the geese and the ganders proudly waddling back and forth, among and around the fluffy ducklings and goslings, and the bull-pup sound asleep by the side of the tortoise-shell cat. Probably he will think of some particular milking-time when the calm, contented serenity of the barn-yard was suddenly disturbed by the unexpected descent in its midst of a neighboring peacock, who, apparently unconscious of the consternation produced by his entry, proceeded proudly to spread his dazzling plumage to convince every one, from Uncle Cy, on the milking-stool, and mild-eyed Bess, down to the white fan-tailed dove, that he was— It.

Conjure up the picture—the peacock at milking-time in the farm-yard; thus Addicks came to Boston—though it is far from my intention to identify the bucolic background I have drawn with the Hub of the Universe.

Boston, up to this time, had been singularly free from the mushroom variety of millionaire which had sprung up overnight in such numbers in New York and Philadelphia. Proudly defiant of a product so alien to all her traditions, her citizens would have sworn that no votary of modern high finance could exist over one curfew-toll within her gates. For Boston had her own financial eminence, of a character in keeping with the chill conditions of conservatism and rectitude appropriate to the metropolis of the New England conscience. She had her Stock Exchange, her numerous great corporations, her scores of single and multimillionaires, and it was her boast that her capital had played the greatest legitimate part in the country's growth. She had furnished a large percentage of the money which had created our vast Western railway system; she had found and made the superb copper-mines of Michigan and Montana, and in all parts of the land branches of her sturdy institutions were vitally assisting the miracle of America's development. Notwithstanding what these wide-flung enterprises imply of commercial push and audacity, Boston, at the time Addicks discovered gas there, was one of the most trusting wealth-investing communities in the world. She had her simple rules of business conduct which years of usage had consecrated into all-powerful precedent, but her brokers and capitalists, however fearful of all things quick or tricky, had never previously figured as candidates for what in Western parlance are described as "come-ons."

CHAPTER XI

HOW ADDICKS CAPTURED BOSTON GAS

At the time Addicks "lit" in Boston that city numbered among her proudest possessions several extremely rich gas companies, and they were owned by her "best people." To do business with Boston's "best people" is no easy task, and up to the advent of Addicks, to do business with her "best people" without doing it through others of her "best people" who could absolutely vouch for you was an unheard-of thing. The manner in which the ex-flour merchant of Philadelphia managed to slip by the barriers and into the heart of our blue-blooded citadel affords the most unparalleled example of audacity of which I know.

In many ways Boston is unlike other great American cities. Some of her institutions through antiquity or association have acquired a positive sanctity. Pedigree is important. The average inhabitant spends much of his time watching the grandson of his neighbor's father, to see the old man's characteristics crop out in him. The boy's failures will be remembered against his own offspring fifty years hence. It is a city of long memories and of traditions. In 1887 Boston, as now, consisted largely of her traditions, her blue-glass window-panes and her Somerset Club.

Now the distinction, sanctity, and antiquity of the Somerset Club are quite beyond peradventure. Since Boston has been Boston she has had her Somerset Club, a club distinctively of grandfathers, fathers, and sons. The right to membership in the Somerset Club is as much the inheritance of a Somerset man's son as his name or as the proud title which always will be found affixed to his signature when he reaches man's estate, "of Boston." For a man to get into the Somerset without long years of waiting and intense scrutiny, not only of his own record but of his parents' before him, is a rare event. Yet the name of J. Edward O'Sullivan Addicks was up for full membership, with Boston's picked best for his sponsors, a few days after he "lit." How Addicks got upon the Somerset list Boston will never tell, and the mention of the fact nowadays within the club-house will empty its sideboard instanter.

The campaign of arrangement for the advent of Addicks in Boston was more elaborate, more astute and expensive than was ever organized for exploitation of prima donna or great pianist. For months an advance agent had been preparing the way for his chief's arrival in a blaze of glory. There was talk in the papers and among the financiers about the wonderful water-gas process which enormously enhanced the profits of gas-making, and such rumor was always linked with the name of the brilliant

Philadelphia Gas King, for so the press had already dubbed him. A wonder and magic immensely provocative of curiosity were woven about the identity of this J. Edward O'Sullivan Addicks, who it was said might be persuaded to visit Boston to work marvels with the stocks that had been "in the family" long before the present generation could remember. When it was sure that the great man was really coming the agent sought the advice of Boston's best in selecting quarters for him. In the Tudor, a beautiful family hotel adjoining the Somerset Club on Beacon Hill, a magnificent suite of apartments was taken, and though the great man could remain in Boston but a brief space, the furniture, the hangings, and even the carpets were all changed for him.

Eminent financial tricksters have various ways of handling their victims. Some believe that the most skilful mode of attack is the slow, confident, dignified approach which allays the subject's fears by its solemn display of deliberation. Others (and Addicks is of this creed) are persuaded of the superior efficacy of the "rush-in-and-drag-out" method. The subject, they say, "gives up" more and quicker when the hurry call is sounded. It was a winter's day when Addicks "lit" in Boston, and circumstances had arisen, the suave advance agent told various Boston's best, with whom he was in consultation, that would make his chief's stay much briefer than either had anticipated. So when the great man arrived at the club just before dinner, quite an array of important people were congregated there.

Addicks ran the gantlet of the critical glances of as critical a group as you'll find on earth, and the word went round—no one could remember afterward who started it—"Typical Southern gentleman! Breeding sticking out everywhere!" So well had the astute advance agent done his work that a little dinner was arranged on the spot, and Addicks made such rapid progress with these reserved and conservative Bostonians that, by the time coffee was served, conversation had reached the stage where it was natural for him to send the waiter to the coat-room for his bunch of gas papers. The emissary returned bringing the fur overcoat with which Addicks always envelops himself in chilly weather. Addicks searched the pockets, and, apparently to his surprise, discovered that they did not contain the required documents, but where they should have been he found a small bale of 1,000-dollar government bonds, containing, one of the party said afterward, at least one hundred certificates. "How careless of my secretary!" said Addicks, nonchalantly replacing the packet in the pocket and motioning the waiter to take the overcoat away again.

It was, of course, due to the admirable work of his advance agent that these Monte Cristo effects impressed the cultured little set who would have laughed to scorn such a display on the part of one of their own kind. In Addicks it was the dazzling eccentricity of the wonder-worker, and so excusable; and the free, flash, careless exhibit of wealth made the man's conversation and subsequent demands seem natural. Next morning, in discussing the work of the previous evening with his lieutenant, Addicks delivered himself of the wise remark: "Finance, my boy, like theatricals, is dependent for success on the staging, more even than on the actor. My experience has shown me that men the world over are alike—if you properly surround them, they will hiss at hissing time and clap at applauding time; yes, upon the way you stage your finance plays depends their success." The fact is that by no other method could this scenic artist of finance have set his plans moving so rapidly. The man had calculated to a nicety on the romantic cupidity he aroused.

After dinner, Addicks at once "got down to business": "Gentlemen, my project is as simple as it is feasible and conservative, for I will touch nothing but conservative enterprises. Gentlemen, you have three great gas companies supplying this great city with light, the Boston, Roxbury, and South Boston. They are worth at the present time about five million dollars. I am going to buy them and spend three or four millions more on a new company; then I shall consolidate the four and turn them from coal into water-gas companies, which will sell gas to your people at less than they now pay, and at the same time make a lot of money for you and for myself. What do you say?"

This was certainly quick action. Boston's best was breathless for a minute. Then some one suggested that in so weighty a matter it would be necessary for solicitors to investigate, for the families owning the stock to be consulted and agree before a proper basis could be arrived at on which to dispose of their holdings.

Addicks' genius was equal to the occasion. "I regret, gentlemen, any seeming haste, but this is the situation: I am going to invest fifteen or twenty millions, or perhaps thirty or forty, in city gas properties, and as the project will require quite a bit of financiering, I have got to round it up at once, in time to slip over to London to lay it before my associates, , , and " (naming some of the great English lords of finance), "with whom you, gentlemen, are probably well acquainted. I think you will, after you have given the matter a little thought, agree with me that it would be a mistake to postpone the conversion of these magnificent Boston plants to the water-gas system until after other cities I have in mind are reconstructed. You see we can turn over but one city at a time, the system being new and competent engineers and builders few."

The painful thought took shape in the minds of the distinguished little gathering that if they were not careful, Monte Cristo might actually slip out of their town without working any of the promised golden marvels.

"Just what is your idea, Mr. Addicks, of how this gigantic piece of business could be done?" one asked.

"Simple, simple"—the great Colonel Sellers of eye-water fame never looked more cool and unconcerned when calling attention to the facts, "100,000,000 of people, two eyes each, a bottle of my patent eye-wash for each at a dollar a bottle, and eye-wash made at a net cost of a dime a barrel"—"simple, simple; you name your price, I pay it, and the thing is done."

Some one pointed out that the gas properties were valued very high. That in the Boston, for instance, the par value of each share was $500—and that it was improbable Mr. Addicks could buy it for less than—than eight hundred.

"Of course, of course; I am not buying gas companies that are not well thought of by their present owners," returned Addicks. "I think you underestimate the value of the Boston Company's stock when you say $800. Naturally, as a conservative business man I wish to buy as reasonably as possible, but as I know what the future of your company will be under the water-gas change, I consider $1,000 a share cheap; and if you say so, will take it now—majority, minority and all—at that price."

This was strong talk. In spite of their proverbial frigidness under all conditions, Boston's best began to get fidgety.

"Indeed," went on the Monte Cristo from Philadelphia, "I'll do better than that. On second thought I will give you $1,200 a share. Think it over and we'll have another sit-down to-morrow."

It took Addicks but a few days to trade, for at each sitting the staging was more enticing and the call from his associates in London more insistent. Minor difficulties were magnificently waved away. A number of scions of Boston's best families had good paying positions in the different companies; what would Mr. Addicks do with them?

"Simple, simple," he replied; "double the time of contract and the salary; no favor to them or you; good men are very hard to get, you know."

One episode that occurred about this time was allowed to get into print when the stocks and bonds were being floated, by way of showing what a tremendous fellow Addicks was. In a hired hack he had driven up to the club from State Street. A snow-storm was raging. After Addicks had been in the club a few moments word was brought in to him that the driver had found his sable overcoat inside the carriage. Addicks stepped into the vestibule to speak to the driver, and next day it was all over the club-house and through the "Street" that the prodigal Philadelphian, overcome at the thought of the unfortunate driver in his scanty clothing exposed to the cruel storm, had said: "My good man, take that coat as a present from me."

For the truth of the story I do not vouch, nor for that other which explains that the door-boy who spread this tale of generosity said afterward, when discharged, that Addicks himself had told him what he had done, and at the same time had given him a five-dollar bill. He would have sworn the moment before that he heard Addicks tell the driver to take the coat to his apartments.

Addicks got what he came to Boston for—the Boston, Roxbury, and South Boston Gas companies. He did what he said he would, built a new one, the Bay State of Massachusetts, and turned them all into the Bay State of Delaware, and the Bay State of Delaware turned them out on the public in exchange for their savings to the extent of $19,000,000 in the form of bonds and stock. Addicks, to use his own language, "cleaned up around $7,000,000," and turned to new fields, fields suited to his peculiar genius.

As he looked over the United States he found but one great city which had not already been captured by "Standard Oil" or some of its disciples—Brooklyn, N. Y. To the present day Rogers swears Addicks' only reason for coming to Brooklyn was to hold up the "Standard Oil" "trustification." Addicks retorts with: "I saw it first." Whatever the facts, in 1892 Rogers in the midst of tagging the different companies was surprised and angered to find that Addicks had slipped in ahead and had secured one of those necessary to the success of his plan. He quickly served notice on the man from Delaware to "git," and Addicks, flushed with an unbroken chain of victories, as promptly returned the notice with, scrawled across its face, a variation of Rogers' pet phrase—for it must be remembered Addicks never "cusses"—"I'll see you in heaven first."

If there is any one time when Henry H. Rogers is quicker of action than any other, it is when his notice to "git" in a stock deal has been returned with "sass."

The ink was hardly dry on Addicks' answer before the Master of "Standard Oil" and his hosts were upon him, but not where the Philadelphian looked for them. While he awaited their attack in Brooklyn, N. Y., he received a series of hurry-up calls from his lieutenants in Boston. Rogers had bought the insignificant Brookline Gas Company, which supplied gas to one of the suburbs of Boston. It was only a $300,000 affair, but it possessed charter rights to come into any and all of the streets of Boston. This was a characteristic "Standard Oil" attack. It came out of a clear sky, and before the public had even a warning of it they were witnessing a war which looked as though it had been years in maturing. Rogers let it become public knowledge that the entire "Standard Oil" forces were to be brought to bear to crush Addicks and that untold millions would, if necessary, be spent in the effort. In reality he had most carefully mapped out a cyclonic campaign which he believed would not call for an expenditure of over $500,000, and which he was sure would in a few months drive Addicks out of Brooklyn, N. Y., and bring him to his knees in Boston. His fight began in earnest in 1894. Gas in Boston was $1.25 per thousand cubic feet, and the rate yielded a good profit to the Addicks companies. Rogers served notice that he would parallel with the Brookline Company every pipe of the different Boston companies and would reduce the price of gas to $1. Simultaneously he attacked the Addicks stocks and bonds in the market, his charters in the Legislature, and took away from him the contracts to supply the municipality of Boston with gas. For a time Addicks struck back savagely. Then, as the fight became hotter, he gave it up in Brooklyn, and concentrated all his resources on repelling the savage inroads Rogers was making in Boston. By this time the contest had grown to such proportions and so much bad blood had been engendered that Rogers declined to be mollified by Addicks' surrender in Brooklyn and refused to retire from Boston unless Addicks repaid "Standard Oil's" entire outlay and got down on his knees in public—a demand that called forth one of Addicks' sardonic smiles.

Addicks had at this time additional difficulties to face. He had spread out his financial commitments, and now he found his stocks and bonds all declining. It was obvious to State and Wall streets that Rogers was in a fair way to drive the buccaneer from Philadelphia to the wall.

It is at this stage that I come into the story.

CHAPTER XII

STOCK-BROKERS NOT ALL BAD

Right here, before plunging deeper into the current of events which led to the organization of Amalgamated—for what has gone before is only that which I deem necessary setting for the story, necessary in order that my readers may clearly take in its meaning—it is only fair to them and to myself for me to say that my life has been spent in the stock-market for the purpose of gain. I have never in my stock operations set myself up for a philanthropist nor in any way posed as a reformer, nor pretended to be a bit better than the business I had chosen for a livelihood. From the first day until now I have endeavored to keep strictly to the principle that I would never knowingly deceive any man, woman, or child who, out of confidence in me, risked their money in speculation or investment. At the same time it should be remembered that the stock-brokerage business often makes queer bedfellows. Moreover, the true stock-operator is sometimes tempted to buckle on his armor and get into an exciting fight solely for the combat's sake, and then he may not be over-concerned about the rights and wrongs of the contention, if upon both sides are lined up professional captains of finance. The minister, the college professor, the dry-goods merchant, may exclaim against this, but they have never known the delicious tingle which, since the abolition of the tournaments of old, can be felt only on the great financial battlefields. If the critics of the stock-gambler could be put through a single minute of a thousand I have known they would be less brash in their denunciations. And let it be remembered that in these terrific dollar-wars there is as much opportunity for heroism, for generosity, for kindly deeds, as ever physical fighting affords. I read here in the papers of the noble act of a captain in the navy who has taken his life in his hands; in another place of a rich man who has given a million to create a charity. On the same page that these men are eulogized I will find references to "Jim Keene, the stock-gambler," etc., "heartless, soulless stock-sharp," etc. "Jim Keene, Stock-gambler," keeps no press agent to flaunt his kindly acts, but from the noble things I know he has done, and the things others with whom I am personally acquainted know he has done—men, women, and children saved from misery, pain, and death, at the risk of ruin to himself—I'll warrant the celestial scroll shows to his record as many deeds of mercy and noble daring as are credited to any soldier or philanthropist who has achieved worldly fame in recent years.

The desire for sudden wealth is strong in all parts of our American community. Men want money, and women too, for a score of reasons—some good, some bad—and the stock-market is the magical place where miracles occur and dollars multiply themselves overnight. The agent for all the cupidity of the world is the stock-broker, and he sees life from a strange angle.

Hundreds of letters come to me daily from all kinds of people, who have no other call upon me than their belief that, having at some previous time profitably followed my advice or advice credited to me, they have a right, when "the papers say" I am doing or going to do this, that, or the other thing in stocks, to come to me with their troubles. In 1899 there reached me from a woman a picture of her husband, herself, her three children, and the aged father and mother of her husband. I wish I might print it, but I dare not through fear that they would be recognized. The letter accompanying it was one of the most touchingly pathetic I have ever read. I investigated the case. The statements made were absolutely true. The woman's husband was the cashier of one of the small national banks in one of the old towns in a New England State. His father's brother had been cashier before him. The family's past was thickly strewn with all those simple honors and good things which are so often the heritage of families of the old, self-respecting, God-fearing, middle-class communities of New England and like long-settled sections of the country. On his death-bed the uncle confessed that for years he had carried upon the books of the bank a shortage which had arisen from mistakes. Her husband, to keep the family's name from stain, had continued to keep this buried, which was an easy thing to do, as when he was moved up from teller to cashier at his uncle's death the two positions were combined into one. The wife explained that her husband had let her into the fearful secret, and together they had carried it until it had eaten its way into their hearts. At last the man could no longer stand the strain. He had followed my printed sayings about the market, and now had made the fatal plunge. He had bought upon margin 2,000 shares of Sugar stock to see if it were not possible to make up quickly a shortage of over $20,000, because I had said Sugar was going right up; and then horror of worse than death had seized the wife and she had given me the awful secret, and a description, a word picture of what would happen if I had made a mistake.

She could go no further. She did not need to. I read the letter. I saw the picture, and even I, who believed myself from long years of experience with such affairs immune—I, too, became horror-stricken. It was no affair of mine. I had not said Sugar was going up; as is often the case, some newspaper had printed what another operator had said and credited it to me. I was not even operating in Sugar, nor at the time particularly interested in it. I could not return the letter nor have any communication with these persons without in a way becoming their accomplice. The woman had said that with the purchase her husband had given orders to sell the stocks at twelve points' rise.

Try as I might to look at the matter in a cold-blooded business way the picture haunted me—the old gentleman proud of his family's long record of sturdy honesty, the old mother's faith in her boy, the wife seeing on each of her children the brand of a felon father, and the husband watching each day's market prices to see whether they had brought him a verdict which meant State's prison or permanent relief from the haunting fear which had become his never-absent shadow; and I read and reread the closing lines of the faithful wife: "Mr. Lawson, you will put Sugar up?—you surely will, just this once—and we will teach the children to pray for you and yours, and God answers this kind of prayers, you know He does."

The picture haunted me; I saw it in the market prices; I heard the story in each tick of the ticker and each rustle of the tape; and every time my eye caught "SUG," the stock-exchange abbreviation for Sugar, I winced, as one does at the dentist's probe—well, I could not stand it. I determined to put up Sugar—that is, I determined to try. Little the woman knew what she asked when she wrote: "You will put up Sugar?" She had read that a stock operator works magic, but it had never entered her head that his wand was a stick of dynamite a thousand times concentrated—a stick of dynamite that the law of stock-market averages shows goes off in his hand nine out of every ten times it is handled, and that when it goes off there is nothing more for the handler but the minister, the flowers, and the head-stone; indeed, often the explosion leaves nothing with which to buy even a head-stone! Little she thought that it might strain the wealth of the Bank of England to move Sugar up twelve points. I moved it up, and it went so easy—oh, so easy! that—well, I will let the first description I pick from my scrap-book from among a hundred from the daily press tell the story:

[From the Boston Journal, March 17, 1899

LAWSON'S LUMP

HIS COFFEE SWEETENED WITH QUARTER OF A MILLION—MADE IT IN SUGAR THURSDAY IN TWO HOURS' TRADING

A quarter of a million in a day!

That was Thomas W. Lawson's record for March 16, 1899.

The celebrated "Unthroned King of State Street" was on top of the Sugar market; that is the reason of it all.

Sugar was the big card of stock speculation yesterday.

Indeed, the stock had one of the wildest days in its history, and its high price—$170—reached amid great excitement—is the highest on record. The speculation was something tremendous, and it has been through the speculation that the people who have been under the impression that the markets were drifting into a dull and uninteresting condition have had a sudden awakening.

From the opening it quickly advanced to 149, receded a point or more, and shortly after noon started sharply upward. The demand for it came so rapidly that the tape could not keep up with it, and the excitement grew as the demand increased. The scenes on the floors of both the New York and local boards were most exciting. Blocks of 500 and 1,000 shares changed hands frequently, and at one time the quotation in the Boston market was fully four points behind that of the New York list. The small army of shorts scrambled to get covered up, and everybody was in a fever of wild excitement over the marvellous movement. Before it had culminated the price reached 170, or a gain of twenty-nine points over the opening—the most remarkable display of strength in so short a period of time that this remarkable stock has ever shown.

Broker Lawson did the buying, and while the excitement was running high he bought freely. He had taken 20,000 shares all told before the advance had fairly gotten under way at from 143-1/2 to 144. At 170 he gave an order to sell 20,000 shares at a limit of 155, and obtained an average of over 160, thereby netting an estimated snug profit of $250,000 or more within two hours. Asked as to whether the strength in Sugar meant a settlement of the Sugar war, Mr. Lawson smiled and said: "There has never been any Sugar war."

The conservative people on the Street are disposed to regard the whole movement as a piece of clever manipulation.

[From the Boston Herald, March 16, 1899

Mr. Thomas W. Lawson was the mover in the deal, and his orders for 20,000 shares early in the day excited other buying, which encompassed the astonishing rise. What point Mr. Lawson had to trade upon is his own asset, if he had any point, and it would not matter so far as the event was concerned whether he had a point. The market was in a position to respond to orders of these dimensions, and it did respond.

[From the New York Journal, March 17, 1899

The frenzied brokers fought like madmen around the Sugar post. The wildest sort of excitement prevailed throughout the day. The rest of the floor was practically abandoned, and brokers crowded, pushed, elbowed, and yelled frantically in their efforts to fill orders. There was no warning. The sudden jump of the stock almost threw the brokers into a panic. Men became ferocious in their efforts to fill orders. Those on the outside made wild rushes to get into the whirlpool. Men who are generally calm fell over each other in their excitement. Scores of arms whipped the air, and men yelled themselves hoarse. So great was the din and so compact the yelling crowd that those on one side of the post did not know the bidding on the other. At one point Sugar was going at 159, and five feet away it was bringing 164. While almost at arm's-length farther away it was going at 160, and farther around the post at 162.

The excitement became general among the offices of stock-brokers as the news flew on the ticker. Members of firms who were not on the floor gathered about the tickers in excited groups and watched the pyrotechnic fluctuations of Sugar to the exclusion of all other stocks. The quotations came out at two and three points apart. One minute the stock was away up, and the next it seemed to fall hopelessly. Then it would as suddenly soar upward again. It reached 170, and in five minutes it was down to 152.

[From the Boston Post, March 22, 1899

Late in the afternoon Mr. Lawson was induced to give the following explanation of his movements in Sugar: "You know it is not conducive to the health of an active operator to talk on what he is doing, for if he expects to retain his hirsute adornment he must either keep jumping so lively that none of the expert scalpers who haunt the jungles of Wall Street can find him long enough in one spot to cut the floor from under him, or he must envelop himself in mystery so dense that all seeking for him will grow color-blind; but on this particular commodity—Sugar—I can depart from the standard formula.

"I have been twenty-nine years dodging the scalping-knives of Wall Street Comanches, and, although I am still here, I have many places on my head where the hair refuses to grow, and, strange to tell, almost all the bare spots are labelled 'Sugar.' I suppose that I have, during the past ten years, contributed money enough to Sugar to endow a fair-sized asylum for tailless bears. It has never seemed to matter whether I bought or sold, went long or short, the dollars which I secured by the employment of pick and shovel, brawn, muscle or gray matter, all seemed to follow one another into the relentless maw of that modern Saccharine Titanotherium.

"Way back in 1890 I invested the profits of my Lamson deal—$700,000—in 10,000 Sugar at 84, and in a few days, amid brilliant fireworks, I bade it adieu, when it gracefully dropped below 50. Again, four years ago, I decided I could make no better long-time investment of $700,000 or $800,000 Electric profits than to short Sugar from 61 to 70. In eleven days it took $1,500 more than my profits to even up my accounts.

"Thinking these things over of late, I determined to make a final demand on astute and relentless Wall Street for my accumulated deposits—a kind of please-give-me-back-my-losses demand. I carefully loaded up two weeks ago to the extent of 20,000 Sugar in the thirties, and feeling the atmosphere was redolent of opportunities, last Friday I bought 20,000 more, the last 5,000 of which in a rather open and frank way that seemed but fair to my scalping New York friends. Well, you know the rest. It took fire. I cleaned up something over $700,000, and put out a short line of 30,000 shares, the last of which I have covered to-day at something over $350,000 profit. Strange as it may seem, I was quit. I have struck a balance with Sugar, and it gets no more of my money.

"I am one of the few Bostonians who are contented to live in the knowledge that Wall Street is too big and bright and cute a metropolitan centre for country boys to monkey with, and you can say I am so tickled to get back my bait that I will never again, never, wander away from home. There is one moral that may be drawn by Wall and State streets from the last few days in Sugar. It is this: It is not necessary to-day, any more than it was in old days, to work deals with false stories or fakes. In doing what I did in Sugar I depended on no fakes nor stories. I simply followed Charley Osborne's old admonition: 'If you want to bull stocks, buy 'em. If you want to bear 'em, sell 'em.' I bought 'em and I sold 'em. These are Sugar facts as far as my movements have affected them!"

For years after, even up to to-day, this yarn turned up in the press in different parts of the world, and every time I read it I chuckled to myself, for I see a big manly fellow, president of a bank now and asking no odds of any, for he can buy 2,000 shares of Sugar at any time and draw his check to pay for it against a bank account honestly earned since the day his wife wrote that letter.

And I see a grateful mother teaching three youths to say a certain prayer, and then I forget the critics' scathing sermons against stock gamblers. It does not pain me when my own children ask, "Why do they say such awful things about the stock operator?" I answer: "Oh, they mean no harm; they don't know the stock gambler they write about."

ONE OF THE SYSTEM'S SHADOWS

That my readers may not drop this chapter with a false idea of the results of the stock-broker's efforts to "live and let live," I will give them an illustration of one of the counterbalances of the law of compensations.

In the same year with the Sugar transaction, in an evil moment my mail brought me the following letter:

Dear Sir: I have read with interest your proclamations about "Coppers." I am not a rich man, but I have about $20,000 lying idle which I should like to add to, and will put it into anything you advise.

The writer received the following answer from my secretary:

Mr. Lawson instructs me to say he received your letter of and he knows no better investment than the stock of the Amalgamated Copper Company, which will be offered for public subscription next week. In the advertising which will accompany the offer you will note that it is to pay 8 per cent., is now earning 16, and should sell at $150 or $200 per share. It will be offered at par. Not only does Mr. Lawson personally believe in every word in the advertisements, but they are vouched for by such men and institutions as the National City Bank of New York, Henry H. Rogers, William Rockefeller and others, whose names are synonymous with success in business affairs. Mr. Lawson does not hesitate to advise you to invest your $20,000 in this stock, provided you are not looking for an investment that is absolutely safe, that is, one that should not, in these times, pay you over 3-3/4 or 4 per cent.; but if you are looking for a semi-speculative investment, that is, one that will pay you over 6 per cent., and where the chances are good for large profits, he recommends this stock.

Later I received the following:

Upon your advice I purchased 200 shares of the Amalgamated stock at $100 per share. When the stock dropped to 80, remembering your strong advice I purchased 300 shares more, and after it had advanced to 120, thinking it was surely going to the 150 or 200 you mentioned, I bought 1,000, putting up my 500 shares as margin. It has now dropped back to 100, and the many stories I read in the papers are causing me much anxiety. Do you still believe as you first wrote me?

To which he received the following answer:

Mr. Lawson instructs me to say he received yours of . His faith in the Amalgamated property, the men who control and manage it, and the stock is the same as it always has been. He, like yourself, added to his holdings at 120, and as high as 129, and knowing what he does about the property, and what the men who control and manage it, and with whom he is intimately associated, say to him, he cannot believe the yarns which are appearing in the press are other than the vaporings of those stock-market critics who must write their opinions of prominent stocks even though they have no means of actually knowing anything about them.

While Mr. Lawson regrets that you have spread yourself out, as you say in your letter, he can only answer your question by the above, to wit, his faith in Amalgamated is the same as from the beginning.

Later I received the following from one of the penal institutions of the country:

You will observe by the postmark on this letter my present place of residence. You probably knew that before, as the press has had much to say about me of late.

I trust you and your associates are satisfied with yourselves when you observe the hell you have caused others. When I first wrote you about the Amalgamated stock I was an honest, prosperous man. I had never committed a crime nor done any great wrong to my fellow-beings. Relying upon what you said publicly and the well-known record of the Rockefellers and their partners, I committed acts which I now know to my everlasting sorrow I should not have committed. I had no intention of doing wrong, but when I saw ruin staring me in the face I used, as I supposed only temporarily, funds intrusted to me to protect my stocks from being slaughtered at declining prices by the sharks of brokers whom I dealt with. The rest is the old story. My wife and children are disgraced and oppressed with poverty, and I am serving a five years' sentence in this institution, buoyed up only with the hope that I may live to face you and your kind, that you may have the pleasure of seeing the wreck you have wrought—in the hope that I may satisfy a desire which night and day gnaws at my very soul, a desire to say to you, face to face: "Look upon a man who, although a branded criminal, is as much better than you and your associates as it is possible for one to be," and to ask you how your wife and your children enjoy the luxuries they have when they know at what price they were secured, for I shall surely, if I live, insist upon your wife and children hearing from my lips what agonies a wife and children, who are as dear to me as yours are to you, have suffered because of your baseness.

CHAPTER XIII

THE "SYSTEM" VERSUS WESTINGHOUSE

In 1894 I had just wound up one of the most strenuous and successful financial campaigns I ever engaged in. This was the Westinghouse deal, of which the papers were full at the time. George Westinghouse, to whom the world owes the air-brake and countless improvements in electrical machinery, having surmounted the difficulties that clog the early steps of the inventor who would be his own master, had taken rank, some years before, among the prominent public figures of the day. The various corporations in America bearing his name had prospered amazingly; his ingenious appliances had displaced home products in the European market; and titles and decorations had been conferred on the inventor, though these last, like the sturdy American he is, Westinghouse had put aside.

This great success was wholly the fruit of George Westinghouse's personal endeavor. It owed nothing to extraneous influences. It had been accomplished along those manly, independent, Yankee lines which have made that name synonymous with hustle and success in every part of the civilized world. Above all, the man had organized and developed his companies without the aid of the "System" or without truckling to its votaries. In consequence he had incurred the deadly hatred of some of its lords paramount.

In the business world Westinghouse's great rival was the General Electric Company. To mention "Westinghouse" and "General Electric" in the same breath was to speak of a thing and its antithesis. Everything George Westinghouse was or had been the General Electric was not and had never been. The General Electric had been and was by leave of the "System"; in fact, was one of the very foremost examples of its methods. Its high-priest was J. Pierpont Morgan; its home, Wall Street; its owners, the principal votaries of the "System." It had grown because of their favor and by means of the rankest exhibitions of knock-down-and-drag-out methods of consolidation of all competitors but—Westinghouse.

Just previous to 1894 Westinghouse had rejected a dazzling scheme of uniting the two institutions on an immense capitalization which would have absorbed millions and millions of the people's savings and earned millions in commissions for its projectors. Wall Street's indignation at his hardihood knew no bounds, and at the time of which I write the yegg-men of the "System" were laying for him with dark-lantern and sand-bag.

To appreciate the story of what the "System" tried to do to George Westinghouse and what he withstood, one must know the man. He embodies in many ways the conception of what the ideal American should be. His remarkable six feet and odd of physique and his fertile, powerful brain are the admiration of all true men with whom he comes in contact. In spite of his unparalleled success and the accumulation of a great fortune, he retains the same simplicity of manner and conduct that characterized him when working at the bench for weekly wages, and with all his shrewdness and force of character he has preserved a simple, honest, childlike belief in humanity. Single-handed he conducted all his great enterprises on a plain, patriarchal basis, using their revenues for extensions, and depending on his faithful and well-satisfied stockholders for such further accessions of capital as the business might in his judgment need. About the time General Electric was most anxious to bolster up its jerry-built structure with the solid Westinghouse concern, the latter institution had begun the erection of some big new plants which required immediately several millions additional capital. Westinghouse prepared to apply to his stockholders for the required funds, and the announcement was to be made at the annual election soon due. Suddenly the financial sky became overcast. The stock-market grew panicky and money as scare in Wall Street as rain in Arizona in May. It was just such a situation as the "System" might have brought about to accomplish its fell designs had it possessed the power to work miracles.

And the "System" took care of its advantage. At a tense moment in that soul and nerve trying period, with Wall and State streets full of talk about General Electric's probable absorption of Westinghouse, General Electric being then at its highest price, $119 per share, the Westinghouse companies held their annual meetings and the big inventor, confidently facing his stockholders, quite regardless of conditions which he thought could have no possible bearing on his concern's splendid prospects, came forward with his demand for the millions required to complete the projects already under way. This was the signal. From all the stock-market sub-cellars and rat-holes of State, Broad, and Wall streets crept those wriggling, slimy snakes of bastard rumors which, seemingly fatherless and motherless, have in reality multi-parents who beget them with a deviltry of intention: "George Westinghouse had mismanaged his companies"; "George Westinghouse, because of gross extravagance, had spread himself and his companies until they were involved beyond extrication unless by consolidation with General Electric"; these and many more seeped through the financial haunts of Boston, Philadelphia, and New York, and kept hot the wires into every financial centre in America and Europe, where aid must be sought to relieve the crisis. There came a crash in Westinghouse stocks, and their price melted. From amidst the thunder and lowering clouds emerged the "System." "Notwithstanding the black eye the name of everything Westinghouse had received, it would stand by and consolidate and save the day!" But the "System" and its everything-gauged-by-machinery votaries had reckoned without their host. George Westinghouse was too strong a man to be thus easily shaken down. He threw back his mighty shoulders, shook his big head, and flung his great private fortune into the market to stay the falling prices of his securities. The movement was too strong against him at the moment, and his millions were but a temporary help. He got on the firing-line himself and did a thousand and one things that only a brave, honest, and democratic Yankee would or could do—everything but accept the cunning aid offered him by the "System" or its votaries. He knew too well that the friendly mask concealed a foe and that the kid-gloved hand extended him had a dagger up its sleeve.

These were the conditions when I, as an expert in stock-market affairs, was called in for assistance. Here was this sound, sturdy institution standing for everything that was best and self-supporting in American finance adrift on the Wall Street shoals, and it seemed almost a hopeless task to attempt its rescue. But it was a task eminently worth while, and I undertook it with all the energy I could command.

The problem was to restore the Westinghouse stocks to their former high price, and, confidence being re-established, to sell the new treasury stock at such a figure as would pay for the plants and other projects the company had under way. The completion of these meant greatly increased earnings and such an advance in facilities and economy of manufacture as would surely seal the fate of General Electric if it competed with Westinghouse under the new conditions. Small wonder "Standard Oil's" whole strength was bent to force the alliance.

My fight had hardly begun when I saw it was to be opposed by all the forces of General Electric and the "System," and I concluded defeat was sure unless by a counter movement on their stock I could keep them so busy that they would have no time to interfere with Westinghouse. Thereupon I laid out that attack on everything connected with General Electric which created so much consternation at the time. To this day, if my enemies are asked to name the act which most conclusively justifies their hatred of me, they will point to my terrible General Electric raid. They will tell you I broke the stock from 118 to 56 in a day, and thereby caused one of our most disastrous panics; that I continued to hammer it to 20, that I compelled reorganization, and then did not let up. They will show you that the misery and ruin I wrought were beyond calculation. I will only say that, of any of the things I am proud of having done, I am proudest of what I did in General Electric, and, willingly, I would give over five years of my life to go through the experience again.

It was a most arduous campaign, and our fate trembled many times in the balance. By dint of hard, overtime work, and what my enemies were pleased to call rank manipulation, we drove Westinghouse stock back to its former price, after which a strong syndicate was formed to take the new stock, and the righted institution at once magnificently swept on its international career which to-day is at its height.

Though I had taken up the Westinghouse cause as a business venture and its successful termination was most profitable to me, I had entered into the campaign with the ardor of a lawyer defending a client unjustly accused of a heinous crime. But there was this difference—if in spite of his efforts the lawyer fails to convince the jury of his client's innocence it means no detriment to his fortune or his reputation, whereas all I had and was were involved in this stock-exchange struggle. The great rewards that are the guerdon of success in financial fights are balanced by the terrific consequences of defeat. The broker general engaged in surrounding his enemy requires every dollar he and his principals can pledge or beg, and where great forces are in conflict millions are burnt up to seize any vantage, as Kuroki sacrifices a regiment to gain a hill. I had won for myself as well as for Westinghouse, but if the fortunes of the war had been on the other side, I must certainly have been wiped out.

CHAPTER XIV

THE ALLIANCE WITH ADDICKS

It was part of my method of conducting my stock-brokerage business to expose through the medium of the press or through market letters the stocks of corporations I thought rotten. It was also my way to work up bull campaigns in stocks that seemed to be selling for less than they were worth. With Addicks or the "Standard Oil" I had no connection. I had watched the Philadelphian's operations and had my eye marketwise on his bonds and stock, particularly on his stock, which was 100,000 shares of the Bay State Gas Company of Delaware, of a par value of fifty dollars each, and which became very active in the market shortly after it was created, at just under par. I thought I saw in the scheme the ordinary, cold-blooded, stock-jobbing, unloading-on-the-public affair. I had heard recounted the man's wonderful doings, particularly his recklessness in the purchase of the Boston companies; I "sized up" his mighty effort to be the tremendously rich good fellow as inspired by the idea and the purpose of giving his "stuff" in the stock-market a good send-off; and from the start I had put his property on my "to-be-watched memoranda" as one I might at the proper time let daylight into.

I was tearing large strips from its values when Addicks' bankers, who happened to be business friends of mine, sought to enlist me on their side of the gas war. I remember expressing frankly my opinion about the contestants and their contest at the time, stating that so far as morality, fairness, or justice went I could see little to choose between Addicks and "Standard Oil." I continued to "bear" the stock until one day my banker friends brought me an earnest request from the Delaware financier that I go to New York and talk things over with him.

On reaching New York—the two bankers and myself—we went directly to Addicks' apartments at the Imperial Hotel. Although the fortunes of war were rapidly crumbling this worthy's brilliant financial structure, there were as yet no outward signs of disintegration. His beautiful estate at Claymont, Del., his stock farm in the same State, his town-house in Philadelphia, his $30,000 apartments in the Knickerbocker on Fifth Avenue in New York, and the superbly furnished suite in the Imperial, close by, all seemed to testify to the man's boundless prosperity.

Memorable though this meeting was destined to be to both of us, my chief sensation in approaching it was a certain curiosity as to the personality of Addicks, whom I had seen, but had never spoken to. I knew him to a "T" in my mind, but here was my opportunity to compare my mental "sizing-up" with the real man. The apartment into which we were ushered was of the low-burning-red-light, Turkish pattern. Addicks rose from a great divan disturbing a pose which his white cricket-cloth suit and the scarlet shadows made so stagy that I guessed it was for my benefit. I looked him over, and he returned the inspection. After the introduction he at once unlimbered his business gun.

"Let's get right down to business, Lawson," he began. "I wanted to meet you to see if we could get together on any satisfactory basis."

I told him that that was my understanding of our meeting. Then he wanted assurances that I had no connections with "Standard Oil" and that I was free, sentimentally and commercially, to enlist in his fight. I replied that I was a stock-broker and operator, and was looking for opportunities; no one had strings on me, and provided he made satisfactory terms I was free to join him; further, that when it came to enlisting in a fight between two such financiers as Addicks and Rogers, sentiment seemed to me out of place.

"That's right," he said. "That's what I like to hear. Now, Lawson, will you take this fight of mine against 'Standard Oil'?"

"If you meet my terms, yes."

Addicks looked at me. "What do you want?" he asked. "Perhaps, though, you'd first like to have me tell you how my affairs stand."

"I know sufficiently where you stand," I replied, "to name my terms right now. If they are acceptable, I'll hear you tell where you stand afterward. I'll take your fight for a cash commission of $250,000 and a cash capital of $1,000,000, to be used in the market on joint account, we to divide the profits of all operations."

Addicks smiled. "You are too high," he said. "I'll pay you $50,000 commission and give you $250,000 capital, and after I show you in what good shape my fight now is and how near I am to victory, you'll agree that the terms I offer are good pay and fair."

"Mr. Addicks," said I, "I have just time to get dinner, look in at the theatre, and catch the midnight back to Boston. It is my business to keep posted on such scrimmages as you are engaged in. If you and your affairs are where I believe they are, the terms I offer are exceptionally low. If your affairs are as you would have me believe, you need no one to captain your fight."

Addicks asked where I thought his affairs stood, and I answered: "I don't think—I know, or, at least, I feel quite sure I do. You are at the end of your rope and are practically bankrupt."

At once Addicks grew indignant. "You are absolutely wrong," he asserted. "I'll admit I have had a hard fight, and that it has cost me, so far, considerable money; but I give you my word I'm worth between six and seven millions clear and clean right now."

I bade him good-night and left. Our interview had consumed not over twenty to twenty-five minutes. I said to his bankers:

"Addicks is the Addicks I have sized him up to be, only worse."

We got back to Boston next morning, and at the opening of the Stock Exchange I sailed into the Bay State stock in earnest, for I felt surer than before that Addicks was nearing his finish. A few minutes after the Exchange opened, Addicks' banker rushed into my office and said the Delaware financier begged that I would return to New York at once, and whispered to me that in a conversation just held on the telephone Addicks had stated that he would accept my terms. I informed the banker I was not anxious for the job, but as he urged his own interest, I jumped on the noon train and in the evening was again in New York.

It was a warm day and I was pleased to get a wire on the train from Addicks asking me to meet him at the pier, as we should hold our conference on his yacht, the Now-Then, at that time one of the fastest steam-yachts afloat.

It was a night of memorable beauty. In the golden light of a dazzling sunset we flew up the majestic Hudson. From under the awning I watched the serried edges of the Palisades as we slipped swiftly by them to the broad reaches of tinted waters above Yonkers. Every natural influence conspired to make acute to me the warning whisper of my soul, which flashed the caution as I crossed the gang-plank, "Watch out!" But, as I said before, Fate hangs no red lights at the cross-roads of a man's career, and I plunged recklessly into the toils my Mephistophelian companion so artfully wove around me.

The Now-Then was hardly in mid-stream before Addicks had got down to business. His demeanor had changed since the previous evening. All his bravado had disappeared; he was simple, frank, direct, and, in the manner of one who has made a mistake and regrets it, he commenced without any delay:

"I didn't think last night I'd pay your price, Lawson. It staggered me a bit, but I gave it considerable thought after you left, and when this morning's prices showed me you were again on the war-path, I saw my error."

"Mr. Addicks," said I, "let's have no fooling about this matter. If we do business together, it will only be after there is some plain—brutally plain talk between us. It will do no good to trick, because some one will get slaughtered when the trickery is discovered, as it surely would be, after we hitched up together."

Then, straight from the shoulder, free from all attempt to gloss over the raw truth, I detailed to him the things I knew he had done to his former associates, and it was a tale of unbroken duplicity and double-dealing on his part, loss and misery for his lieutenants, and profits and curses for him. I ended by saying: "If we get together, Addicks, it will be upon my terms, and I'll see to it that you never put me in the position in which you have put all the others you've been connected with. I don't trust you and I'll watch you all the time."

When I had finished Addicks looked at me sadly with a wounded, "how-this-man-has misjudged-me" expression in his eyes.

"Lawson," he said, "you were never more mistaken in your life, but it's a matter I don't want to argue about. You'll tell me you were all wrong after you know me better. I'll do business with you—yes, and I'll allow you to make your own terms. I'll agree to them whatever they are, and I'll live up to the very letter of them, however hard."

I may mention that it is a peculiar characteristic of Addicks that one may talk to him as though he were a pick-pocket, and he will not resent it, if it is "business." Where H. H. Rogers would flash into a Vesuvius of wrath, the Delaware statesman only smiles.

Addicks by no means convinced me of his sincerity. I decided I would test him pretty thoroughly before I went further. So I said: "This seems the proper time for a clean statement from you as to just where you and your companies stand."

I did not believe this man could make an absolutely truthful statement on any subject of importance, but I knew enough of his real position to protect me from being fooled. What was my surprise, therefore, when in the most open way possible he calmly spread before me a condition of affairs far worse than the worst I knew. He was, indeed, bankrupt and his corporation was in little better shape.

As soon as I could catch my breath I said:

"No wonder you refused my proposition last night. If your bankers had dreamed of this state of affairs, they would have had a receiver to-day. You cannot meet my terms. You cannot even carry out the ones you yourself offered."

Addicks leaned back on the cushions of his chair in the easiest, most insouciant way imaginable. He grinned. "That's true," he replied, "but I never give up a ship till I feel her bump the bottom, and I am sure that, bad as things are, you and I can pull them out and whip Rogers to a standstill."

It was a remarkable situation. Here was one of the most ruthless financial schemers of the age cornered for slaughter, and he had put himself absolutely at the mercy of the man who had bitterly fought him and whom he knew hated his kind. Yet he was as cool and collected as a bunch of orange blossoms at a winter's wedding.

The man's supreme nerve astounded me, yet I could not help admiring him. I saw through his game, yet his assurance fascinated me. I thought a minute. I said to him: "Addicks, I'm really sorry for you, and I'll promise you here now to keep what you've told me sacred. What's more, I'll stop fighting you. I'll cover my shares and without doing any one any harm I'll help make prices a bit better for your securities."

He smiled, said "Thank you!" and continued looking at me as though he awaited something further, a quizzical, expectant smile on his face.

There was an interval of silence. Finally I said to him—and there were neither red lights nor warning intuitions to signal my peril: "Just what do you expect me to do, Mr. Addicks?"

"Whatever you think best," he replied in a mild tone. Then, rousing himself a bit, he went on: "They say in the market that you like a fight and the harder it is the better. Well, I certainly have an uphill fight. Do as you would have the other fellow do to you."

After that I had no further doubts of Addicks' slickness. I said to him: "You are certainly the shrewd man they describe you as. Now continue to be frank long enough to answer this one question: Did you figure this out as the last card to throw at me, knowing that the very desperation of the case might warm me up and tempt me to tackle it for the sake of the fight there's in it?"

Instantly Addicks knew his game was won. He straightened up and was the able, shrewd, and cunning financier who had tricked conservative Boston. His facts chased his figures in marvellously rapid succession, and he showed a knowledge of conditions, relations, and corporation tricks that dazzled me. For an hour he rushed on, and when at last he came to a stop I said to him:

"It's unnecessary to say any more. I see the situation as you would have me see it, and it comes to this: If I refuse to link up with you it means another 'Standard Oil' victory and another wreck for Boston. Rogers' success means that New England speculators and investors will again, for the three hundred and thirty-third time, be robbed of their savings. If I get in, we may either avert all this or I may be ground up at the same time you are. However, it's too good a fight to miss, and so here goes. I'll link up."

At some particularly hazardous halting-place in after-years Addicks and myself have often laughed as we have talked over that August evening on the Now-Then. I was easy, he asserts, and I must admit that he is right—I was easy. Yet no one knew Addicks better than I did then. Looking back along his extraordinary career, one is obliged to allow a certain magic as a factor in his men-and-dollar tussles. We had absolutely nothing in common, Addicks and I. We thought and felt differently about every relationship of life. A dozen other ventures, sure, easy, and promising infinitely greater profits, were ready at my hand—but he appealed to my sense of adventure, he promised me abundant and glorious fighting, and I forgot everything else and went with him.

When the Now-Then touched her pier and I stepped ashore, it was as captain of Addicks' corporation and stock-market forces, with absolute power to wage war, make peace, and use in whatever way I thought best such resources of his as I could lay hands on. I lost no time. Within forty-eight hours of my return to Boston I had mapped out my campaign, reconstructed Addicks' broken lines, and gayly set forth on about as forlorn a hope as ever operator or fighter tackled.

Nothing more desperate could be imagined than the condition of the Delaware financier's affairs when I assumed control. All the resources of his companies were pledged for loans, and the constantly falling prices of his securities, coupled with the discrediting stories Rogers' agents kept in circulation, made it difficult to keep these going. To pay would mean ruin, for Addicks had no further thing of value to pledge. At the same time, Rogers' company, which had now paralleled many of the Bay State Company's pipes, had secured a large slice of that corporation's business, and had a corps of up-to-date solicitors working overtime to secure the balance. Boston, in the meantime, having decided that Addicts' star was of the shooting variety, and on its return trip, was throwing up its hat in the wake of the "Standard Oil" band-wagon. The city government and the Massachusetts Legislature had awakened to the enormity of Addicksism and were boiling over with that brand of virtue which the "System" and "Standard Oil" know so well how to rouse in American breasts by way of American pockets. By this time Rogers' investment in Boston had grown from the half-million he had in the beginning estimated as sufficient to annihilate Addicks to three and a half millions, a million and a half of which represented real property, and the balance, all kinds of expenditures made in the fight to crush the Delaware financier, a large part of it being invested in the votes and favor of State and municipal authorities.

Chief among the enemies of Addicks at this period was the young and brilliant boss of Boston, its reform mayor, the Hon. Nathan Matthews, and thereby hangs a swinging tale. When the Addicks-Rogers gas-fight broke out in Boston this Nathan Matthews was at the zenith of his political career, and was rather a greater man than even reform mayors generally fancy themselves. He was at that state of development in the lives of aspiring persons which compels the average spectator to debate whether the swelling of the cranium should be met by a larger hat-band or by a sweeping haircut. En passant, Addicks' Panama had had its fifth enlargement to accommodate the successive bulges of his brow.

Now, the city of Boston's contract with the Bay State Company for gas at a dollar and twenty-five cents, which had run a long term of years, was just expiring. One bright June morning the mayor's secretary telephoned the secretary of the Mogul from Delaware that His Honor of Boston, desired converse with the Gas King. If those who overheard the dialogue can be credited, the parley was of this character:

"This is the mayor of Boston, the Hon. Nathan Matthews."

"This is J. Edward O'Sullivan Addicks, Gas King and United States Senator-to-be. What would you with me?"

"I would hold converse with you in regard to a contract of much moment which will expire in a few days."

"Well and good. My office is in West Street. Give your card to my first, second, or third secretary and I will not keep you waiting long."

"The office of the mayor of Boston is at the City Hall and my first or under-secretary will make things agreeable while you wait. When will you call?"

"I would have you understand, Mr. Mayor, that any one to talk gas with J. Edward O'Sullivan Addicks, Gas King and United State Senator-to-be, comes to his office."

"Good-day to you, Mr. Gas King and United States Senator-to-be."

"Good-day to you, Mr. Mayor."

I do not, of course, guarantee that the conversation took exactly the form here given it, but no injustice has been done its substance, nor would it be possible to estimate in miles the breach it created. From that telephonic encounter date the earnest efforts of Matthews and Addicks to do up each other, in which both were successful to a degree that filled their hearts with Indian pleasure.

A few days later public announcement was made that the Brookline Gas Company, Rogers' corporation, had been awarded the contract for lighting Boston, and that henceforth the legal price of gas to the consumer was to be $1 per thousand feet. This was due notice to all concerned that "Standard Oil" had captured City Hall, and Addicks realized his error. He sought the mayor's office, but the mayor had no time to see him. His companies met the new rate. There was nothing else for them to do.

CHAPTER XV

THE GREAT BAY STATE GAS FIGHT

It was to this condition that I had to adapt my campaigning plans. I determined first to raise the market price of Addicks' securities; to turn the tide against the "Standard Oil" by that most potent of stock-market weapons, publicity; and then to attack Rogers from the rear through the City Hall. For Addicks to attempt to match pocket-books with Rogers and "Standard Oil" in corrupting city or State officials I knew would be useless; and besides a fundamental stipulation in the agreement with the Delaware financier on the Now-Thenhad been that under no circumstances should bribery or corruption be allowed to enter into any of our plans while I was connected with the enterprise. I had always held, do now, and always shall hold, that the meanest crime in the calendar of vice is bribery of the servants of the people. I felt pretty sure, moreover, that I could play a card that would more than offset the dollars of "Standard Oil." Nathan Matthews was on the high-road to the governor's chair, but I happened to know that, however ambitious he might be for political preferment, his temperament rendered him more avid for distinction in business. Addicks had within his gift the richest plum in all the Boston commercial world. As controller of the affairs of the Bay State Company of Delaware, which controlled the nomination and consequent election of the officers of the old Boston gas companies, he could award to any one he pleased the presidency of these corporations, together with the large salary that went with the office.

My plans in shape, I rushed to the firing-line. I began with a statement to the investors of New England and the gas consumers of Boston brimming over with facts and figures. Then I fired a volley of candid details as to the manner in which city and State officials had recently betrayed the public's interests. Lastly, I discharged at "Standard Oil" a broadside which my attorneys and friends assured me meant jail on a libel charge. I put my banking-house and my personal guarantee behind the old and new loans, and proceeded to roll up my sleeves in the stock-market. I got results at once. A change became apparent in public sentiment—the rottenness of Addicksism was overcome by the stench of "Standard Oil." The prices of Bay State stocks and bonds shot up; loan funds were offered freely and at lower rates of interest.

There were, however, reprisals. Rogers met my onslaught by a manœuvre new in "Standard Oil" tactics. He came into the open, issuing a proclamation over his own signature which gave me the lie, at the same time tearing off a yard or two of my skin and throwing on a bucket of brine to remind me I had lost it. This attack was just off the press when I was out with a rejoinder which he, in after-years, referred to as quite the hottest thing of its kind he had ever read. In it I calmly, but in that "chunk English" which those who really wish to convey the truth naked can always find handy, told him plainly who he was, explicitly what "Standard Oil" was, and exactly who and what I was. I opine that about either assault there was nothing dignified, generous, or refined, but in stock-exchange battles one has not time to scent shrapnel. The immediate result of this interchange of deckle-edged insults was to daze the public. "Standard Oil" attacked and actually replying; Rogers assaulting Lawson and Lawson sending back worse than he got—almost anything might happen next. It was right here I got to Rogers' solar plexus. I came out with another plain public talk, and gave him the choice of haling me into court—in which event I pledged him my word I would send him and his associates to jail for bribery and other crimes—or of acknowledging to the world he was licked and on the run. He was silent and I loudly claimed victory. The price of Addicks stocks quickly emphasized our success by a further advance.

Thus far the campaign appeared to be working smoothly, and I turned my attention next to my rear attack. I began negotiations with Mayor Matthews for the withdrawal of his support from Rogers. It was a difficult task, but after much manœuvring I landed my big fish. I promised him the presidency of the Boston, South Boston, Roxbury, and Bay State gas companies for the term of three years, at a salary of $25,000 per annum, with the explicit understanding that he was to allow me, as his vice-president, to see that the bargain between us was lived up to. When the trade was made it was understood that the fact of Matthews' change of base should be kept secret, and that he should not assume the office until the end of his term as mayor of Boston. With that agreement the deal was clinched, signed, sealed, and delivered.

In order that my readers may comprehend the events that follow, it is necessary that they understand something of the complications in which Addicks' manipulations had involved that corporation.

When Addicks purchased the several Boston gas properties he organized a company, the Bay State of Delaware, in which this ownership was vested. In order to facilitate the financing of the new corporation and for other manipulative purposes of his own, Addicks created an inner corporation, the Bay State of New Jersey, owned by the treasury of the Bay State of Delaware, to which he turned over the stocks of the Boston gas companies. These the Bay State of New Jersey transferred to the Mercantile Trust Company of New York as collateral for the twelve million Boston Gas bonds which had been sold to the investing public. While to all intents and purposes the Bay State of Delaware was owner of the subsidiary properties, the contract with the Mercantile Trust Company was made with the Bay State of New Jersey, and it was to the president of the latter corporation (Addicks) that the Trust Company was bound to deliver the proxies for the gas stocks in its possession, three days before an annual election. Knowledge of this subcutaneous corporation was confined to Addicks and his immediate associates, and the Delaware financier alone quite grasped its potentialities.

Hitherto Addicks had used the proxies to elect himself president of each of the subordinate corporations, drawing the several salaries which went with the offices. To prevail on him to give up these places and their emoluments to a man he hated as bitterly as he did Matthews was a difficult task, but his situation was desperate. Finally, he agreed. I did not know till long afterward that this reluctant compliance was yielded only after Addicks had had a secret session with his Bay State directors, at which they voted him, by way of salve for his resignation, a sum equal to three years' salary, $75,000.

The mayor, who was a lawyer, prided himself on his shrewdness, and was fully alive to the serpent strategy of Addicks. He determined that the prize he had secured should not slip through his fingers for lack of precaution. We had many legal pow-wows in which the most astute lawyers at the Boston bar were called in, and finally the directors of the Bay State made an iron-clad contract with Nathan Matthews, agreeing to deliver over to him whatever proxies it, the Bay State Gas of Delaware, received from the Mercantile Trust Company of New York, on a given day before the annual election, with which he, of course, could elect himself president. This contract was signed by Addicks and his directors and by all the officers of the Bay State of Delaware corporation, and was passed on and approved by the eminent law sharps both sides had retained.

A few days after the document that made Nathan Matthews supreme boss of Boston Gas was conveyed to him, there came an explosion. Like the premature bursting of a bombshell at a Fourth of July celebration, the transaction "leaked," and the press announced in sable head-lines that Mayor Matthews had sold out, that Addicks was on top, and that Rogers and "Standard Oil" would surely be found beneath the débris. Matthews has always claimed that this "leakage" was a piece of Addicks' double dealing; Addicks declares it was a part of Matthews' and Rogers' deep-laid plan to give him the double cross. Anyway, as a hurrier-up of coming events the news was most successful, although its effect was somewhat of the nature of that produced by the throwing in of an overdose of soda at a candy pull—the pot boiled over, and the air for a time was permeated with the odor of burned sweets. In spite of all public and private criticism Matthews budged not a jot, and confirmed the reports. I made the most of our triumph over "Standard Oil," and for a few days the public took to it, too. Then came one of those return waves of sentiment which may always be counted on in any contest in which "Standard Oil" is engaged. From mysterious places and in untraceable ways the report became current that victory was really with Rogers instead of with our side; that the deal was a smooth piece of Machiavelian work; that Matthews when he took the helm was to steer our ship alongside one of Rogers' forts and perhaps drop anchor under a row of his concealed guns.

This rumor alarmed me. I lost no time in running it to earth, and discovered to my consternation that Matthews had spent the night before he made the agreement to come over to us in New York, at the home of H. H. Rogers. Exactly what had occurred there, or what their programme was, I don't know. Long after this episode had slipped into gas history, at the time when Rogers and myself were doing business together, I asked him to enlighten me on this one point, and he did to the extent of saying, "Matthews only did what I approved of." This certainly redeemed Matthews in my eyes from the reproach of having sold out his friends. There is nothing more despicable than a man who, after having consented to be "put" will not "stay put"—even though the first "put" be of a questionable character.

This new complication demanded immediate action. I called on Matthews to make public announcement that I was to be his vice-president, and thus set at rest the reports that were fast destroying the beneficial effects of our coup. I argued that such an announcement would convince the public that victory was with us and not with Rogers. My surprise may be grasped when the Mayor placed this icicle in my hot palm:

"Mr. Lawson, it has long been my ambition to show the public of Boston and gas consumers what I could do with this situation, and now that I am absolutely assured of gas supremacy, I would have you and all others distinctly understand I will run it as I deem best, regardless of the wishes of any one."

Nathan Matthews was destined later to learn that in an Addicks edifice there are secret trap-doors and concealed passageways available for quick escape in emergency, and that the term "absolutely assured" is of relative value when used in high finance, with Addicks to interpret the relativeness. A few days after the mayor had shown his colors the annual election was "pulled off" in an unexpected manner. The Mercantile Trust Company delivered its proxies to the president of the Bay State of New Jersey, who promptly re-elected himself and his friends to their old offices.

Next morning the public, the press, and the ex-mayor were alike surprised to learn that J. Edward O'Sullivan Addicks was still president of all the Boston gas companies; that General Sam Thomas, of New York, and Thomas W. Lawson, of Boston, were vice-presidents; and that the expected and widely heralded Matthews turnover to Matthews had been indefinitely postponed. There was a tremendous "towse" for a few days during which time I tried my hand at public-opinion moulding, and so successfully that all interested saw that the tide had really turned, and was running swiftly against the heretofore invincible "Standard Oil." Rogers tried to stem it by causing it to be known that Matthews was to carry the new complication to the courts, but we quickly disposed of this possibility by reaching a settlement with our man. This was brought about by the payment to Matthews of a number of thousands of dollars, which Addicks afterward informed me he had entered in the gas-books as "balm salary." From this event until August, 1895, it was one continuous running fire with Rogers and his crowd, with a constant gain to our side in public opinion, though final victory was still far off because of the unlimited money resources of "Standard Oil." In fact, it gradually became evident that, though we might hold out, it was impossible to whip "Standard Oil" to an open acknowledgment of defeat.

The phase of the problem that gave me keenest cause for uneasiness was the possibility I recognized of treachery in my own camp. I had become painfully aware that Addicks was getting impatient and was ready at any favorable moment to make one of his quick Judas turns, which would land him safe with Rogers as the price of the slaughter of the rest of us. True, I had taken all possible precautions to safeguard my own and my friends' interests against his craft by securing from him and from the subsidiary companies iron-clad power to act for them without consultation. To get this I had had to use great pressure, for he had balked long and hard against giving it. This was the condition of affairs when I decided to stake everything on one move.

* Certain of my critics have seized upon the transaction with Mayor Matthews, narrated in this chapter, to say: "He bribed the Mayor and is no better than other bribers."

The fact is, that the only thing the Mayor of Boston could do in the gas war—take sides with Rogers, grant a permit to the Brookline company to open the streets and come in competition with our companies, thus compelling, in the interests of the people, a reduction in the selling price of gas from $1.25 to $1.00—the Mayor had already done. There was nothing more in his power, and the only object we had in securing his services was to put him between our companies and Rogers, in the belief that Rogers, owing to his former relations, would not dare fire through him.

I never, directly or indirectly, bribed Mayor Matthews; but, on the contrary, only induced him to do what he had a moral right to do and I a moral right to ask him to do.

CHAPTER XVI

PEACE NEGOTIATIONS WITH ROGERS

Having made up my mind that the time had come for a final engagement, I decided myself to try legitimately to settle with Mr. Rogers, and prepared two letters which, if he were willing for us to get together, would pave the way for a meeting. These letters I sent by my secretary, Mr. Vinal, to Mr. Rogers at Fairhaven. My readers, in weighing this odd correspondence, must bear in mind what the relations between Mr. Rogers and myself had been. We had vilified each other in every imaginable way, and I knew, or at least I thought I did, that the "Standard Oil" magnate would not hesitate to use any written communication of mine that he could lay hold of to bring about a split between Addicks and myself. I had good evidence that he believed that in such a rupture lay his only chance of bringing home the quieting blow he had been trying to inflict on us. Letter I. read as follows:

Henry H. Rogers, Fairhaven, Mass.

Dear Sir: My secretary, Mr. Vinal, will hand you this letter. If after reading it you are desirous of further communication with me, he has instructions, after you have returned this one to him, sealed in the enclosed envelope, to hand you another, which if after reading you return to him in another enclosed envelope, he will bring to me with whatever verbal answer you may care to send.

My secretary knows nothing more of his errand or the contents of either letter. He can, therefore, give you no further information. If you do not call for the second letter, I will consider you do not care to pursue the subject further, which will lead me to notify you that the Boston gas war will end in a most sensational way next Wednesday.

Believe me, sir,

Yours respectfully,

(Signed) Thomas W. Lawson.

Upon his return from Fairhaven Mr. Vinal informed me that Mr. Rogers, after reading this letter twice, folded and placed it in the envelope I had sent and handed it without comment to him, whereupon my secretary delivered to him letter II., which was a type-written communication on a plain bit of paper, addressed to no one, signed by no one, and bearing no marks to identify the sender:

There is a gas war now existing. Upon one side is the "Standard Oil." Upon the other the Addicks Bay State companies.

After a fight has been begun there are but four things possible:

"Standard Oil" can sell out to the Bay State.

The Bay State can sell out to the "Standard Oil."

They can come together by consolidation; or

They can continue fighting until one or the other has been annihilated.

Nothing else is possible. Therefore, one of these four things is to be the outcome of the present war.

If you can be shown now that if one of the first three is not settled upon before next Wednesday the fourth will be impossible beyond that date, and that it is absolutely in the power of one man, without consultation with any one, to bring about the accomplishment of any one of the first three, you will meet that man before next Wednesday and make your selection.

I can absolutely prove to you that this war will not continue after next Wednesday, and that it is absolutely in my power, without consulting any one, to do any one of the three things you signify you desire done.

Mr. Vinal reported that Mr. Rogers also read this letter a second time, but slowly and carefully, as though he were weighing each word, and then, sealing it in the envelope, passed it back to him with: "Say to your employer I return to New York to-morrow, Sunday night, and shall be at my office, 26 Broadway, from 9.30 on Monday morning till five in the afternoon; that I shall dine at my house, 26 East 57th Street; that I shall be through dinner at eight o'clock, and that I go to bed at 10.30. Tell him that any man who has an important communication to make to me affecting a matter in which I have large interests will be welcome to call on me between the hours I have named, provided he notifies me a little while in advance."

When my secretary, whose practice it was to give me the minutest details of such affairs as this errand, had reported all that had happened, I at once sent a message to 26 Broadway stating that I would be at Rogers' house at eight o'clock on Monday night, and on the stroke I pushed his electric latchstring. His man had hardly taken my hat when Mr. Rogers himself came down the hall with outstretched hand.

CHAPTER XVII

A MEMORABLE CONFERENCE

If the years of my life are protracted beyond the Psalmist's threescore and ten, even though the events that chance in the comparatively long future seethe and struggle as strenuously as those that befell in the eager, vivid procession of yesterdays which makes up my past, my memory's picture of this meeting will always hang where the lights cast their kindest reflections.

I had left Boston on the noon train, and got down to my hotel, the Brunswick, on Fifth Avenue, by six o'clock. In those kind days of good memory when New Yorkers really lived instead of looping-the-loop through life, the Brunswick was head-quarters for Southerners and Bostonians of the old school. To-day its bricks and mortar and the picturesque iron balconies, from which two generations of America's celebrities reviewed the marching armies of peace and war, are heaps of refuse; for the old Brunswick has had to give place to yet one more of the twenty-storied, emblazoned hostelries, whose alabaster halls, frescoed walls, mosaic floors, and onyx and silver bathtubs are designed to minister to the comfort of our great and free people when they needs must wander from the luxury of their homes. When I had dressed I crossed over to the old Delmonico's opposite, and, in a secluded corner beside an open window which gave full view of the passing show on Gotham's great boulevard, I sat and listened to old "Philip," who, time out of mind, had been high-priest of the famous Frenchman's temple of appetite, as he posted me on the latest doings of the town where no one remembers further back than yesterday, and to-morrow doesn't count. Ordinarily I should have lingered for hours with "Philip" and his tidbits, but that night my mind was a mad steeplechase of memories and hopes, all starting and finishing at 26 East 57th Street, and I fear he must have thought he had failed in the plump little duck which I left unpicked, and in the bottle of Chianti which I hardly sipped.

At 7.30 I lit my cigar and started for what I felt was to be the tomb or the forcing-house of all the air-castles I had cherished from boyhood. At last I was to meet the real champion; I was to tussle hand-to-hand with the head of the financial clan, the man of all men best fitted to test to the utmost the skill and quickness which I had picked up in the rough and tumble of a hundred fights on State and Wall streets—Rogers, wary, intrepid, implacable, the survivor of bloody battles in comparison with which mine were but pink skirmishes.

I had carefully put aside that half-hour between dinner and the moment for my appointment to run up and down my mental keyboard under what to me are the most favorable conditions possible—an evening walk through the streets of a great city. Some men can invite their souls only in sylvan solitudes, but the flare of light, the clash of traffic, the kaleidoscopic procession of humanity, with its challenging contrasts shifting and seething on great metropolitan highways, breed in my mind a sense of calm, cool remoteness in which all the glitter and excitement of the spectacle suggests only its appalling transiency.

From the gay carnival of Broadway I cut across through the brownstone gloom of 27th Street into Sixth Avenue, where the tired men and women of the toiling millions sat in their doorways or at their windows over the shops resting after the heat and travail of the day. Some watched the sidewalk antics of their children—perhaps speculating on the possibility that this or the other among that merry throng of urchins might rise to be an alderman or even a city boss—perhaps President of the greatest republic on earth—or—transcendent bliss—a Rogers or a Rockefeller.

From 42d Street I turned up Fifth Avenue, lifting my hat and exchanging a word with Mr. and Mrs. Russell Sage, and for an instant, as I left them, my wandering thoughts took a new twist, for Mrs. Sage had informed me that "Father and I are on the way to prayer-meeting"—early evening prayer-meeting in New York! For an instant I was in one of those tiny New Hampshire villages, a forgotten haven of rest and simplicity, innocent as yet of steam, machinery, or trolleys, for the sweet lady and the angular man with the pained gait which spoke in loud tones of the unbroken store-shoe could belong in no other than a rural place. But the image of the New Hampshire village only flitted across my mind's film, for my truant senses seized on a message over memory's telephone: "Russell Sage has $100,000,000." One hundred millions, and I was back on earth again, but as I walked the thought was buzzing in my brain: "Is it possible that that countryman has MADE one hundred million dollars, when the expert carpenter who started at the birth of Christ to trudge the world until from his honest labors he had accumulated $1,000,000 by laying aside each day all the wage he was entitled to, one dollar, had at the end of 1,900 years only a little more than half that sum?"

At last I turned the corner of 57th Street, and when I looked down Mr. Rogers' home-like hall and grasped his outstretched hand and heard his "Lawson, I'm glad to see you!" I would have sworn it was hours and hours since I left the little table in the corner of Delmonico's.

The chief impression I recall of my experience that night is gratitude for Henry H. Rogers' unexpected kindness, and admiration for his manliness, ability, and firmness. When this memory rises in my mind I regret "Frenzied Finance" and all the consequences with which it is fraught for him and his connections. When the American people are aroused, as they surely will be, to demand restitution and are in the act of brushing, with a mighty sweep of indignation, back into the laps of the plundered the billions of which they have been robbed, and "Standard Oil" and the "System" break and fall like trees before the gale, I doubt, even if Henry H. Rogers be brought face to face with ruin, that he will feel half the pain I shall, for I know that the picture of that memorable night will surely come back to me with all the vividness of reality.

But as my mind harks back, there clashes with this another, a hellish picture, which the same Henry H. Rogers painted with the brush of Amalgamated, and a procession of convicts and suicides trail slowly toward me out of the canvas. Then I realize that my pen is but the instrument of a righteous retribution and that no personal feelings, however tender, must be allowed to interfere.

"Come this way," said my host, striding ahead of me along the hall. "In here we can have our talk and our smoke undisturbed." He led me into the big, empty dining-room and closed the door.

"Mr. Rogers," I began, "it is kind of you to be so friendly after the mean things we have said of each other. Am I to understand you don't lay any of all that has passed up against me?"

"Lay it up against you, my boy? Drop that all out of your mind. You probably know I talk to the point and mean what I say. If you had hit below the belt as that—Addicks has, Iwould lay it up against you and a hundred years would not make me forget it. I know what you've done and why you've done it, and it was as much your right to do it as mine to do what I have done. I have nothing against you, and if events place me in a position where I can do anything to make your job easier without hurting my own interests—mind that, without hurting my own interests—I will do it. You have my word for it."

We sat within a few feet of each other, and I looked squarely into his eyes as he said, "You have my word for it," and they were honest eyes—honest as the ten-year-old boy's who with legs apart and hands in pockets throws his head back and says: "Wait until I am a man, and I will do it if I die for it!" I looked into them and I knew "My word for it" was all gold and a hundred cents to the dollar. For a minute we gazed steadily into—through each other, and I knew he was reading away into the back of my head. Inwardly I said: "If I do business with this man for a day or for a lifetime, I will never face him and give him my word for one thing and mean another," and in the years after when we did millions upon millions of business, with only each other's word for a bond of fair treatment, not once did I depart from the letter of my resolution. Up to the recent famous "Gas Trial," where our roads suddenly shot off at right angles, owing to a foul act of perjury, Henry H. Rogers never tired of meeting all his associates' attacks upon me with: "Lawson's word is gospel truth for me."

When we dropped our eyes, both evidently satisfied, he said: "Now, what have you to say to me?"

I spoke my piece rapidly and without interruption: "There are four things possible, as I wrote you—only four. I will take up the fourth first. I have absolute power to speak for all our local companies. If we, you and I, come to no settlement by to-morrow night, I will, without warning to any one, confess a default to the notes of our different companies and have a receiver appointed. As our stocks and bonds are held by our best investors all over New England, and as no such move is suspected, there will be a terrific rumpus. In the crash I shall go down with Addicks and the rest, for we have all put our personal resources behind the enterprise. I will see that the howl following the crash shall be such as all must hear, and I will call attention to the illegal acts of every one—your companies, Addicks' companies, and the city and State officials that have made such conditions possible. I don't think you will be able to stand against the cyclone this crash will raise; but even if you do, the receiver, having no interest to pay on bonds, will be in a position to smash the price of gas to seventy or seventy-five cents, and make it impossible for you to get possession of our companies for so long a time that the consumers will never allow you to get the price back to a profitable one. Have I made it clear that you cannot, as you were counting on doing, continue this fight till you have us tired out and crushed?"

His answer came as clear, quick, and sharp as the click of a revolver: "Perfectly, provided you can do the thing you say."

"I will prove to you I can."

"It is not necessary," he clicked back. "Do you give me your word that you can?"

"Absolutely."

"I am satisfied. Go on."

"That leaves only three possibilities," I continued. "You buy us; we buy you; or, we consolidate. I will take the third first. Under any circumstances or conditions will you join forces and do business with us?"

"Under no circumstances nor conditions will I do any business with Addicks. He has played me false, broken his word, and lied to me when there was no necessity for doing so, and no man who has done this once can ever do business with me a second time."

I once stood by a mechanism through which passed a strip of metal. Click! 'Twas cut. Whir! 'Twas a cylinder. Click! Whir! Click! A corner, an edge, an end, and b-r-r-rr! It was dropped, a metallic cartridge, to do its part in peace or war. Even more fascinating was it to see this human machine eject the product of its whirring brain.

"Then we have but two possibilities. Will you buy us out at the price we must have?"

"What is the price?"

"Sufficient to make good the promises that I have made to Addicks, my friends, and the public since I have been in command," I replied.

"Pass that by as an impossibility."

"Then, Mr. Rogers, we are down to this: You must sell and we must buy you out."

"Right. Now, how do you propose to buy?"

For months the ablest financiers and business men of Wall Street and Boston had striven to start up negotiations with Mr. Rogers with a view to settlement, and all had dropped them without even getting in an opening wedge, and here was I at the end of fifteen minutes of my first meeting, with my task half accomplished. I went on:

"There is something more you must do, Mr. Rogers. You must assist us in buying, which means you must sell at the terms you and I agree are the only ones we can meet. Therefore I will run over our situation. You have certain property, consisting of the Brookline Company and miscellaneous investments in connection with it. What cost does it stand you?"

Frankly, he went over what his Boston gas-war equipment consisted of and what it had cost, which, boiled down, amounted to $3,500,000. He then said:

"Let us figure what it will be worth to you when, it being known you have won out, you will have additional prestige and no competition."

We agreed upon $2,000,000 as representing the probable appreciation in what we were to acquire from him over and above any increase to our own securities.

"I'll take cost, $3,500,000, if it is cash or the equivalent, or I will take $4,500,000 if it is to be credit of a nature that assures me my money eventually, and I will divide my profit of a million equally with you. This sum will of course be in addition to anything you may be paid by Addicks."

Instantly, as if we had agreed upon it in advance, our eyes met—his cold, clear, and steely business—mine, I hoped, the same. For a second neither of us said a word. Then I said: "Thank you for the offer of the $500,000 profit, but we will cut all such offers out. My pay comes from my side. I never yet have known the man who could take pay from both sides and do his work properly." I slowly drew out the word "properly," and he in the same tone of voice said:

"'Properly' is better than 'honestly.' You know, Lawson, there is much cant in these times of which 'honesty' is the refrain."

"You and I will make no headway discussing moral ethics, Mr. Rogers, although we may in discussing business practices," I said, and I chalked up on my mental black-board: "Test One." Then I went on:

"I agree that $4,500,000, in anything we can pay in, is as fair a price as $3,500,000 cash, provided we find a credit guarantee satisfactory to you; unless indeed you are willing to allow us the $500,000 you just offered me."

"What I offered you was part of my profit. I will not allow any of it. My price is the same whether I pay you anything or not."

"Very well, Mr. Rogers, then the situation is this: In any trade that is made it will first be necessary for you to turn your property over to us to manage in conjunction with our own. When the public see it in our hands, our securities will advance and we can, by issuing additional Bay State stock, sell it and secure whatever sum it will be necessary for us to have beyond what we can borrow on your securities. Do you agree with me?"

He saw it as I did.

"I imagine you will never consent to turn your property over to us on our say-so that we will later pay you for it?"

"You are right there. I would not take J. Edward Addicks' guarantee in any form he could possibly put it. Once he got his hands on my company, for even thirty days, he would so far misuse it that he would deliberately default for the purpose of returning it to me in a damaged condition, and, in addition, would play some of those tricks which are second nature to him."

"It will be necessary for us then," I went on, "to give you some forfeit bond so large that, even if we misuse your property while it is in our hands, you will be repaid for the damage done, and it must be at the same time something of such value to us that even Addicks will be compelled to play fair."

"Well, what can you put up?" Mr. Rogers asked.

"Addicks has a right, through the Bay State Company of Delaware, to issue, through the Bay State Company of New Jersey, a million and a half new bonds for the purpose of acquiring new property. He and I have discussed the scheme as a last resort should any settlement seem possible."

"Do you mean to tell me there is anything Addicks can get his hands on which he has not yet used for his companies nor stolen for himself?" replied Mr. Rogers incredulously.

"Yes, he has time and again assured me of this, and he would not dare to lie to me under existing conditions."

He arose from his chair and stood directly in front of me and straightened up for what I could see was to be an unusual effort. Then with the force and the fire which in all hissupreme moments make Henry H. Rogers wellnigh irresistible he said:

"Lawson, I have listened to you. Now listen to me. I have taken you at your word, and have talked frankly and shown you my hand as I have seldom shown it to a stranger. To do the business I want to do, I see I must talk even more frankly than I already have, and I want you to weigh carefully what I shall say to you, for it may have a great bearing on your after-life. How old are you?"

"Thirty-seven," I replied.

"I thought you were about thirty-seven," he said. "Well, I am fifty-six and in experience am old enough to be your grandfather, so you can afford to give weight to what I am about to say, especially as I give you my word that I speak for your benefit first and my own afterward. I watched you before you hitched up with Addicks, and always thought that if the opportunity arose, we might do business together. We, or as you and others like to call us, 'Standard Oil,' have money enough to carry through whatever business we embark on and we know where there is all the business to be had that we care to engage in. We have everything, in fact, but men. We are always short of men to carry out our projects—young men, who are honest, therefore loyal; men to whom work is a pleasure; above all, men who have no price but our price. To such men we can afford to give the only things they have not got, or, if they have already got them, to give them in greater quantities—I mean power and money. You made a great mistake when you joined forces with Addicks, because no man can afford to be associated with the kind of a rascal Addicks is, the lowest I have yet come across. He is the type of man who cuts his best friend's throat with as much ease and satisfaction as he does his worst enemy's, if not with more. I fully expected that by this time he would have sold you out. If he had, where would you have been? Now, here you are from sheer desperation driven to me to avoid utter failure. Suppose you can do all you hope to—get the bonds, put them up and secure my property—do you not suppose that by that time Addicks will have some mine dug under you which will blow you to destruction? But grant even that he plays fair, and you bring the Boston situation up to a paying place, what good will it do you? You surely have more sense than to believe a man of Addicks' make-up can be permanently successful?"

Mr. Rogers halted. I had risen, and we stood facing each other. I felt that I was right here playing for that greatest of all stakes, my self-respect, the loss of which to any man, I had long before discovered, means ebon failure.

"What do you want me to do?" I asked.

"Say you'll come with us, and we'll fix up the Boston situation in some way that will forever eliminate Addicks from our affairs—your and my affairs. I would not insult you by asking you to sell Addicks out. It is unnecessary. He has no real rights in Boston. You and I can figure out a scheme that will take care of every other interest, and we'll give Addicks a lot more money than he can secure in any other way and show him the door. As for you and me, we'll make a lot of money and make it fairly and above board. But I am not thinking so much of the immediate situation as I am of the possibility of you joining us and working on some of the deals we have on hand. I shall put you in a position to make more money and secure more real power than you could possibly obtain in a like time under any other conditions. You know corporations and the stock-market, and you can readily see what the combination of our money and prestige and your knowledge of the market and investors will mean."

Heaven knows I could see what it all meant. I had even at that time in a chrysalis state those plans for destroying the "System" which now in a rounded out and matured form I intend to be the superstructure of my story of "Frenzied Finance." I had, a year before in Paris, outlined those plans to some of the brightest financial minds of Europe, and while they had marvelled at their radicalness, they had pronounced them sound, and had offered to furnish the hundred million of dollars required for their execution. Then I realized that to take this money from bankers would hamper me in the execution of my plans, and I postponed putting the project in force until I could furnish the necessary money through my own connections. Again, I had big ideas as to the copper situation—ideas that only awaited unlimited capital to be brought before the people, and which, if carried out, would do for them what had as yet never been done—give them tremendous profits upon their savings. And here were the unlimited capital and unlimited business prestige right at hand, but

"Mr. Rogers," I said, "don't! Please don't! I appreciate your proposition, and I thank you, but I can't accept. I agree with you about Addicks, the position I am in, and the mistake or foolish recklessness I was guilty of when I linked up with this Boston mess, but that doesn't alter the case an iota. I am enlisted with this man. I knew what he was when I consented to take charge of his affairs, and I should hate myself if I sold him out, even though I knew he would without hesitation sell me out. I must be true to myself."

Mr. Rogers remained silent. I went on:

"This, if I accepted your proposal, I could no longer be, even were Addicks and Boston Gas out of it. The man who is 'Standard Oil' wears a collar, and if I did what you ask I should expect to wear a collar and—and—I can't do it." I stopped; I was not excited; it was impossible to be so with that calm figure, apparently cut from crystal ice, so near me, but I was very much in earnest. I wondered what would come next. Mr. Rogers raised his hand and held it out to me, mine grasped it, and without a word thus we stood long enough to put that seal on our friendship which none of the many financial hells we jointly passed through in the after-nine years was hot enough to melt.

But that friendship is ended now. Henry H. Rogers' evidence in the Boston "Gas Trial" was the spark that kindled the dead leaves of the past into the conflagration which, now spread beyond the control of man, has brought to light the hidden skeletons of forgotten misdeeds and exposed them for all the world to see.

He at last broke the spell. "Lawson, you're a queer chap; but we are all queer, for that matter, and we must work along those lines we each think best. I once stood, just as you do now, in front of a man whom I looked up to as all that was wisest and best. He made an earnest effort to induce me to choose the ministry for my life-work, but I chose dollars instead, and I sometimes wonder if I chose wisely; but, as I said, we all must select our pack and, as we are the ones who must carry it, I suppose no one else should complain."

After a moment's pause I shot ahead into business again as though we had never left it. It took me but a short time to arrange the details of our trade. The Bay State of Delaware was to buy all of Mr. Rogers' Boston investments and to pay for the same $4,500,000—$1,500,000 in six months, $1,000,000 in a year, the balance in a year and a half, with interest at five per cent.; the Bay State was to put up, as a pledge of good faith, $1,500,000 new Boston bonds; and as soon as such deposit was made, Mr. Rogers was to transfer his securities and corporation to us. I was to go to Philadelphia that night and arrange all details with Addicks and report the following day.

It was 10.30 o'clock when I left 26 East 57th Street. I hurried down to the Brunswick, where I had time only to shift my clothes and catch the "midnight" for Philadelphia. After breakfast next morning I tackled Addicks. It goes without saying that I was a cyclone of enthusiasm as I minutely ran through what I had done, beginning with my letter to Rogers and finishing up with my visit of the night before. I omitted not the slightest detail, and when I wound up with my request that Addicks get the lawyers together and prepare the necessary documents for the turnover of the bonds and acceptance of Rogers' properties, I felt that my share in the Boston gas war was almost ended.

CHAPTER XVIII

THE DUPLICITY OF ADDICKS

Addicks looked at me in a cool, aggravating way, as though my enthusiasm was a joke.

"Lawson, you have done a big thing, a big thing, but you put up too many bonds, altogether too many. It looks to me as though that old trickster had got the best of us at last."

By this time I had learned all the moods of this man and knew that when he assumed that air of cold, saturnine jocularity it was safe to look for the uncovering of some vaporized trickery. My enthusiasm oozed. I hastened to ask:

"What do you mean by 'too many bonds,' Addicks? I gave him all we had. Sorry it was not more. We are to pay him four and a half million dollars, and the sooner we do it the better. Now out with what you've got in your mind; I won't stand any trifling."

Addicks continued to look at me with the same insolent, critical air. He said slowly:

"The reason I say you've given too many bonds is that we haven't a million and a half to put up. Where in the world did you get the idea we had?"

In an instant I realized that this sharper had tricked me into apparently tricking Rogers. I was boiling with rage.

"You have told me over and over again that you retained the right to issue a million and a half bonds, that you had never parted with it, and relying on your assurances, I have done business with Rogers. Let's have the truth now at once."

Addicks is a master in the management of just such tangles as had developed here. I had expected him to give way before my indignation. He looked me square in the eye and turned the tables on me. He got mad first.

"You have taken too much on yourself," he began vehemently. "You had no right to go ahead without consulting me. Because I've given you full swing you think you are the whole thing, but you're not. And as for your rushing in on me without warning and expecting me to let you turn all the assets of this corporation over to your new 'Standard Oil' friend, I won't stand for it. You can't do this corporation's business that way."

He poured on for five minutes without giving me a chance to interpose a word. He seemed to be consumed with anger and paced up and down the office. Then suddenly he stopped:

"We cannot afford to have any trouble, you and I, Lawson. I'm sure you did only what you thought best, but the fact is, I pledged some of those bonds for our war supplies a few months ago, and though I'm not going to dispute it with you, I'd swear I told you at the time."

As Addicks talked I had been mentally reviewing the situation in which I found myself. I saw myself dropped out of Rogers' consideration as the same kind of a financial trickster that Addicks was. For the moment, I had no fight left; I was knocked out.

"Don't feel bad, Lawson. You got as far with Rogers as it is possible to get, and you are dead right when you say that once we get hold of his corporation so that every one knows we've licked him, we can easily sell stock enough to pay him in a few weeks." As he talked he was again the master financial trickster, full of device and strategy. Finally I answered:

"Don't say any more, Addicks. Words won't help us. I've got to face Rogers as soon as a train can take me back to New York, and after that—then I'll have something to say to you." I started to go.

"What are you going to say to him?" he asked.

"Say to him? What can I say to him? At my solicitation he gave me a hearing—at his own home—treated me best in the world. I told him certain things, and pledged my word they were truths, and I've got to go back and tell"

"Tell what?"

"That I'm either as big a liar as he says you are or a fool—a doddering fool."

"You are going to do nothing of the kind," Addicks declared peremptorily. "You're going to tell him that you were not posted up to date, and that I, being pressed for money, had pledged some of the million and a half I had told you we had. That's all. He'll see it all right, and he'll trade for—for—what we have left."

I suddenly remembered that he had not told me how many bonds he had on hand. Just a ray of hope in the fog.

"How many free bonds have we to offer, Addicks, suppose he is willing to overlook this ugly piece of trickery?" I asked anxiously.

"I'm not quite sure," he answered, "but I can find out from the books." He rang for Miller, his right-hand man, the dummy treasurer of the Bay State Company, and said to him: "Harry, Mr. Lawson has got mixed up about the bonds. He thought we had a million and a half. You remember we've pledged some in the loans. Just how many have we now on hand?"

"Harry" looked it up and said: "Just $904,000 worth."

"There you are, Lawson," cried Addicks. "There's plenty to assure Rogers we'll do what we agree to."

Fool that I was, I did not see his game. No one ever does see Addicks' game till it is too late, for no one but a moral idiot would play the game Addicks plays, and, thank heaven, moral idiots are so rare in life that it is not worth while figuring out the formula from which they work.

By one o'clock I was at Mr. Rogers' office at 26 Broadway.

He greeted me warmly. "Well, Lawson, did you get things finished up all right?"

"Mr. Rogers, I have a most humiliating admission to"

"Hold up right there. Cut out all explanations and excuses. Have you brought those bonds as you agreed to, or not?" His eyes were snapping and shifting from one color to another.

"No, I have not got them."

"Why not?"

Had I been a woman I should have clapped my hands to my ears and screamed, so sudden and bomb-like came those two words.

"He had used some of them and has only $904,000 on hand."

"Only $904,000!"

It is impossible to convey the concentrated scorn and sarcasm Mr. Rogers infused into these words, and he continued to glare at me for fully a minute, his eyes as searching as x-rays. When that glare shifted I had a presentiment it would leave me forever a stranger to him, and I made up my mind to turn on my heel and leave his office without a word. I felt that he was in the right, and that if I were in his place I'd glare, too.

Suddenly the expression changed. He said peremptorily: "Lawson, get on the first train for Philadelphia and bring back those agreements executed and the $904,000 instead of the $1,500,000."

"Mr. Rogers," I began, but he stopped me with an imperative gesture.

"Don't say a word, but do as I tell you. I warned you you were dealing with a dog, but you wouldn't have it. Now I'm going to put this trade through even if I make a fool of myself thereby. You've done your work and that whelp shall not keep you out of its results. I'm in this now, and we will see if Addicks can outplay me as well as you. Not another word. I understand the whole thing."

I returned to Philadelphia deciding once and for all certain things in regard to Mr. Rogers and others affecting the future of J. Edward O'Sullivan Addicks; and that night Addicks and I "had it out." I shall not attempt to reproduce our talk. Suffice it to state that when I called for the bonds Addicks began to hem and haw, and then I realized that he had a second time lied to me. We were in his Philadelphia office, and it was night and we were alone. I demanded the truth, and finally he told me he had no $904,000 of bonds. As a fact he had not a single bond. He had used them to the last one and had deceived me for months. In regard to this interview Addicks has always maintained that I laid hands upon him, and that he was on the verge of doing some awful thing, but this is false. What I did was to turn the key in the door and then, without undue regard to his sensibilities, draw a word-picture of the position he had placed me in. Also I said what I thought of him. That is all.

The vast profits which the stock operator makes apparently overnight are often subjects for the world's wonder and envy. But if the gains are great, the road is muddy. If those who covet the golden rewards will participate in a deal or two, wallow in the filthy double-dealing which is an inevitable part of the cost price of success, they will quickly realize the dark side of the glittering game, and that the sacrifices are in proportion to the winnings. If I had been asked that night what price would recompense me for the hell Addicks' shabby deceit had stirred up in me, I should have said—that night—that no number of millions would pay for the bitterness of the experience.

It was after midnight when I left Addicks' office, and as I walked to my hotel I was steeped in gloom and bitterness. Before me was the most humiliating ordeal with which Fate had ever saddled me. I had to confess failure a second time, and under such circumstances that Rogers would be justified in believing me either a swindler or a dupe unworthy of respect or consideration.

I was at 26 Broadway by ten o'clock the same morning. Mr. Rogers was in his main private office. His secretary was with him. He was full of business, and, I thought, preoccupied. As I entered, and before a word of greeting passed, he gave me one of his keen, appraising glances.

"Well?" was all he said.

"Your estimate of Addicks was correct. He has no bonds," I said, giving him the worst of it at once. I was desperate and certainly in no mood for apology. Rogers looked at me. I thought he gasped. He rushed—whether he pushed or pulled me, or we both slid, or how we got there I don't know—but in an instant after I had said "He has no bonds" we were in one of the number of 8 x 12 glass-sided pens he calls waiting-rooms, but which the clerks have dubbed "visitors' sweatboxes." He put both hands on my shoulders and he yelled—fairly yelled: "Say that again! I did not get it."

In after-years I became on rather playful terms with the extraordinary bursts of wrath to which Henry H. Rogers occasionally gives way, and which sweep through the "System's" shrine like a tornado; but this was my first experience, and it was a shock and a revelation. Just what was going to happen next I could not imagine. I remembered afterward that the most definite of the impressions that chased each other through my mind was that Henry H. Rogers would surely have a stroke of apoplexy. Then that he would "bust." However, I pulled myself together and began:

"Mr. Rogers, what's the use of getting excited?"

I got no further. He jumped backward. The next second I was in the storm-centre. The room was small. Suddenly it became full of arms and legs and hands waving and gesticulating, and fists banging and brandishing; gnashing teeth and a convulsed face in which the eyes actually burned and rained fire; and the language—such a torrent of vilification and denunciation I have never heard, mingled with oaths so intense, so picturesque, so varied that the assortment would have driven an old-time East Indiaman skipper green with jealousy. I was horrified for an instant, then surprised, and after that, if it had not been for my position as the cause of it all, I should have been interested in the exhibition as a performance.

I could hear a stirring and a movement outside. The clerks were evidently aware of the scene. Forms passed rapidly across the ground-glass walls.

After a time Rogers controlled himself. Then he said to me in a voice still vibrant with passion:

"Lawson, tell me—put it in short, plain language—do you mean to say that after coming to me of your own accord and agreeing to do certain things, and then returning here to this very office, admitting that you had tricked me; after my overlooking that breach of faith and agreeing to take half the collateral simply because it was all you could raise, and because I desired to assist you—do you mean to say you have the audacity to tell me to my face that the whole thing is a lie and you have imposed on me?"

"I mean, Mr. Rogers, to tell you that Mr. Addicks has just proved to me that he has no bonds; that he is a liar and worse."

"Oh, he is, is he? But does that justify you in coming?—oh!----"

Again he was off. When he stopped for breath I raised my voice and made it loud and emphatic enough to convince even a man temporarily insane that my part as audience and victim had ended. I said:

"Mr. Rogers, I can't say more than that I apologize for the part I've been made to play in this transaction, and I'll leave your office prepared to take any kind of medicine, however harsh it may be, that you will deal out on account of all this. Not only will I take it, but I'll think you are right in administering it."

Rogers once more got himself under control. I stepped toward the door.

"One minute, Lawson—one minute. What are you going to do? Go back to your associate, that gentlemanly, square-dealing fellow in Philadelphia?"

"Mr. Rogers," I replied, "I ask no mercy at your hands, but there's a limit to the things a man will stand under the mess I'm laboring with. I'm going to do the best I can. What it will be I don't know. There's a deal of money at stake—my friends', the public's, my own—I'm responsible for it. I've made a terrible blunder. I am paying for it, but nothing that has happened has altered my idea of the duty I owe myself and others."

He was about to say something sarcastic. Then he choked back the words. His manlier nature rose to the surface.

"Lawson," he said, "I'm sorry for you. Upon my soul I am."

"You needn't be, Mr. Rogers. It's all right; it's part of the game, but I'm awfully sorry I came near you." I opened the door.

"One second more, Lawson," he said, stopping me and putting out his hand. "I'm not only sorry, but I give you my word I have not a doubt—no, not a suspicion of your good faith throughout this business—and if at any time you see your way to open up negotiations, you're welcome. Do you understand? You're welcome to come in here or to my house at any time you think you see your way out."

I said "good-by" and bolted before my feelings overcame me.

CHAPTER XIX

ENTER H. M. WHITNEY

It is not surprising that there should now have ensued an interval of silence and peace in the Boston gas war. Disheartened, disgusted, disappointed, I had to take stock of our position. However enraged I might be at the new revelation of Addicks' extraordinary veniality, the other elements in the situation remained as before. I could see nothing for me to do but to resume the tactics I had employed previous to the meeting with Rogers. My friends' interests had to be protected, and to do that war must be waged until a vulnerable spot in Rogers' armor had been found. But it was some days before I could screw my enthusiasm back to fighting-pitch. In the mean time Rogers did nothing. He, too, was waiting for new developments.

To this extent the situation had altered, however: I knew just where I stood with Rogers, and he realized the consequences of pressing us into a corner. I knew he would sell his company and retire from the field if I could find a way to pay him for so doing. He knew that if he turned the screws too hard I would as a last resort turn the tables by throwing Bay State Gas into bankruptcy. I tried many times and in many ways to find means to bring about a termination of the struggle, but to no purpose. Our extremity was such that it was impossible to do more than protect our companies from a receivership. To raise new capital to deposit as collateral with Rogers was out of the question, for the public, looking on at what was evidently most disastrous warfare, was in no temper to buy new stock.

The lull in our hostilities was only a pause between battles. It suddenly came to an end January, 1896, when a new enemy appeared in the field. Henry M. Whitney, who had built up Boston's electric street-railway system, and who, from his frequent dealings with the Massachusetts Legislature in obtaining franchises, had the reputation of carrying that body in his waistcoat-pocket, came before this Legislature with a proposition for a charter for a new and independent gas company. Up to this time Whitney had had no relation with the gas public. He based his new departure on the claim that he had come into possession of a patented device through which it became possible to turn the low-grade sulphuric coal of Nova Scotia into coke without sacrificing either the valuable by-products, such as ammonia, tar, etc., or illuminating gas. This was a very remarkable pretension, for we had long ago eliminated these low-grade coals from consideration as material for gas-making; but if Whitney's device actually was what he claimed, undoubtedly he would be a dangerous competitor. Whitney's petition set forth further, that because of the exceedingly low price of this Province coal and its richness in by-products he could afford to sell gas to consumers at 50 cents per thousand feet (the legal charge was then $1 per thousand feet), a price which would enable the great manufacturing institutions and all the steam and heating plants to use gas economically for fuel purposes.

The thing was sprung one day and was all over town before night. There were interviews and pamphlets floridly setting forth Mr. Whitney's good intentions toward gas consumers.

Mr. Whitney was, and is, one of Boston's most important citizens, at the present time president of the Chamber of Commerce, and a brother of the "System's" most Machiavelian votary, the late William C. Whitney. The application, backed by his prestige, and the roseate dreams of cheap gas it conveyed, created a sensation in Boston. Evidently he intended to have it seem that the people were in favor of the new charter, for simultaneously there appeared notices in the press calling for three distinct citizens' meetings. There seemed to be general rejoicing that at last the odious Standard-Oil Addicks-Bay State Gas outfit with all its corruption and unwholesome wrangling was to be deposited outside the city walls.

The experience of any man who has had to do with political and financial affairs invariably shows him that nothing ever happens of itself. Thunderbolts do descend from clear skies, but an enemy and not nature has hurled them. A clever tactician will always look for his antagonist's hand behind any isolated or detached fluctuation of public feeling which bears in the slightest degree upon his problem. In going over the circumstances, looking for the correct interpretation of the appearance in our field of this second Richmond, I took into consideration the fact that H. M. Whitney was deep in a speculative venture, Dominion Coal, which owned vast tracts of these low-grade coal lands in Nova Scotia, and it was known he had been trying vainly to utilize their products in the locomotives of the Boston & Maine Railroad and several other ventures in which he was a controlling factor. In one way it seemed reasonable that if Whitney really had found a way to get something out of his coal, he was justified in making the best possible use of it. On the other hand, I could not but see how the new project brought about the very situation at which Rogers had so long been aiming. Selling gas at 75 or 50 cents, the new company would absolutely command the business; the old companies must go bankrupt, pass into a receiver's hands, and in due course would be absorbed by the Whitney corporation. That would leave but one gas company in complete control of the Boston field, and it would not be bound to continue the low prices when competition had disappeared, but would be legally free to go back to the old rates of $1 and $1.25. In a combination which so completely went Rogers' way, surely his fine slim Italian hand might be perceived at the throttle.

Once I had made up my mind by what we were confronted, I lost no time. Inquiries revealed that Whitney's alleged control of the Legislature was not exaggerated. In fact, it seemed eager to do his bidding in any direction. There was no space for negotiation or deliberation, so I returned his bomb with another, which, exploding in his breastworks, created as much of a sensation as his own had done. I did not believe Whitney could do with Nova Scotia coal the things he claimed, but, whether or not, if he got his charter, Rogers' object would be accomplished. If he were absolutely bound, however, under heavy bonds to do exactly as he had promised, his proposition would be so loaded that it might go off in his own hands and blow him to pieces. The next day I went personally before the Legislature and agreed to pay the State of Massachusetts $1,000,000 for the charter Whitney had applied for, and offered to give bonds to do all the things Whitney would give bonds to do on receipt of it.

This proceeding caused a halt. It startled the public and set the Whitney forces agape. My proposition was decidedly novel, and on its face absurd—the State could not under the law accept a million dollars or any other sum for its charter—but, on the other hand, it was the quickest-acting horse-sense producer that could possibly have been brought to bear. It was discussed everywhere. Men said: "Why not? If the State has a valuable thing to give away, why should it not go to the one who will pay the people the most money for it?" I had outflanked the enemy, and if he gave battle it would have to be on my conditions. Whitney was furious, and his privately owned Legislature cursed me for interfering with its plans; but he and they recognized my advantage, and that night I had a call from Mr. Whitney and his attorney, George Towle.

"What are you trying to do, Lawson?" Whitney asked.

"Only trying to protect from destruction the Boston gas companies of which I am vice-president and general manager," I replied.

"But my proposition is a perfectly legitimate one," Whitney objected. "I have got hold of this invention, which enables me to utilize my Dominion coal in such a way that we can make coke out of it, and at the same time get all the gas. This coal is cheap to produce and costs little per ton to bring in. So I can sell gas cheaper than you can make it."

"And we have a plant for the manufacture and distribution of gas which has cost us seventy years and millions of dollars to get together, and we have also the customers to whom you must sell your cheap gas," I returned. "If you can really do what you claim, why not go ahead, make your gas, and sell it to us? We will distribute it to the people and we will divide the profit, and you will make as much as though you did it all, for you will not have a fight on hand nor be obliged to build up a duplicate plant. That's all you can do now; you cannot get a charter to duplicate our plant, because whatever price you offer the Legislature for it we will go you a few hundred thousand better."

We argued for hours. I showed him that if he finally prevailed and got what he was after, his charter would bind him to the absolute fulfilment of his promise under bonds that would make it unprofitable and dangerous. He finally made up his mind that such a victory was not worth winning, and he said to me:

"What kind of a hitch-up can I make with you and your companies?"

"Any fair one," I replied. "This is the situation as I see it, and I'm going to be frank: You say you have a good scheme, but you certainly have a Legislature, and you have evidently entered into a compact with Rogers whereby he is to utilize what you have, to knock us on the head. Now we have fairly checkmated you, and Rogers is out. Seems to me you owe it to us and yourself to give us the same chance you offered him. Let us utilize your plans to save ourselves and to knock Rogers on the head. But first, are you free to go on with us without explaining things to 'Standard Oil'?"

Whitney assured me that his arrangement with Rogers was tentative, depending on whether he could get the charter and could carry out his other plans.

After some further manœuvring we agreed that we should withdraw our offer from the Legislature, that Whitney should secure the new charter, and that it should be so worded as expressly to allow his company to lay pipes, manufacture, buy or sell gas, and to consolidate any or all of the existing or new gas companies in the State of Massachusetts; and that when the charter was granted it should belong equally to the Addicks Boston gas companies and to Whitney. Upon their part the Boston gas companies would buy of the new company all the gas it produced at something less than it was costing them to manufacture it under the old process. That bound us to nothing dangerous, and we were not forced to take Whitney's gas unless he actually got the results he promised.

At this time I knew nothing whatever of the workings or the wire-pullings of State legislatures. My business life had been engaged at the stock end of corporate transactions, and I had not troubled myself about franchises, or how they were obtained, being content to play my part with the manufactured product with which we dealt on the market. In a general way I knew political corruption existed. That Rogers had obtained favors for his Brookline Company through bribing officials I had good grounds to believe; I had read of strange doings in connection with H. M. Whitney's West End Railway franchise obtained from the Massachusetts Legislature amid an accompaniment of much public scandal; but being quite without personal experience I had no clear conception of how things were done and, innocently enough, I asked Whitney before we parted:

"How is it possible for you to get this valuable charter from the Legislature, particularly with such a strong and honest man as Roger Wolcott in the governor's chair, when Addicks has been trying continuously for four or five years, regardless of expense, to secure an ordinary one under which he can combine our gas companies?"

George Towle answered for Whitney:

"Lawson, that part of the transaction is no affair of yours. Mr. Whitney will absolutely guarantee to deliver all those goods, and should it prove necessary to override the governor in getting them, he will guarantee to do that too. You can call all that done the minute we sign papers."

There was no doubt the new combination was a winner for both of us. If Whitney got the charter, he would be in a position to make a lot of money out of his Dominion Coal stock, which would surely go up with a bound in company with Bay State Gas stock when it became known that our companies were in the new deal. Besides, all the talk he would make over the value of the charter would help create a market for new stock which we would issue for the purpose of obtaining funds to buy Rogers out. Later, if Whitney's invention was what he imagined, his own profit would run into millions and our properties, having the sole right to distribution, would be stronger than ever. That meant resuscitation of Bay State Gas, and that all the stocks and bonds held by my friends and the public would return splendid profits.

I tested the scheme in all its aspects and found only one weak spot in it. We, the Boston companies, were to "go snags" with Whitney in the results of a legislative game in which he was to bear the expense of getting a charter, and as Whitney and Towle said it was to cost them $250,000 to $300,000 to get it, it looked as if there would be some nasty business done at the State House.

I do not set up for a saint, nor to possessing exclusive virtues which distinguish me from the ordinary American citizen who does business for gain. In reiterating that the bribery end of our "hitch-up" with Whitney did not appeal to me, I am neither pluming nor crowning myself; I am merely stating a fact. This was an emergency, however, I could not regard as a mere personal concern. It was my duty to care for the interests of a great property which must not be endangered by my scruples, and I was willing to be advised by my business friends in the matter. I went round among my most conservative banking, business, and newspaper connections and put hypothetical questions to them bearing on my difficulty. In nearly all instances the replies were the same, and the subject seemed to be regarded as a joke—what were legislatures for, anyway, but to be "fixed"? All who did business with legislatures "fixed" them, and Whitney was certainly the star "fixer." I frankly stated that I considered bribing a legislator as a low-down crime and that I did not believe it was done in our strait-laced old Commonwealth as freely as they all seemed to imagine. Thereupon I was sarcastically referred to my Bell Telephone, New Haven, and Boston & Maine Railroad friends, to the organizers of trust companies, and to many other representative pillars of social and business society who had had occasion to deal with the State. I started at once a round of investigation among men who would talk frankly to me, and discovered that a most iniquitous condition existed. Massachusetts senators and representatives were not only bought and sold as sausages or fish are in the markets, but there existed a regular quotation schedule for their votes. Many of the prominent lawyers of the State were traffickers in legislation, and earned large fees engineering the repeal of old laws and the passage of new ones. Agents of corporations nominated candidates for office, and paid the expenses of their election in return for votes for a favorite measure and promises to "do business." The Legislature was organized on the same basis; its executive officers were chosen because of their subservience to certain corporation leaders; committees were rigged to do given things and prevent other things from being done. Above all, I learned that the chance of a citizen of Massachusetts obtaining a charter from the Legislature of his State, unless he had money to put up for it, was about as good as a hobo's of securing a diamond and ruby studded crown at Tiffany's by explaining that he wanted it. In fact, the citizen's request would be regarded by senators and representatives very much as Tiffany's would regard the hobo's—as a joke first, then as an impertinence.

Right here I desire to say to my readers and especially to all those hypocritical and ignorant people who, imagining any strong statement must express a strong prejudice and not a fact, will cry, "He overstates! He exaggerates!" that in years after when I had full opportunity to study at close range the Massachusetts Legislature, its workings and those who worked it, all the impressions I had received at this time were absolutely confirmed. I do not hesitate to state, then, that:

The Massachusetts Legislature is bought and sold as are sausages and fish at the markets and wharves. That the largest, wealthiest, and most prominent corporations in New England, whose affairs are conducted by our most representative citizens, habitually corrupt the Massachusetts Legislature, and the man of wealth connected with such corporations who would enter protest against the iniquity would be looked on as a "class anarchist." I will go further and state that if in New England a man of the type of Folk, of Missouri, can be found who, after giving over six months to turning up the legislative and Boston municipal sod of the past ten years, does not expose to the world a condition of rottenness more rotten than was ever before exhibited in any community in the civilized world, it will be because he has been suffocated by the stench of what he exhumes.

To return to my story, after my investigations I again saw Whitney and Towle, and they, not relishing my remarks on the subject of bribery, told me frankly to attend to my own part of the affair and leave their part to them. At this stage I called in Addicks, our corporation counsel, and some of the largest holders of Bay State bonds and stock, and put before them the bargain I had arranged with Whitney. They all agreed it was an excellent combination, and ratified the terms I had proposed to Whitney. It was further agreed that Whitney should make over to us one-half ownership in the new company, which we were to transfer to the Bay State Company after the charter had been granted.

There was every reason at this stage in the deal to regard victory as assured, for it did look as though the flapping sails on our much-buffeted and battered craft were at last to be filled with a lusty breeze strong enough to carry us to the harbor we had so long been trying to make. Besides what we ourselves could do and had already done, we now had Whitney for an ally in the deal, and certainly he was a stock-selling power throughout New England. He had agreed to go before the Legislature and the public, and pledge his word that his scheme would do all the wonderful things he had promised for it. And when amid acclamation the charter was awarded and it became known that we were its beneficiaries, I could see our stock soaring.

CHAPTER XX

AN AWKWARD ATTACK OF APPENDICITIS

In no walk of life is that head-light axiom, "Man proposes, God disposes," so often flashed plump in the eyes of enthusiastic travellers for their bewilderment or befuddlement as in finance. At this very moment of success I was, without knowing it, on the brink of ruin, owing to causes and conditions which were beyond human power to calculate or foresee. Here is what happened:

All the details of our bargain having at last been agreed upon verbally, it was proper the principals should get together and formally execute the documents which should bind the trade. We arranged to meet on a given Saturday at the beautiful stock-farm of Parker C. Chandler, Esq., the Bay State's general counsel, and as secrecy was important, a special train was to take the party the twenty-five miles out of Boston. By an unavoidable accident I missed the train, and in driving over the road in a bleak rain-storm, caught a violent cold. I was about three hours late, but when I arrived we went to work with a will and by seven o'clock, shortly before dinner, our contracts had been dictated to the stenographers and would be typed, ready to sign, by the time we came to our coffee.

That dinner was a thing to be remembered. No one in New England understands more admirably the art of dining than does Parker Chandler, and he gave us a feast worthy to celebrate the brilliant new combination which was to end all our troubles and lead us out of darkness into the light. As the cheese was being served I was seized suddenly with a terrible pain, which was followed by convulsions. They carried me to a bedroom; lawyers and capitalists went scurrying after doctors, and in the confusion the documents which were all ready awaiting execution were put aside. It was obvious that at that moment I could not O.K. them. At last specialists from Boston arrived and it was diagnosed that I was suffering from an aggravated attack of appendicitis. At two o'clock in the morning, after a prolonged consultation, the consensus of opinion was that my next field of operations would be in another world.

It must have been some time a little later that I, awaking to a brief interval of consciousness, witnessed a tableau, the memory of which invariably rises to my mind's eye whenever I try to mitigate or subdue my feelings of hatred and disgust for Addicks. The room was dimly lit; the two doctors were at the foot of the bed; Addicks, standing beside them, was looking fixedly at me. I caught his eye; doped as I was with opiates I saw the cold, calculating expression of his face, which told me as plainly as words that he felt it was all up with me, that my usefulness to him was at an end, and that without a thought for my interests or a scintilla of regret, he was calculating how to turn my death to his advantage. An amused conviction of the man's heartlessness crept over me, and then I passed out into the land of dreams.

From that night until one bright morning ten days later, I was visiting other worlds than those of finance and gas; but on the tenth day they told me I had eluded the grim ferryman and, barring accident, might get out into the world again in five weeks. A suspicion which owed its origin to that glimpse of Addicks on the first night of my illness awakened in my mind, and the following day I sent for my principal attorney and demanded an exact statement of what had happened in the interval of my illness. He had kept close track of all that had occurred, and the facts he revealed, calloused as I was to the thought of Addicks' baseness, horrified me by their cold-blooded villany. My associates had gone ahead with a vengeance, without waiting a minute to see whether I should live or die. My offer to the Legislature had been withdrawn; Addicks had substituted his name for mine in all the documents, and then he had traded with Rogers. It had been arranged between them that Whitney should go on and get the charter, which was to allow the company to sell gas at any price, for it was not to be under the supervision of the gas commissioners, who had pledged the public that the price of gas in Boston should not ever be more than $1 per one thousand feet. This obtained, a new corporation was to be organized, into which Rogers would merge his companies, and Addicks our Boston properties, in such a way as to leave Bay State stock and bondholders high and dry, while Addicks, Whitney, and Rogers reaped tremendous profits. These amiable plans were being hammered into shape at top speed, and unless I could get into harness at once, my friends and I would most certainly be ground up. Head-quarters had been opened at the Algonquin Club, and there Addicks, Whitney, Towle, and the lawyers and lobbyists were holding day and night sessions.

There was but one thing for me to do, and I lost not a moment. I sent for my doctors and said: "I will devote to-day, to-morrow, and next day to getting well; but on the fourth day I will be moved in a special car to Boston and then to the Algonquin Club." I explained the situation and showed them that regardless of all consequences this must be done.

I shall never forget the expression on the faces of these loyal associates of mine—Addicks, Whitney, and the others—when I dropped in upon their deliberations Saturday morning, four days later. My doctor, a nurse, and my lawyer accompanied me, and I was swathed in flannels and shawls. I got to a chair, dismissed my attendants, and launched in. What little I had to say would be brief, I told them, but "edgy." It was all that. I insisted that we should go right back to our old bargain exactly at the place we had left it the night I was taken ill. If they did not comply, I would make application for a receiver for the Bay State companies and give to the afternoon papers the inside facts of the affair from beginning to end. No one doubted either my ability or my determination to carry out my threat. We sent for the documents that had been prepared at Parker Chandler's, and inside of three hours these had been substituted and the several agreements entered into with Rogers formally renounced. I retired to bed that night with a chuckle of self-satisfaction, and a convincing appreciation of the truth of the axiom I have referred to.

The low-down treachery and double-dealing characterizing this transaction, the utter callousness to sacred obligations it exhibits in men of presumed high standing and personal honor, may surprise my readers. I assure them that several such episodes will be told in the forthcoming pages of this history. Indeed, among a certain school of eminent financiers, loyalty is no more than devotion to the opportunity of making the highest profit. If circumstances shift this from the side of their enlistment to that of an adversary, their arms and hearts go where their pockets lead. It must be remembered that the Hessian who "down-town" is steeped in perfidy, trickery, and fraud, may appear before the "up-town" world as a Christian citizen and an example of domestic virtue. The type is not uncommon nowadays of the pleasant and proper gentleman, prompt to knock down any one daring to asperse his veracity after five any evening and all day Sunday, but who considers himself free to engage in any dirty juggle or misrepresentation from 9 A.M. to 4.45 P.M. In office hours you run no risk in calling him a liar, for then he'll laugh at the joke and tell you business is business. However, the foregoing episode was an experience that left an indelible impression on my mind, and the hatred and disgust it engendered precipitated events out of which in the course of years came the offences and injuries that are responsible for the story of "Frenzied Finance."

The immediate results of my reappearance were not startling. Rogers raved at Addicks and especially at Whitney, but he was too old a student of men, and the monkeys Dame Fortune makes of them, to sulk over the facts he could not remedy. He soon resumed his former attitude of waiting for something to turn up, which indeed he had maintained ever since my unsuccessful effort to make terms with him.

Fate had not yet tired, however, of playing shuttlecock with our hopes. The world learned one morning of a new gas called acetylene, clear, brilliant, cheap, and simply made from calcium carbide. It would surely revolutionize gas-making the world over, and the company which could secure the right to it would have those who could not at its mercy. Addicks moved like a flash to gather in the advantage, and the announcement that the new gas had been proved a success was coupled in the press with the news that the Bay State Gas had captured the invention for New England, and was to pay millions for it. This did give a boost to our securities, and for a time it looked as though we had clinched our success with another rivet. What Addicks had done was this: He had bought the right, subject to the test of a big public demonstration. For this demonstration a fine flare-up was arranged. Eminent mayors, counsellors, and gas magnates were to attend in multitude, and if the invention met its engagements, there would be such a blaze of publicity and congratulations that we felt sure our new stock would go off like hot cakes. The demonstration proved in a most sensational way that acetylene was a failure—a tremendous explosion occurred; three men were killed, many others injured, and next day back went our stock to its old figures.

All this time I had sought most diligently for the real solution of our troubles—a method of purchasing Rogers' companies. A substantial guarantee there must be, not only for the performance of our financial engagements but to insure to Rogers the integrity of his properties while under the domination of Addicks. The difficulty was, in the weakened condition of the company, to put together any satisfactory guarantee. Others in our group had wrestled with the problem as strenuously as I had. Suddenly, a few days before May, 1896, the light came to me. All the time the solution had been in our hands, and, beset as we were, it had never occurred to any of us. We absolutely controlled the old Boston gas companies. They were intrinsically among the richest corporations in Massachusetts, and although their stocks were pledged for the $12,000,000 of bonds held by the public, they did not owe a dollar. Though the terms of the agreement between the Bay State Company and the Mercantile Trust, which held their shares, precluded them from contracting any debts, they were empowered, through us, their officials, to buy or sell gas, and all their great wealth was behind such contracts. If, then, we agreed on their behalf to buy gas of the Brookline Company for a term of years at such a price and in sufficient quantities to give the latter concern a profit equal to ten per cent. dividends on its stock, surely we had complied with the very letter of Rogers' exaction. Testing the idea in one way and another, I found it sound as a bell. The problem after that was to get into shape for the substantial issue of new stock we must make to pay for our purchase. The banks and trust companies were loaded up with our securities pledged for loans, and before there could be any conviction behind our prosperity it behooved us to get all our valuables out of pawn. I went to Mr. Rogers and frankly told him I had solved our problem and his by a financial invention of my own. I entered into the details of our plan, explaining it would not even be necessary for us to buy any gas of him, because we would turn over a sufficient number of our own customers to the Brookline Company to secure to it the required profit. He saw in an instant the scheme with all its far-reaching possibilities, and assented. Then I broached the rest of my plan—we would pay him four and a half millions in six months. To do this we must sell stocks and bonds. Before we could do that it was necessary that he help us still further—he must buy of us all the bonds now in pledge and the stock of the Dorchester Gas Company, another Bay State asset up for security, all for the sum of a million and a half dollars. For this amount these securities would at once be released and turned over to him. Then he should resell them to us together with the Brookline Gas Company for six millions of dollars. There would be a formal turning over of the management of his properties so the public should be convinced that we really were the victors in the strife. Mr. Rogers saw my point, quickly ran over the details in his comprehensive way, and closed the trade without further bargaining. That time, thank Heaven, it was not within Addicks' power to thwart me.

On May 1st we made our settlement in compliance with the terms I had arranged. The six millions of dollars were to be paid November 1st. As the necessary options and sales could not legally run to our company, they were made to Henry M. Whitney, and he simultaneously transferred them to us, and we elected him a director of our different corporations. Rogers publicly resigned and turned over to us the control of the Brookline Company, and we elected our own management. To all intents and purposes we had won.

The settlement was the sensation of the day in financial circles, and I was the recipient of many generous congratulations. I had neither time nor inclination to take care of bouquets at that moment, however. I was too keenly aware of the difficulty of raising six millions of dollars in the limited period at our disposal. Times have changed since 1896. Then six millions was quite a large sum, larger than sixty millions now. That was before the halcyon period of "Frenzied Finance."

CHAPTER XXI

BRIBING A LEGISLATURE

That six months between May 1st and November 1st was the most crowded period in all my experience up to that time. Events of consequence tumbled over one another in startling succession. We actually lived on sensations. In exercising the historian's right to choose the order of setting down incidents I am puzzled as to which to give precedence. Shall I begin with the sensational bribery of the Massachusetts Legislature which occurred within this period, or with the episode that was the exciting climax of that interval of trial? About this time, too, occurred the laying of the foundation of "Coppers" and Amalgamated, but that certainly requires a chapter to itself. However, as all are starry examples of what made "Frenzied Finance" possible, and as any one fits into my story as well ahead as behind the other two, I'll take them in the succession above set down.

The Whitney machine for the manufacture and moulding of legislation was complex but efficient. It achieved its wonders in broad daylight. Considering all it did and how that all was accomplished, the astonishing fact is that no outcry to speak of was ever raised at its performances. It was vastly bolder than Tammany and made fewer excuses for its grabbings. It must be remembered, however, that its chief engineer was a leading citizen, and his assistants all gentlemen of great respectability and admirable antecedents, and, in Boston, social and civic distinctions are shields behind which much may be concealed.

Corrupting a Legislature is not something a man may do with a fillip of his finger and thumb. However bold the operations, the convenances must be observed. When really large designs are entertained, the manipulator sets to before the preceding election and has his "lawyers" at work throughout the country interviewing candidates and ascertaining their feelings. Thus a certain percentage of votes are signed and sealed in advance, ready for delivery at the proper time. But there is always a crowd of new men who must be taken care of on the spot, and these must be approached with tact. Some amateurs have fanatical notions of honor which interfere with both their own and the interests of franchise-grabbers. To deal with all contingencies, to take care of captured votes and to shape legislative proceedings along safe lines, requires the services of almost an army of men.

At the head of Whitney's forces was his lawyer, George H. Towle, big of brain, ponderous of frame, and with the strength of an ox. A man of terrific temper, he knew not the meaning of the word fear. Nothing aroused him to such frenzy as to have to do with a legislator who unnecessarily haggled over the price of his vote or influence. On occasions when a lieutenant reported that Senator This or Representative That would not come into camp, Towle, with an oath, would say: "Take me to him, and I'll have his vote in ten minutes or there'll be occasion for a new election in his district to-morrow!"

Second in command was Mr. Patch, Towle's secretary and factotum, his exact opposite in every way. Where Towle was brutally straight to the point, Mr. Patch was as smooth an intriguer as ever connected himself with secrets by way of keyholes and transoms. It is a Beacon Hill tradition that for years Towle on final-payment day would have the members of the Massachusetts Legislature march through his private offices one at a time, and, handing each of them their loot, would proclaim: "Well, you're settled with in full, aren't you? That represents your vote on and on ." Then he would loudly identify the bill and the particulars of the service, while behind a partition with a stenographer would be Mr. Patch, who after the notes had been written out would witness the accuracy of the stenographer's report. When the Legislature assembled again, old members, the same story goes, would be requested to call on Towle to renew acquaintanceship. Then he would allow them to look over his memoranda "just to keep them from being too honest," as he gently phrased it.

Subordinate to Towle and Patch was a long line of eminently respectable lawyers known over the Commonwealth as "Whitney's attorneys." These men assisted at nominations, orated at elections, and took care of the finer preliminary details. The first line of attack was composed of practical politicians of various grades—ex-senators or representatives, and local bosses, who were known as "Whitney's right-hand men." Below these were the ordinary lobbyists, the detectives, and runners, who kept "tabs" on every move and deed, day and night, of the members of the Legislature. This was the Whitney machine, and it worked together with that fine solidity and evenness which can be attained only by constant practice and much success. In comparison with this competent organization, an average "Tammany Gang," a "Chicago Combine," or a "St. Louis Syndicate" would look like a hay-covered snow-plough in August.

It is seldom the public is given an opportunity of seeing a picture, drawn to life, of the Legislature of one of the greatest States in the Union in the act of being bribed to grant the votaries of "Frenzied Finance," for nothing, those things which should and do belong to the people, and for which the "System's" votaries would willingly pay millions of dollars if they were compelled to. I shall dwell on the performance that ensued at this juncture of my story long enough to present an outline of such a proceeding.

Head-quarters for Whitney's Massachusetts Pipe Line were opened at Young's Hotel—Parlors 9, 10, and 11, Rooms 6, 7, 8, second story front. Parlors 9 and 10 were the general reception-room, while 11 was reserved for the commander himself and for important and "touchy" interviews. The rooms 4, 5, 6, 7, 8 were used for educational purposes. In the morning the place was deserted, but at noon the parlors began to fill up with the different officers of the "Machine" and their friends, trustworthy members of the Legislature. A little later an elaborate luncheon would be served, the supernumeraries eating in one room, Towle and his chiefs and the legislators in the other. At table the gossip of the morning session at the State House was exchanged and the work laid out for the afternoon legislative and committee sessions. Another interval of silence and peace until at 5.30 the real business of the day began. Mr. Patch was generally on the ground first, carrying the books in which the bribery records were kept, for be it remembered that the efficiency of the Whitney machine was largely due to the thoroughly systematic manner in which its operations were conducted. Nothing was left to chance or to any one's memory. In turn, the subordinates presented careful reports of the day's transactions. At 6.30 Mr. Towle would go over these documents, "sizing up" the actual results for submission later to the chief himself. Between 7.30 and 8.30 the "Machine" dined; the remains of the feast having been removed, the doors were locked and the books brought out.

If an outsider could possibly have obtained the entry to the head-quarters of the Whitney Massachusetts Pipe Line, say at nine o'clock any evening during the session, he might easily have imagined himself at the Madison Square Garden or at Tattersall's on the evening of the first day of an international horse-sale. This is what he would have seen: In Parlor 10, seated at a long table a dozen of Mr. Towle's chiefs, all in their shirt-sleeves, smoking voluminously; before each a sheet of paper on which is printed a list of the members of the Legislature; against every name a blank space for memoranda; at the head of the table Towle himself, frowning severely over a similar sheet having broader memoranda-spaces. One after another the chiefs call off the names of the legislators, reporting as they go along. The outsider would have heard droned monotonously: "..... from ..... not my man; ..... from ..... my man and .....'s man; seen to-day, stood same as yesterday; ..... from ....., raised price $20, making it $150; agreed; $10 paid on account, total of $90 due; raised because ..... told him that he had got $20 more from ....."

As each man reports the other chiefs and Towle discuss the details, and when a decision on disputed points is arrived at, Towle makes a memorandum on his blank, and the chiefconcerned records the order in the little note-book which each carries. All reports at last in, Towle retires to Room 11 and speedily returns with the "stuff," consisting of cash, stocks, puts, calls, or transportation tickets, which he deals out to the chiefs to make good their promises for the day. It would have been obvious to the outsider, as soon as he had learned what was being dealt in, that a large proportion of the members of the Great and General Court of Massachusetts had bargained with the different members of "the machine" to sell their votes not only in committee but in full session of the Legislature, and that the price was to be paid when the votes were cast, though something was invariably exacted on account, to tie the bargain. Payment was made in cash, calls on Bay State Gas or Dominion Coal, or transportation on any of the railroads in the United States or Canada. The latter appears to be a class of remuneration Towle favored, probably because it cost nothing.

The conference seldom closed for the day without Towle admonishing his subordinates: "The old man's getting dead sore at the way his leg is being pulled, and if you fellows don't get those countrymen to play a more liberal game, they'll just drive the boss out of the business, and then there'll be a slump in prices that'll make them prefer to stay home and farm."

You may ask here, Could such things happen without attracting public attention? Or are the citizens of Boston so habituated to the corruption of their Legislature that they could witness unmoved this wholesale bribing campaign conducted in full daylight from Young's Hotel? Thank Heaven, this is not so. There are in every American community honest, sturdy souls who can be depended on to come forward in emergencies and cry out aloud against a threatened political crime. Above the brute hubbub of a city's roar their voices are heard like the voice of conscience, and the hurrying throng pauses a second in its mad rush after dollars to listen to their tale of the Commonwealth's wrong. But what's in the air is not on earth. The practical politicians, whose affair it is to heed and counteract these honorable protests, laugh contemptuously at the vanity of any contest between theories and the "stuff." They know the overpowering logic of gold.

There were public meetings in Boston; good-government clubs throughout the State met and "resoluted"; citizens' organizations howled robbery and malfeasance. For a few weeks all Massachusetts seemed wrought up. From the space the papers gave the protestants one might have imagined that there was a chance for virtue, but the results of the clamor were more apparent than real. Day by day, night by night, the "machine" ground away at Young's, and as its product fell into the hopper Whitney and Towle only smiled at the clamor and awaited the moment when, as Towle coarsely put it, "the reformers would have yawped themselves to a standstill."

That day came at last. One by one, all in a perfectly orderly and methodical manner, the giving-bonds-to-compel-promises clauses, restrictive amendments and other people's safeguards had been voted down and the "Are you ready for the main question?" having been put in both houses, the Massachusetts Pipe Line Charter was duly passed and sent on to the governor. It required his signature to make the bill a hard-and-fast law, and that once appended, all Towle's "promises to pay" became due.

As the campaign neared a finish Whitney had, a number of times, informed his chiefs, and they the members of the Legislature, that the governor had given personal assurance that if the bill passed both houses, he would sign it. On this score all interested had been relieved of doubt, and immediately upon the Senate's favorable action Bay State and Dominion Coal shares advanced in price. During the period the governor had the bill under consideration there was an active and rising market and a great volume of transactions on the Stock Exchange. Apparently the day of our peace and prosperity had dawned at last. But we were not yet out of a gnarled Fate's clutches.

In the midst of a strenuous forenoon of trading, suddenly, without the slightest warning, both stocks began to sink in price like pigs of lead from a capsized boat. At once I was on the defensive. To prevent a wild market panic during the few minutes consumed in getting telephone connection with the State House, I had to purchase thousands of shares. I knew that something disastrous had happened, but was not prepared for the startling information that came over the wire: "The governor has vetoed the Whitney bill with a savage message." My informant told me that Towle and his men were making for head-quarters on a run. As I hung up the receiver, the bell rang again. In a second my telephone with Whitney's office was in the middle of a spasm.

"Have you got the news, Lawson?"

"Have I got it? The tape is screaming it. Bay State and your stock are racing for the bottom," I replied.

"What shall we do? This is a thunderbolt."

"Do?" I replied. "It's for you to say what to do. That's your end, not mine, but from now until three o'clock one thing you must do, or there'll be no further thinking on the subject—protect Dominion Coal—have your brokers on the floor every second and tell them to buy all that's offered. Beat a slow retreat if you must, but prevent a wild break. Things at the Exchange are bad now. I'll take care of Bay State. Look out for Dominion at once, and when you are through I must see you—where?"

"At Young's in ten minutes."

"I'll be there."

Ten minutes later I was in Whitney's head-quarters. There pandemonium reigned; all the cocksureness and bluster of the "machine" had vanished, and it was a horde of clamorous and excited men I found struggling round Towle and Whitney, who vainly sought to stay the panic. It was not disappointment at the governor's message that had so stirred these hardened practitioners of politics, but the terror of impending loss. The majority of the Whitney band, lawyers, lieutenants, and water-carriers had bought one stock or both on margin, and had assured their friends it was safe to plunge to the limit.

On earth there is no more pitiable sight than the panic of a herd of novice stock-speculators suddenly awakened to a realization of their ruin. The ticker clicks a sort of death-watch as the merciless tape, without hitch or let up, reels off destruction. To such desperate beings the stock operator—the market-maker—is the straw to save them from drowning, and to him they turn as the one possible source of aid and hope. I only knew these men at sight's end, but they knew me and were sure in their abject plight that I could help them—by what wizardry they never stopped to think. They were terribly certain that unless the market turned, their brokers must have additional margin or their stock would be thrown overboard, sinking prices still lower and bringing down their friends' stock, and so on, like a row of falling bricks.

From their comfortable viewpoint of out-of-temptation virtue, my readers may regard these lawyers, lieutenants, and water-carriers of Whitney as bad men, deserving of no sympathy, meeting here a righteous punishment; but, my word for it—and I know the world and the human ants and spiders who inhabit it—while they bore no marks of immorality, they were the average men one meets in one's journey over the bridge between the two unknowns.

My talk with Whitney and Towle was brief and pointed. It was no time for pow-wow. It was the moment for action. Men who do things in stock-markets never waste time over milk that is in the gutter. How to get new milk to replace that spilt is their care.

"What are you going to do, Mr. Whitney?" I asked.

George Towle started to explain. I stopped him.

"The market is bad," I said, talking quickly. "If time is dribbled, it will be worse, and—and Boston will be a warm place for you, Towle. It would not surprise me if it got warm even for Mr. Whitney, when the desperate men who are filling the brokerage shops and the corridors outside demand a reason why they were egged on to buy stocks on Mr. Whitney's word that the governor would sign. No excuses now; I want to know from Mr. Whitney just what he proposes to do. You both told me the legislative end was none of my business, and, thank Heaven, it was not. You said it was your business. Now, how about it?"

Henry M. Whitney is a great general. He also can light his cigar, when the battle's on, with the friction of a passing cannon-ball.

"I'm going to pass it over the governor's veto," he instantly answered.

"Can you do it?" I asked.

"I can, for I must." He meant it. It needed but one look into his and Towle's eyes to see they both had read the message on the back of To-morrow's visiting-card.

"All right," I said. "Let your people have the word, and it must have no doubtful ring; tell your brokers to buy Dominion Coal, and don't let them stand on the order of their buying. Dominion Coal must be put back, regardless of how much it costs or how little you want what you must buy. I will turn Bay State before three if it is necessary to trade in the whole capital stock to do it."

As I came out of Parlor 11 to rush back to my office I said to the despairing men who crowded the corridor outside the head-quarters, and who had in their desperation thrown all caution or thought of concealment to the winds: "Coal and Gas look to me like good buys." The sudden revulsion of feeling was pathetic. In a minute the news had spread by way of them to their brokers and their suffering friends: "It's all right; Whitney and Lawson are buying stock." It got to the Exchange almost as soon as I did.

We turned the market.

That night Whitney and Towle's plans were mapped out to the army and their orders despatched with a vicious snap that plainly said: "Whoever attempts to put the Whitney machine in a hole will be shown no mercy." The morning papers announced that Whitney had picked up the gantlet Governor Wolcott had thrown at his feet, and—all roads led up Beacon Hill.

It was a quick, sharp set-to. Every man was lined up with a jerk, and when the line was tallied up and tallied down and Towle had consented to the last raise in price of votes and given away to the final squeeze, the word went up and down the ranks that the Whitney bill would, on the approaching last day of the session, go flying through both Houses over the governor's veto with a vote or two to spare. Again the prices of the two stocks shot upward.

Then, sharp and quick as a bolt of lightning, Fate, who apparently had been camped on the trail of Bay State Gas and Addicks from the first, let fly another of her quiver's contents. On the morning of the closing day of the session (the one selected for the Whitney coup), there slipped in and out amongst the Whitney legislative ranks a man with a story. As each legislator listened, his brow knitted and he nodded assent. The story was a simple one: In one of Whitney's former campaigns, desperate like this one, on payment-day Towle had gone back on his promises and forced the acceptance of a fifty-cents-on-the-dollar settlement; and, so the story now went, he, Towle, had put the saved fifty cents, a matter altogether of some $75,000, in his own pocket. Probably he was now going to repeat the operation on an even larger scale. In an hour there came to Young's Hotel a trusty messenger who delivered to Towle himself the ultimatum of the Great and General Court of the dear old Commonwealth: "Money in advance or no bill!"

Consternation reigned. The army was quickly recalled to head-quarters, and despatched back to the State House to put through every manœuvre known to the two veterans—but to no purpose. The Great and General Court stood its ground, openly defied the army and hurled back into Towle's teeth all his frantic threats. It was the last day, and the Great and General Court was intrenched inside the protecting walls of the State House, and it knew that before it could be compelled to come forth to face Towle he must come to a decision. A terrible dilemma, surely, for the amounts promised had run up to such an enormous aggregate that it was impossible to pay all in so short a time, even if such had been Whitney and Towle's intention. Yet to pay one or a few of the dangerous malcontents meant to pay every one; the gang had firmly banded themselves together.

This was the real moment of panic. Even Whitney and Towle were at their wits' end. Finally, in desperation, and as a last resort, Whitney rushed to the governor, threw up his hands, and asked for mercy. "What would the governor sign?"

Massachusetts' able and fearless Governor Wolcott, who seemed to have been expecting some such outcome of the battle, gave his answer clear as an anvil-blow:

"You have told the people your company would give them cheap gas. Bind yourself to do it by amending the charter so that the highest price your gas can be sold at will be sixty cents. Then I will sign."

There was nothing else to do. At the last minute the amendment was inserted. The governor's representative gave the word that it was satisfactory, and it passed.

I was in my office taking care of the market. Of the stampede I knew nothing. Suddenly came the word: "The Whitney bill has passed on the governor's recommendation." Both stocks started to jump; then a halt, then—I didn't try to stop the decline, for I saw something terrible had happened. In a few minutes the news was on the Street: "The charter was not worth the parchment upon which it was engrossed."

The biter had been fatally bitten.

The market closed with the tape and ticker fiercely, exultingly shouting "Ruin!" with each tick and slip: and that night Whitney's head-quarters was little better than a mob. Frantic men demanded money, money due to them for votes, money they had promised for margins to the brokers before the Stock Exchange opened the next day, and swearing desperate consequences to Whitney and Towle regardless of the effect upon themselves.

Early next morning there came to my office two wild-eyed, desperate creatures, Towle and Mr. Patch.

I had spent the night going over my accounts and those of which I had charge, and in addition to a quick, real loss of over a million dollars, I realized that the immediate future was so hung with dark clouds that I dared not anticipate what the coming day might mean to me and mine; but when I looked upon the big, powerful man, who had always seemed in any light in which I had heretofore beheld him to fear neither man nor God—when I looked and saw his plight I pitied him deeply, sincerely. He carried a large travelling-bag, and Mr. Patch two others.

"Lawson, for God's sake, don't do what they are all doing—don't upbraid me! I've got to get out into the world and be dead to all I know—family, friends, every one. If I stay, it's State's prison or worse, and Whitney says I must go. I've got all the papers together and Whitney has given me what cash he had on hand, and this check of $10,000. Do me one last favor, get me gold for it. I know I have no right to ask any favors of you, but think if you were in my place. I have a wife and children, and—" and the great, strong man wept like a child.

I called my secretary, and in a short time George Towle with the $10,000 in gold and the bags of "evidence" faded out of my life and into the gray mist of eternity.

A few days after, a vessel dropped anchor off the island of Jamaica; George Towle's body was carried ashore and buried, and Mr. Patch was escorted back to the ship. A few days later, with weights of lead to carry it to its last resting-place at the ocean's bottom, the latter's dead body was dropped over the vessel's side. And somewhere floating the high seas are a venturesome sailor-captain and a crew, who when in their cups tell, 'tis said, strange tales of bags of gold and mysterious documents.

As for the members of the Great and Good Court of the old Commonwealth of Massachusetts for the year of our Lord One thousand eight hundred and ninety-six, they received, none of them could tell from where, their promised vote-money in the form of a yarn that the "stuff" belonging to them had been delivered to George Towle, but that Towle had decamped with it to foreign shores, where he was living in luxury with Mr. Patch.

'Tis writ that some crimes are so black and foul that they will not down, and when I read over what is written here, I wonder if there will not some day be another chapter of "Frenzied Finance" written by another pen than mine.

I sent two police officials to the island of Jamaica, and had the contents of the coffin marked "George H. Towle" photographed. I could not photograph the contents of the ocean's depths.

CHAPTER XXII

PLUNDERED OF THE PLUNDER

So extraordinary a happening as the disappearance of George H. Towle and Mr. Patch, you think, should have furnished a national sensation. And this is the first you have ever heard of it. Bear in mind that here for the first time the facts of this case are set forth in their proper relation to one another, and without the fear or favor that has hitherto prevented them from being understood.

In Boston after the adjournment of the Legislature, however bitter the feeling of the men who had sold themselves, and those others who had lost their all in the crash of stock values that had followed Whitney's defeat, their own complicity enforced silence and prevented outcry. It was given out that George H. Towle and Mr. Patch, tired by their labors, had gone to the country for a brief sojourn. On their return there would be a settlement. And with these assurances, both legislators and lieutenants had, perforce, to be satisfied. Gradually, betrayers and betrayed drifted back to their own homes and their erstwhile avocations, and when the strange story of the disappearance and death of the chief actors in the Whitney drama came from over the seas, it fell on the heedless ears of men who had written off a loss and desired to forget the experience. A conspiracy of silence is easily organized among accomplices.

I myself was the greatest sufferer by the disaster. Banking on Whitney's assurance of success I had loaded up heavily with Bay State on my own account; and my customers pinning their faith to my predictions of a rise, had also bought heavily both of the gas stock and Dominion Coal. In my attempt to support the market when the first decline occurred, I had further increased my holdings, and, at the final break, thousands of shares purchased for my clients were left on my hands. So my loss was very large, many times larger than Whitney's. Like the others, I said nothing, crediting the expense to education, while Whitney silently tucked his emasculated charter into a crypt already furnished with other corporation derelicts, to await some fair opportunity of legislative or other resuscitation; for the instrument, shorn though it had been of its immediate availability, was by no means without real value. Probably in view of prospective contingencies, perhaps with a sense of what his error had cost me, he said to me: "Lawson, the Pipe Line charter is worthless now, but if at any time in the future it becomes valuable, you or your company shall have half of it."

If Henry M. Whitney had kept that promise, what a world of disaster and bitterness might have been averted. Generated in corruption, perhaps it is not strange that this charter has since been so fertile a breeder of dissension and ruin among all who have attempted to handle it. It may be accepted as an axiom of finance that double-dealing is as dangerous to the dealer as to his victim. The fierce conflicts that at intervals burst out in the financial world and like a cyclone spread dishonor and destruction broadcast, invariably are caused by some one man's treachery.

To return to my story. To all appearances, the gas war was over. We bore the palm of victory, but looming up before us was the task of getting together the six millions which Rogers must have by November 1st. That paid, the companies became permanently ours. It was a period of unremitting effort, but the prospects of success were excellent. Addicks had got ready a new lot of Bay State stock, and I had prepared the public to take it. With the proceeds of this stock and the securities which Rogers would turn over to us, we should have money enough to meet our engagement, always provided no slip-up occurred. Since the May 1st settlement our relations with Rogers had been satisfactory—I should say, my relations—for he persistently kept Addicks and his crowd at a distance, refusing to have anything to do with them. But it's hard to keep a big pot boiling in the open without some intruder smelling the savor of your soup and sneaking up for a mouthful. Though secrecy had been solicitously preserved regarding the details of our bargain with the "Standard Oil" magnates, certain of the camp-followers of "Frenzied Finance" had nosed out the facts, and at the very moment when our position and prospects seemed most secure a plot was being laid, which, as after-events will show, came close to bringing about the destruction we had thus far managed to escape.

As the time of settlement drew near, it became necessary for me to have frequent conferences with Addicks and his directors, and we opened headquarters at the Hoffman House in New York. It was my habit to come over for a short time every week, when we got together, reported progress, and discussed future moves. It was at one of these gatherings, on Friday, October 16th, that we had intimation of our peril. I had come down on the midnight train from Boston and was brimming over with pleasant news and agreeable anticipations. The day and all other things seemed good to me. The air was crisp and the morning sun gleamed brightly on the red and yellow autumn tints of the trees in Madison Square. For a moment I stood on the corner beside the naval monument watching the down-townward procession of cabs and coupés in which the spider aristocracy of finance makes its way to its webs in Wall Street and lower Broadway. In the parlor of Addicks' suite at the Hoffman the directors were gathered when I entered, and with them was Parker Chandler, the Bay State's general counsel. We got down to business at once. I told them how well our affairs were moving in Boston and listened to their tidings of progress elsewhere. We were all in the merry mood of success. The past was nothing but a bad dream; our thoughts were on the rich moments beyond November 1st when we should handle and know the real currency of our victory.

The telephone bell rang. Some one wanted Addicks quick.

Addicks stepped to the instrument. We all heard him say: "Hello." Then—"Is that you, Fred?" (Fred Keller was his personal secretary.) Then—"Yes, I hear you plainly. Repeat it." Then—a minute's wait while we listened. Then—"When will they get up there?" Then—"Send every one home, lock up and go over to the house, and call me on my wire." All this in his ordinary, well-attuned, even voice, without the emphasis of a word to show that the subject was a hair more important than any of the hundred and one ordinary messages which went to make up a large part of his daily life. The talk was so commonplace that we were none of us interested enough to even stop our chatter.

Addicks stepped from the telephone and in a "bring-me-a-finger-bowl" tone of voice said: "Tom, come into the other room for a minute; I want a word with you."

He passed ahead of me through a small parlor into his bedroom. I followed. He went straight to the bureau, took something from a drawer, slipped it into his pocket, turned and dropped upon a lounge. But a minute had elapsed since he had gone to the telephone. Could this gray ghost be the same man who a short time ago had been smiling so contentedly at Parker Chandler's last story? His face was the color of a mouldy lead pipe and seared with strange lines and seams. The eyes that met mine were dim and glazed, lustreless and dead as the eyes of a fish dragged from watery depths.

Courage is not character; it is temperamental. There is an impression that the man truly brave is he who can face sudden, unexpected misfortune or calamity without a tremor or a flicker to suggest his hurt. That is but a single phase and indicative of physical rather than moral qualities; or, perhaps, merely the callousness born of long exposure to danger. One of the bravest men I've ever known stood watching the ticker one day during a downward run. Suddenly I heard "My God, I'm ruined!" and he fell in a faint on the floor. And a certain bank officer, whom I knew to be an arrant coward when arrested for stealing a million, smiled at the policeman who had tapped his shoulder and asked him for a light for his cigarette. Addicks had not turned a hair as he hung up the telephone receiver, and here he was cowering in a mortal funk, abjectly hopeless.

"Lawson, the game's up," he said in a trembling voice. "That was Fred. He says Dwight Braman has had himself appointed receiver of Bay State; that he raided the Wilmington office immediately after he was appointed, broke open desks, and took all the papers he could find, and that in an hour or so he will be in Philadelphia and in possession of all my books and papers. He has a court order for the bank accounts and the right to take charge of our funds."

"This is a startler," I said; "what are we going to do?"

"The trap is perfect, and I'm in it. They've caught me with every bar down. Before, when they attempted to get a receivership, things were ready for them—books and papers packed for Europe and cash in charge of an unserved officer prepared at the first word to start for Canada. But now, a few days before election, when if I don't throw a lot of money into Delaware for my followers, they'll turn on me like wolves—they've caught me napping. It's a plot, sure—a receiver in possession, particularly Braman, and appointed in a way that shows deliberate calculation, proves it was done by some one who knows our situation to a 'T.' It means ruin for me and the company. You know I won't have a friend left on earth, and enemies now will rise up like snakes before a prairie fire."

It was indeed a stiff, tough turn, yet I was watching the man rather out of curiosity to note how he could take a reverse than out of sympathy. I don't believe there was another man on earth who, similarly placed, would not have aroused my pity; but Addicks—no man or woman has pity for Addicks.

"Well," I repeated, "what are we going to do?"

He did not reply for a moment. I continued to look at him. The eyes haunted me. I noted that the lines round the lids had deepened into furrows. He half raised himself from the lounge.

"I've said they would never get me, and they won't." Instinctively his hand sought the pocket into which he had dropped what he had taken from the dresser's drawer. Then I knew. The yellow streak showed plain at last. I had guessed from the start it was there.

The stock manipulator in common with the successful general must have the capacity to deal with the unexpected. The faculty to see a situation whole must be his, to focus instantly the lay of the land, the enemy's plans and strength, his own resources, the strategic possibilities of his position; and instantly, if necessity demands it, he must be ready with a new plan of campaign fitted to the first emergency. The more rapidly his mind works the safer are the interests he is guarding. But if he has not this capacity, he can never be a market manipulator.

For a moment I could not but pause to admire the devilish ingenuity of the trap that had been sprung on us. The state of affairs that Addicks revealed was about the worst imaginable. I had been on this particular war-path so long that my mind instantly grasped the possibilities of destruction that lay in this new attack. I saw November 1st—no money to pay Rogers; everything forfeited; Addicks in a nauseating scandal; and all those friends of mine who had put their funds into Bay State because of their confidence in my ability to win out slaughtered. No, it should not be if I could prevent it. Other storms we had met and weathered, why not this? Even if it were a tornado, we would "ride her out." Perhaps we should not be afloat when the rollers subsided, but at least we should be at rest—on the bottom. I turned to Addicks, who, heaped up on his lounge, was staring into vacancy.

"Brace up, Addicks," I said. "We are not knocked out yet. At least let us find out what has struck us."

I was some moments in arousing him from his condition of despair, but finally he pulled himself together, and piece by piece we went over the situation. I had to agree with him that he was in an end-to-end-center-pull trap. The cunning machinery he had set up to meet just such an emergency, now that it was in hostile hands, was rather a source of danger than of safety. There was but one way out of the complication—we must undo this receivership and release our properties and funds before November 1st. Addicks, when he got his thinking loom running, declared the receivership was all a "Standard Oil" plot to ruin him. I felt sure it was an independent operation, but there was no time for controversy.

The telephone bell rang again. It was Fred Keller, talking from Addicks' house. We soon had all the details of the raid. This is what had happened. Dwight Braman, a former Boston broker, now a New York capitalist and promoter, had suddenly appeared in Wilmington, Del., accompanied by Roger Foster, a New York attorney representing Wm. Buchanan, one of the original holders of Bay State Gas income bonds. He held $100,000. They had gone before Judge Wales, and pleading that the interest on the bonds was in default and that Addicks was dissipating the assets of the company, had succeeded in inducing the judge to appoint Braman receiver. The whole performance was put through with such marvellous rapidity that not one of Addicks' innumerable henchmen had had a hint of it, and so no warning could be given in any direction. Braman, an adept in corporation try-outs, lost not a moment, for the instant his receivership appointment was signed he pounced down on the Delaware offices of the Bay State and seized everything they contained. He was waiting there for the first train to Philadelphia for the purpose of capturing the head offices of our corporation, which were located there, adjoining Addicks' private offices.

It was the moment for rapid action. We had an hour before Braman and Foster could reach Philadelphia, and in finance in that time continents' have been submerged and oceans pumped dry. Addicks instructed Fred Keller to rush the books of the company into a trunk, together with all the private papers in Addicks' safe, and to come at once to New York, where he would be beyond the jurisdiction of the Delaware court. We returned to the large parlor and hastily explained to the waiting directors what had occurred. Addicks instructed the Bay State secretary, who was present, to connect with the trunk upon its arrival and disappear. In the meantime the company's counsel advised that Addicks and the other directors barricade themselves in their rooms at the Hoffman to frustrate any attempt to get legal service on them, for we well knew that Braman and Foster, as soon as they realized they were balked in Philadelphia, would go to the New York courts for additional powers—which afterward they did.

This line of defence having been fully organized I hurried down town to 26 Broadway. I felt certain that Mr. Rogers had nothing to do with the Braman-Foster affair, but to satisfy Addicks and make assurance doubly sure I determined to see him. After being with him for five minutes I knew I had not been deceived. Rogers agreed with me that the situation looked as though it had been made for his interest, for it threatened to leave us absolutely at his mercy with nothing to prevent his checkmating Addicks at his own game. As I pointed out to him, however, there were disadvantages in the position which he must take into consideration. His acceptance of the opportunity would work such losses to the public and to my friends that though the responsibility might be laid to Braman and Foster, I would fight so viciously that no one would be spared. Besides, between the Addicks scandal and that other which we agreed must unquestionably lurk in the hasty appointment of the receiver, the whole affair must eventually be ventilated in court. It is always hard for Mr. Rogers to forego an advantage, but by this time he was tired of the wrangle and wanted peace, and, moreover, he did not relish the thought of court proceedings, so he admitted that my reasoning was good, and promised to do anything in his power to assist us.

CHAPTER XXIII

TWO GENTLEMEN OF FRENZIED FINANCE

The enemy did not leave us long in suspense. Next day Braman and Foster arrived in New York, bursting with a noble wrath at the failure of their coup in Philadelphia. An outrage had been worked upon them, upon the public, upon the majesty of the law. To hear their ravings one might have supposed them the evangelists of Justice righteously denouncing a desecration of the sacred altar; or, that we had deprived them of an inalienable right they had possessed to our property. It would have been humorous if the conditions had been less tragic.

No defender of property right is so vociferous as the financier who, having appropriated his neighbor's goods, argues that possession constitutes legal ownership. On a country road I once almost rode over two hoboes, who were so busy wrangling with one another that they had not heard my approach. I gathered that one of them, having filched a collection of laundry from a farmer's backyard, had placed it in charge of his mate while he went off for a second helping, and had returned just in time to stop the latter from decamping with the swag. The talk the original purloiner was giving his ungrateful assistant was one of the best expositions of virtue and honesty I've ever listened to.

We met the following Monday and in reply to my request that we talk things over, Foster delivered himself of an exalted exposition of the rights of deluded stockholders, the majesty of the law, and the stern duties of Mr. Braman, who, for the time being, had departed his private self and, until further notice, existed only as a rigid arm of the court. Just as I had arrived at the conclusion that I had got into the wrong shop, Braman took up the lecture by informing me of things I already had made myself familiar with, to wit, how he had at different times occupied similar rôles in other corporations' affairs and how relentlessly he had exposed mismanagement and peculation. I suggested to him that in most such cases the receiverships seemed to have been dismissed in favor of the former managers. He waved his hands and replied that in this particular case there was absolutely no chance of control being returned to Addicks, who had outrageously abused his trust; "although, of course (this as a sort of second thought) you know, Mr. Lawson, if Mr. Foster on behalf of his client should receive the amount of his claim and the proper fee, from whatever source, I should be powerless to prevent the dismissal of the receiver."

Braman and Foster were a delightful combination. As the talented Chimmie Fadden would say: "Dey knew dere biz from de bar to de till an' from de till by de way of de cash register to de wine-cellar, so's dey could do de circuit wid dere lamps blinked and dere hands tied." With their corporation mix-up records I was familiar, and after a few minutes' talk realized that it would be impossible to do anything with them until they had kicked up against one or two of the bricks Addicks was now with renewed energy preparing to cast into their pathway. I left with an agreement to see them the following day, and a parting reminder that all natural history showed that unpicked ripe plums were in great danger of being blown from the tree with every passing breeze.

I hurried back to Addicks. "It's the old game," said I; "they are on the box and have the lines, and know just how badly we need our coach, and it's only a case of how much 'inducement' we can stand."

I left him and went down to 26 Broadway. I had not wasted time, but they had been there ahead of me.

"Lawson," said Mr. Rogers, "this time Addicks is up against a real condition, and phenomenal work will have to be done or his race is run. Braman and Foster have been here and made a strong bid for a partnership with me, but I did as agreed and sent them away with a cold 'I'm in no way interested.'"

Foster and Braman secured an order from the New York courts to take possession of all property, money, papers, and books claimed by the company, and formally laid siege to Addicks' quarters in the Hoffman. There was considerable excitement for the guests and the newspapers. Doors were battered down, but the astute and slippery Addicks led them a merry chase until they finally caught him hiding in a freight elevator which he was using for a private staircase, only to find he had no books, papers, or money.

The week that ensued was full of trouble and incident for all concerned. Addicks led an expedition to Wilmington in an effort to get the court to call off the receivership, but had his labor and the expense of his lawyers for his pains. Braman and Foster dragged us through a weary round of special hearings and demands of various kinds in the different courts, but by Tuesday night of the second week their ardor had cooled considerably and they were as puzzled how to let go of the bull they had captured as we were to find a way to make them do so.

Bright and early Wednesday morning Braman called on me, and when he threw his coat and hat into a chair he must have dropped his receivership cloak too, for after he had carefully closed the door and made sure we were without witness he said:

"If there's any business to be done in this matter it must be done quick."

I admitted no one could possibly appreciate this more than I—but what could be done? After bluffing for an hour and exchanging honest views for fifteen minutes we agreed that the situation stood thus:

If nothing were done before the coming Sunday, the 1st, the receivership would be permanent; the stock, which had fallen to $3 per share, would remain at that figure or go lower; my friends, the public, and myself would be tremendous losers; all the past of Bay State, the doings of Addicks and Rogers, and the appointment of the receiver would come in for thorough investigation; an awful scandal would be aired in public; every one would be covered more or less with mud; and no one could possibly be the gainer but "Standard Oil," for Braman agreed with me that the deal we had made with Rogers would probably stand in the courts.

On the other hand, if an arrangement could be arrived at by which we could have the receivership discharged, the company returned to its officers, or our equities preserved, all would be gainers by the move, for it would be proof positive that whatever the obstacles, we could overcome them, and the stock would go flying upward again.

After we had set out all the advantages, disadvantages, and possibilities of the situation, I bluntly plumped Braman with that inevitable question of all such "sit-downs": "What's the price?" And Braman as plumply and bluntly answered: "Buchanan, Foster's client, must have the face of his bonds and interest, $150,000, and we must have at least $150,000 for our trouble and expense."

My long experience in corporation affairs, and my intimate knowledge of the practices which the "System" with its votaries has made habitual was such that I was proof against shock from anything that could possibly turn up in even extraordinary financial deals, but I was just a bit staggered by the business-like way Braman demanded for himself and Foster $150,000 and the coolness with which he further explained that they must divide their share with certain influential persons without whose hearty cooperation the tangling-up which had been so cleverly accomplished would have been impossible. He made no bones of showing me that once "we gave up" it would only be a matter of the number of minutes required to get details fixed before everything would be as it was before he had interfered. I dwelt upon the possibilities of the judge not following orders to the letter and the minute, but he only smiled and answered: "Leave all that to us; if we don't make good as agreed, we get no pay." He was fully alive to the dangers of the game, and he impressed upon me he would take nobody's word for anything. With him and Foster nothing but money talked, and it must not be of the marked-bill kind either, meaning he would not take anything which could be tied up by injunctions and lawsuits after the receiver had been dismissed. However, he would play fair. He would not ask us to pay on anything but the actual delivery of the goods. He also frankly told me that he had named the very low figure, $150,000, because he expected to invest what he received in Bay State Gas stock at $3 and, upon its jumping to $10 or $20, to make half a million.

But this is outrageous, you say. You call the performance I have described by hard names! Surely our courts are not also the creatures of "frenzied finance"? you ask. I warn my readers that this narrative is no more than a record of events occurring within my own knowledge, and that dark and vicious as the pictures seem they are photographs of actual happenings. Nor should the public conclude that the dishonor and dishonesty revealed in connection with Bay State Gas are exceptional. On the contrary, such doings are the rule in the affairs of great financial corporations. Into the rigging and launching of almost every big financial operation in the United States during the last twenty years, double-dealing, sharp practice, and jobbery have entered; and, what is more, the men interested have participated in and profited thereby. To correct a popular fallacy I want to say that I am not referring here simply to moral derelictions but to actual legal crimes. If the details of the great reorganization and trustification deals put through since 1885 could be laid bare, eight out of ten of our most successful stock-jobbing financiers would be in a fair way to get into State or federal prisons. They do such things better in England. During the past ten years three "frenzied financiers" have practised their legerdemain in London—Ernest Hooley, Barney Barnato, and Whitaker Wright. The first is bankrupt and discredited; Barney Barnato jumped into the ocean at the height of his career, and Whitaker Wright, after numerous attempts to escape, was hauled up before an English judge and jury, promptly convicted and sentenced, and committed suicide by poison before leaving the court-room. I will agree at any time to set down from memory the names of a score of eminent American financiers, at this writing in full enjoyment of the envy and respect of their countrymen and the luxury purchased by their many millions, whose crimes, moral and legal, committed in the accumulation of these millions, would, if fully exposed, make the performances of Wright and Barnato seem like petty larceny in comparison. But freedom and equality, as guaranteed us by the Declaration of Independence, have recently been capitalized, and "freedom" now means immunity from legal interference for financiers, while the latest acceptance of "equality" is that all victims of special privilege are treated alike by those who control and exercise such privilege. If the judges and the public prosecutors of these United States were equal to the sworn duties of their sacred offices, this "freedom" would have been confined long ago, and throughout this broad land there would be jails full of "frenzied financiers" who had imagined themselves licensed to rob the public.

But to return to Bay State Gas: "Braman," I said, "we see the situation through the same glasses, but before deciding as to prices let us see where the coin required is to come from. Until the receivership is dismissed not a cent can come from the Bay State treasury, so that eliminates Addicks. I, personally, am in such shape because of this same receivership that I can do nothing. So, as usual, it comes down to the man with unlimited money—Rogers. The question is, how to get Rogers to advance so large a sum in such a ticklish business? He does not want to get mixed up in a matter in which any one man's treachery might mean State's prison."

"Somebody's word ought to be good," he commented.

"Only two men's words would be of any avail," I interrupted—"yours and Addicks', and you have just made it clear that in this case neither would be worth the breath expended in pledging it."

CHAPTER XXIV

BUYING A BUNCH OF STATES

I left Braman and went down to Mr. Rogers. After a careful canvas of the situation it was settled that the only way out was for Rogers to furnish the money to release the receivership, in consideration of which accommodation Addicks should forfeit the old Boston companies to him through Bay State's failure to comply with the terms of the May contract which matured the following Monday. Rogers would administer these companies in trust, applying their earnings to the liquidation of the bonds, and after these latter had been paid off, would turn them back to the Bay State Company for the benefit of its stock; or he would release the companies to us whenever we could raise the money to redeem them. Thus Rogers would make sure of the amount of his original investment, the million dollars profit the May 1st deal permitted him, while I should have secured for my friends and the public the amount of their investment in the property and a good profit for the stockholders to boot. To secure Addicks' consent to this arrangement would be the difficulty; but there was one consideration that would probably induce him to give way—his terrible plight in case the receivership became permanent.

Having reached this point, the next problem was how to get the money. Rogers refused absolutely to be a party to any payment that could be traced back to him. He pointed out the sources of hazard; first, through treachery on the part of Foster, Braman, or Addicks, he might be accused of bribing a court officer, the receiver; Addicks might blackmail him by charging him with conspiracy, or a conspiracy charge might be brought by Bay State stockholders, and he be held for tremendous damages. He refused to put himself into any such trap. I put forward a dozen ways to meet the emergency, but he would have none of them. Finally he suggested a method which was certainly perfect of its kind. He began by letting me into the secret that the chances of a McKinley victory in the election the following week looked pretty bad, and that the latest canvass of the State showed that unless something radical were done, Bryan would surely win. Hanna had called into consultation half a dozen of the biggest financiers in Wall Street, and it was decided to turn at least five of the doubtful States. For this purpose a fund of $5,000,000 had been raised under Rogers' direction, to be turned over to Mark Hanna and McKinley's cousin, Osborne, through John Moore, the Wall Street broker, who was acting as Rogers' representative in collecting the money. It would be legitimate for the National Committee to pay out money to carry Delaware, and he, Rogers, would arrange it that the coin to satisfy Braman and Foster should come through this channel. Thus he would be completely protected.

"Lawson," said Mr. Rogers, looking at me with intense and deadly seriousness, his voice charged with conviction, "if Bryan's elected, there will be such a panic in this country as the world has never seen, and with his money ideas and the crazy-headed radicals he will call to Washington to administer the nation's affairs, business will surely be destroyed and the working people will suffer untold misery. You know we all hate to do what Uncle Mark says is necessary, but it's a case of some of us sacrificing something for the country's good. Bryan's election would set our country back a century, and I believe it's the sacred duty of every honest American to do what he can to save his land from such a calamity."

The "System's" conscience has its own quaint logic—the logic of self-interest—and this is how it reasoned: "The election of Bryan would disturb our control of American institutions, therefore American institutions would be destroyed by Bryan's election. On us, the 'System,' devolves the sacred if expensive duty of saving the nation, and, however abhorrent to our fine moral sense, patriotism compels us to spend millions in bribing and corrupting the electorate so that virtue, 'Standard Oil,' and J. P. Morgan may continue the good work of caring for the public's interests as their own."

As I listened to Rogers' exordium on the duties of a citizen in an emergency, I remembered the "Standard Oil" code—"Everything for God (our God); God (our God) in everything." It was so essentially "Standard Oil," this willingness to commit even that greatest wrong, subverting the will of the people in the exercise of their highest function—the election of a President—but only that good (their good) might come of it. It was no more than selfish greed tricked out in the noble trappings of morality, an infamous crime disguised as patriotism. Doubtless, the excellent, God-fearing, law-abiding citizens of the doubtful States who read this and learn how the "System" defeated their will at the polls will cry, "Monstrous! Can such things be in America?" and then will resume their interrupted occupation of "letting well enough alone." However, this is aside from my story.

Having clearly set forth the political situation through which we should be saved, Mr. Rogers proceeded to map out my own programme. First, I must perfect an alibi for him by going to Foster and Braman, and impressing upon them the fact that he was absolutely out of the affair, and must under no circumstances be brought into it; next, I must convince Addicks to the same effect, and in addition tell him that Mr. Rogers had angrily refused to get into the mix-up; I should then hold myself in readiness to meet John Moore and Hanna or Osborne as soon as an appointment could be arranged. That afternoon I got the word and went to 26 Broadway, and from there Mr. Rogers and I went over to John Moore's office, slipping in the private door from the rear street.

"John," said Mr. Rogers, "I am going to turn this matter over to you and Lawson, and I am to have nothing further to do with it. What you two agree to will be satisfactory to me, and remember, both of you, every dollar that is paid is paid by the National Committee, but after it's all settled, and if there is no slip-up, I will look to Lawson for whatever is expended. Is it understood?"

We agreed that it was, and Mr. Rogers left us.

John Moore deserves more than a mere passing mention here, for he was at this time a distinguished Wall Street character and one of the ablest practitioners of finance in the country. During the last fifteen years of his life, John Moore was party to more confidential financial jobs and deals than all other contemporaneous financiers, and he handled them with great skill and high art. Big, jolly, generous, a royal eater and drinker, an associate of the rich, the friend of the poor, a many-times millionaire, who a few years before had been logging it on the rivers of Maine, his native State, John Moore well deserved his "Street" name, "Prince John." His firm, Moore & Schley, transacted an immense brokerage business, and numbered among its clients great capitalists and bankers all over the country. Especially were Moore & Schley famed for their discretion, and the highest proof of confidence reposed in the firm was the fact that it did the bulk of the stock speculating for what is known as "the Washington contingent." This is, perhaps, the most peculiar and delicate business that comes to "the Street." A big Wall Street house opens a Washington office and organizes an elaborate system of special wires, wires from which there can be no possibility of leakage. It is then ready for the patronage of members of Congress, United States Senators and national officials, whose honorable positions make them the custodians of national secrets of great commercial value. If, for instance, a new law is to be passed which must favorably affect a given stock, legislators who are on "the inside" often buy thousands of shares in order to reap the profit of the rise in value incidental to its passage. Or perhaps there is in prospect a law which will interfere with the special privilege of some other stock and reduce its price. Those in possession of advance information "go short" of that stock (sell for future delivery) to profit by the drop. There are many other opportunities the Washington "insider" of speculative turn may use to advantage. For instance, if a high official of the Government were about to issue a proclamation against a foreign nation, and should desire secretly to make a million or so out of the panic he knew must follow the announcement, he would cast about him for a broker who would preserve this sacred confidence. It would invariably be through the Moore firm that his secretary or confidential man would do the short selling. There are also the operations of lobbyists who, to affect important legislation for this great interest or the other, buy or sell stock for the benefit of legislators whose votes they desire to influence. Extreme caution is demanded in the execution of such orders, or all hands might by some slip-up find themselves wearing striped suits.

Such a catastrophe seemed imminent some years ago when the Sugar Trust was before the United States Senate for some legislation necessary to bolster up its monopoly. Its agents had either been less cautious than usual in disguising the raw bribery they were perpetrating, or this particular Senate was too brazen to take the usual precautions to hide its greed from the world. In any case, so great an outcry was made in the press of the country that some sacrifice to the people's wrath was called for—one of those familiar sacrifices which, at intervals of ten or fifteen years in this republic, our rulers make to the great god Integrity. An investigation was organized, and a Senatorial inquisition had before it eminent sugar capitalists and many other distinguished gentlemen who could by no possibility shed light on the transactions, and then, realizing that a show of earnestness, at least, was demanded, it was agreed that some member of Moore & Schley's firm must go on the witness-stand, and, on refusing to tell which Senators had speculated in sugar, must be sent to jail. This grandstand play, it was calculated, and rightly, would so hold the attention of the American people that when the committee concluded its investigation with the usual loud acclaim of duty well done, its Draconian punishment of the unsubmissive broker would act as another ten years' stay against outcry.

When this stratagem was decided on, John Moore announced that he as head of the firm should be the sacrifice. But the representatives of the "System" and the Senate firmly refused to assign him that rôle, and instead, to his grief and anger, nominated for jail the associate member who had charge of Moore & Schley's Washington business, whom they declared the logical victim. During the thirty days that his friend and partner spent behind the bars John Moore's hair whitened more than in all the years before, and from that time until his death he refused firmly to take part in his old line of work, or was ever again his old jovial self.

CHAPTER XXV

ATHLETICS OF FINANCE

Entirely apart from his relationship with Mr. Rogers it was a great help in this Bay State emergency to have the aid of a man of John Moore's wealth of vim and wide knowledge of men and affairs. Freely and frankly I explained our situation to him with its innumerable complications until he had mastered its intricacies. A tough job he pronounced our proposition, and he was the authority on the subject. After our talk was ended he called in Osborne, who had evidently already been talked to. He said to Osborne:

"I've been over Addicks' affairs with Lawson, and there is no question in my mind and that of other friends of the party that he should have what is necessary to carry Delaware. You had better have the committee ready to put in between $350,000 and $400,000 if we call for it. I will see that it is kept down as low as possible."

Osborne then spoke his piece and replied that the committee would do whatever was decided best, and asked me to send Addicks around next day to explain just how he was pushing things in Delaware. All this was play-acting for the benefit of Rogers' alibi.

The next thing on my programme was to persuade Addicks to relinquish his hold on the old Boston gas companies, and this was likely to prove my most difficult task. I left John Moore, who agreed to hold himself in readiness at any hour to consult on and approve such settlement as I could arrange, and energetically started in on the Delaware financier. It was a trying ordeal. As soon as Addicks saw I had something to work on he began to demur and object. If he could not have things his way, he would do nothing. He knew that I had joined a conspiracy to ruin him; that I was in league with Rogers, who was in league with Braman and Foster, and that all were banded together to take all he had away from him. In the course of that two hours' wrestle I was tempted several times to throw up the whole affair, and there were some bitter and savage word-passages that left both of us heated. I could do nothing with him; he must hear from Rogers personally. Finally I got the "Standard Oil" wire, and Rogers talked so plainly and coldly as partially to sober him, but ended by agreeing to have his counsel talk things over with Addicks, which was a distinct concession. A little later Mr. Rogers' representative was at the Hoffman and he and Addicks had it hot and heavy. After about fifteen minutes of conference they had wellnigh come to blows. However, the hot exchanges had begun to tell. Addicks grew saner, but he insisted on seeing Foster and Braman. I warned him that he was fast getting our affairs into such shape that no one could patch them up, but to no avail. He must meet his enemies face to face if only to ram into their teeth that they were scoundrels. Finally, I got Braman on the telephone and explained that I was doing my best to quiet a crazy man, who would consent to nothing until after he had seen him and Foster and told them what thieves they were. I heard Braman chuckle. He said: "Bring him along to Foster's house at 10.30," and added: "It wouldn't be a bad idea to have an ambulance along, too." This suggested further complications, for Braman has the reputation on "the Street" of being more eager to face a wild man on a rampage than a sick one in a plaster cast, while Foster, although a little bit of a fellow, was never known to side-step or duck trouble. I slipped word down to Moore at the Waldorf to follow along to Foster's place in a cab.

There are several "spite houses" in New York. Foster's house was one of them. It is a narrow strip of a brownstone dwelling at 79 West 54th Street, built to express the enmity of one property owner for his neighbor who refused to pay an extortionate price for the land. It is about the width of a front door, and inside there is just about room to move around. It afforded a queer background for the scene enacted there that night.

Promptly at 10.30 Addicks and I were at the door, and by 10.32 the tunnel-like walls of the "spite house" resounded with as illuminating a verbal interchange of billingsgate biographies as I have ever listened to. At 10.35 I covered Addicks in a hasty but quite successful retreat which he beat to our cab. Thence to the Hoffman House, where I summoned Parker Chandler to aid in the calming of our raving associate. The next two hours were of the pulse-jumping, vein-tearing kind incidental to "frenzied finance," but they were not without avail, for Addicks finally agreed that he might consent to "something" provided the Bay State equities in the Boston companies were so preserved that he could eventually get them back into his hands by repayment to Rogers or by the redemption of bonds.

Having got thus far, I again went after Braman and Foster, who were at the Hotel Cambridge. We repaired for further conference to the University Club, which was then in the old A. T. Stewart marble palace on the corner of Thirty-fourth Street and Fifth Avenue. I shall never forget that session. It was past midnight, but the three of us battled with our smoky problem, now good-naturedly, now bitterly. At times it looked hopeless because of this obstinate demand or that steadfast refusal. It must have been three o'clock in the morning when I left them and stepped into the Waldorf for a moment to relieve Moore's vigil. Then back again to the Hoffman, where Addicks, Chandler, and some Bay State directors were nodding. By this time I was in no mood to say more than that I would be over in the morning, and that Addicks should go early to the National Committee's head-quarters and explain the desperation of conditions in Delaware to Hanna, Osborne, and their associates. At last I was free to return to the Brunswick for a few hours' rest.

In the country, cock-crow is the signal to be up and doing. In the city, the signal to be up and to do is a hoarse, metallic roar that would drown a million country cock-crows if each particular cock were as big as the mythical rooster of antiquity and could crow in proportion to his size. My readers who dwell on the hills and in dales and wheat-fields, and who are unfamiliar with the wild, weird early morning din of the city, may not know that the metropolitan cock-crow is made up of the jingle and jangle of a million tin milk cans jolted over a million blocks of stone to the tune of thousands of steel-shod feet, the shrill cries of an army of butcher and baker boys and the groans and the moans of countless troubled and tortured human souls. Cock-crow in the country means "Awake to another day of life." Cock-crow in the city is a signal for the slaves of Mammon to arise to another interval of flight and pursuit.

The great city cock was just getting ready to send forth his hoarse cry as I went to bed, and he was still on his roost a few hours later, when I awoke. I looked from my window of the Brunswick across the Square, now flooded with the pure sunlight of early morning, and all the kinks and quirks and hobgoblins which the rush and irritation of yesterday had generated seemed to have vanished, and I could not suppress a smile at the thought of the night before, when this battle—this puny, insignificant battle for a few dirty dollars—had almost raised feelings I now knew too well should only be aroused by real battles, battles in which noble principles were involved, and I felt better able to fight what I had thought, the night before, was going to be a hard battle.

"Pshaw!" said I, as I looked away and beyond the park to the grand battlefields of my better imagination, "what will it matter a hundred years hence what name appears against victor or vanquished in the archives of fame or the records of infamy when the student reads, 'A.D. 1896, Bay State Gas-"Standard Oil" war,'" for I saw that among the countless real deeds there would be no room for any record to mark the existence of any Gas or Dollar war.

With these thoughts still in mind I sat down to breakfast with Parker Chandler, and as I listened to his cheerful gossip of yesterday, I inwardly resolved that whatever the result of the day's effort, I would take it with a smile.

Thursday was another period of strenuous struggle and unceasing effort. I began early, and every moment was taken up with arguments, wrangles, pleadings! Chandler had agreed to see that Addicks kept his appointment with the National Committee and that a quorum of Bay State directors should be on hand in the Hoffman so that we could get quick action on any proposition that came up. This arranged I hurried over to see John Moore, then down for a last word with Mr. Rogers. Addicks came next for a spell; from him to Braman and Foster; back to John Moore; more interviews with lawyers and round the circle again. It seemed as though it were impossible to arrive at any agreement that some one of the principals interested would not kick over. At four o'clock Friday morning John Moore and myself ceased our labors for the day, both of us wellnigh exhausted. With all our efforts many of the vital points to our agreement were still in the air. A few hours' sleep and we were back at our task, and by six o'clock on Friday night the last obstacle had been overcome and the deal was completed.

There remained now the tremendous business of putting all the arrangements concluded into execution. A multitude of legal documents had to be drawn up and executed, first by Rogers and then by the Bay State board of directors and officers. It was a pile of work, but not a second was lost, and by 11.20 that night we were ready for the third act, which was to be performed simultaneously by different sets of actors in Boston and Wilmington. For this our officers were split. With the directors of the Boston corporations, Chandler, and Mr. Rogers' attorney to supervise the legal end of next day's transaction, I left on a special car attached to the midnight train for Boston; while Addicks and the Bay State directors set forth on another midnight train for Wilmington, Del., to be followed in the early morning by my New York partner, John Moore's partner, Braman, Foster, and more counsel representing Mr. Rogers. This contingent was to carry the money.

CHAPTER XXVI

THE CIRCLING OF THE VULTURES

I don't believe there ever was before or since a financial operation in which so many things, each of vital importance, had to be done at one and the same time.

Before I took the train for Boston, just after the last deed had been signed, Braman, Foster, and I had come to a complete understanding in regard to the manner in which the court proceedings the following morning should be conducted. It was understood that no one should take another's word for anything, and consequently that no money should pass until specific performance of all the required conditions. Immediately on the release of the receivership, Foster and Braman were to be paid their "fee," and they asked that the $175,000 cash coming to them should be arranged in separate piles of bills. The two packages containing Foster's and part of Buchanan's, and Braman's $50,000 were to be in the joint custody of John Moore's representative and my partner, who, with Rogers' counsel and Addicks, had been assigned to represent Bay State in the court.

What would happen after the transfer of these several amounts was outside my jurisdiction. Addicks did not confide to me his own scheme of revenge, but of Braman and Foster's purposes I had a clear idea. As Braman had explained, the great winning of his adventure should be made in the stock plunge he and Foster contemplated in Bay State Gas stock, then selling at 3-1/2 to 4; but lest there be some slip-up in court, "buy" orders to their brokers were contingent on the word "go!" from Wilmington. To get this off at the right moment a clerk was taken along, whose only part in the play was to telephone this word "go!" They expected in this way to make at least half a million.

Addicks' intentions, as I afterward learned, were less exalted but much more direct. He had conceived a plan whereby without danger to himself he could punish Braman and Foster for the wrong they had done Bay State, and at the same time meet his election expenses at no cost to his own pocket. In the course of his electioneering campaign in Delaware, conducted as all the world knows how, Addicks had gathered to his cause as tough and rascally a set of "heelers" as ever waylaid aged woman or lame man on the highway. A lieutenant who had been despatched to Delaware early Friday afternoon, when it had become evident that we should get things settled up, gathered the sturdiest members of this precious troop together and solemnly told them that a serious hitch had occurred in Addicks' game and that it looked as though, owing to the receivership, there would be no "stuff" to put in circulation this year. The men responsible for this outrage were to be in Wilmington on the following day and from the appearance of things would get the money Addicks had destined for his followers. He understood they were to receive it in cash, too—$175,000—cash that really belonged to Addicks, who had intended it for his good friends in Delaware. The thugs, properly indignant at the wrong that had been done "the Boss," dispersed rapidly to discuss the information among themselves. That night a group of leaders got together and figured out a little plan of campaign to frustrate the robbery of their beloved master. Court proceedings to release the receivership could not take long, and they calculated that the train schedule would detain Braman and Foster at least two hours in Wilmington after the adjournment. What more easy than the organizing of a little scuffle on the station platform or on the street and in the rush—well, many things happen in a rush. This simple procedure commended itself to all concerned, and that night there was much rejoicing among the Addicks camp-followers at the pleasant things that should be pulled "off" at the flim-flamming bee next day.

All these things were in the air when court opened in Wilmington on Saturday morning. A special telephone line had been run and arrangements made for a clear wire right into the directors' office in the head-quarters of the Gas Light Company in Boston. At the telephone in Wilmington sat my partner ready to communicate to me the exact course of the proceedings, so that I might simultaneously make the agreed transfers of our companies to Rogers. I knew my partner's voice; he knew mine. We, too, were taking no chances.

* NEW YORK, February 21, 1905.

Dear Mr. Lawson: In your article in Everybody's Magazine for January, among other misstatements upon which I shall not now comment—since you have committed yourself too far to make it likely that you will withdraw them—you accuse me of having speculated in Bay State Gas stock with Mr. Buchanan's money; and of having subsequently been sued by him. I hold Mr. Buchanan's receipt for the money collected for him, which I paid him the night that I returned from Delaware. He has never sued me. Please inform me whether you are willing and agree to strike out these statements from your article when published in book form, and also whether you will agree to withdraw the same in your magazine. I tried to call on you and discuss the case when in Boston, January 21st; and I also tried to meet you on the day after last Thanksgiving; but apparently you were unwilling to see me. I remain,

Very truly yours,

ROGER FOSTER.

>THOMAS W. LAWSON, ESQ.,
>Boston, Mass.

FEBRUARY 23, 1905.

My Dear Mr. Foster: I received your letter of the 21st inst., and in reply will say, if I have done you any wrong in my story, "Frenzied Finance," or otherwise, it has been unintentional, and I regret it, and I seek this, the first opportunity, to give my regrets the same wide circulation as my original statements.

As I wrote you previous to the publication of the magazine containing the parts you refer to, I try to exercise the greatest care in allowing nothing to appear in my story but facts—facts I know to be facts, and in addition only such facts as are absolutely necessary to my work, which is the portrayal of those events of the past essential to a proper understanding by the people of the evils that have been done them, and how they have been done, that they may do what is necessary to undo them and to prevent their repetition in the future, and, in addition, such facts as it is fair for me to use. I repeat what I said to you then: I have absolutely no feeling in regard to you other than an intense desire to do you exact justice.

I dealt with you in the entire Bay State receivership affair in connection with Mr. Braman and I thought that I had every reason to believe that his Bay State Gas purchases were for your joint account; but now that you assure me they were not, I hasten to have such assurances chase my original story with the hope that they may speedily overtake it.

My information that you had been sued by Mr. Buchanan came to me in a way that left no doubt in my mind of its correctness—no doubt until I received your letter. Papers were sent to me some time ago by reputable attorneys in a suit of Buchanan against Braman and, I understood, yourself, along the lines outlined in my story, with the request that I allow my deposition to be taken, so that Buchanan could get at the facts in his attempt to recover the moneys claimed.

Your assurances to the contrary in regard to this matter I also hasten to start on the road you point out, and I will see that both statements are expunged from my book.

You are in error in thinking that I did not wish to see you when you were in Boston. I did not know in either case of your desires until it was too late to see you. I certainly would have had a "sit-down" with you if it had been possible.

Again assuring you not only that it is a pleasure to set forth the facts you have called to my attention, but that I am your debtor inasmuch as you have given me an opportunity to perform that duty which I owe to every individual my story treats of—to state facts and only facts with which they have been connected—believe me,

Yours truly,

THOMAS W. LAWSON.

CHAPTER XXVII

COURT CORRUPTION AND COIN

The closing scene of this most significant drama was enacted on Saturday morning in the Wilmington Circuit Court-room. There was nothing in the cold formality of the proceedings to indicate that here was the dénouement of a serio-comedy in which greed and ambition had clashed in a battle for millions; nor in the amiable indifference of the men who got within the enclosed space below the judge's desk to suggest the murderous passions and fierce hatreds raging beneath the surface of the prevailing calm.

The dramatis personæ were gathered in little groups representing the separate interests—Addicks and some of his lieutenants; my partner at the telephone; John Moore's partner and Rogers' counsel with their heads together; Braman and Foster nearer the judge, their eyes wandering toward two dress-suit cases piled before John Moore's partner, which, it was understood, contained the money. At a glance it was impossible to tell the one containing Buchanan's share from the other laden with the receivership loot, but each was tagged, and it was evident that possibilities of a mix-up had been carefully guarded against. Behind Braman was his clerk, and in the rear of the court-room sat as many of Addicks' thugs as could squeeze into the narrow space reserved for spectators. They, too, eyed the dress-suit cases avidly, for the information had been passed around that these innocent receptacles contained the "stuff," of which the "Boss" was about to be robbed.

Court came to order. Foster rose, announced that the claims of his client had been satisfied, and made a formal motion to dismiss the receivership. The Court formally consented, and as the clerk was entering the dismissal in his minute-book my partner telephoned the facts to me. I sent back the word that my directors were resigning—had resigned—that Rogers' directors were being elected—had been elected—that the Boston gas companies were now transferred to Rogers. My partner whispered my words to John Moore's partner and Rogers' counsel. At once the two dress-suit cases, each loaded with currency, were slipped to Braman and Foster. At the same time the messenger who was to telephone to their broker rose and quickly left the court-room. A brief period was consumed in signing receipts, certificates, and other legal papers, and then the performance was over. Addicks rose and went out among his henchmen in the rear, who eagerly surrounded him. In the bustle Braman and Foster, each with his own booty, fled.

Let us see what was happening at the Boston end of the wire while all this dumb show was being enacted in the Wilmington court-house. My directors and officials were lined up against the walls of the directors' room in the Boston Gas Light Company's office like so many members of young John D. Rockefeller's Sunday-school class, inasmuch as they were prepared to listen, sing, or shout "Amen!" at any time they received the nod of the class-leader. In an adjoining room Rogers' counsel had a similar line-up, with the difference that my men were about to shed the crowns which the others were waiting to receive, and which would transform them from humble business men into royal gas kings. Through the open wire I was in such close touch with the scene in the Wilmington court-room that I was almost sure I heard the subdued weeping of the blindfolded Lady of the Scales on the bills which occupied such a prominent part in the disreputable proceedings. Nothing now could impede the course of events, so I concluded to take Time by the headgear and secure what Bay State stock was in the market before Braman and Foster got in their work. Over another wire which was at my elbow I gave the word "go!" to my own brokers in Boston and New York, and when a few minutes later they told me they were securing thousands of shares, and that the stock was climbing toward 10, I could not repress an inward chuckle at the thought that the money we had so reluctantly parted with would spread over only one-half or one-third the surface it was originally intended to cover.

It was all over in a few minutes, and when my partner said, "It's done," and "By Jove, there go Dwight Braman and Roger Foster on the dead run with a dress-suit case apiece!" I held my sides as Parker Chandler in his inimitable way bawled: "Tom, let's leave our straw hats on the pegs, for we'll probably be back next spring figuring out how to pump air enough through the gas-measuring meters to pay for that money we've just loaned Braman and Foster for a day or two."

Braman and Foster, as I have observed before, knew their business. The danger to which $175,000 in currency would be exposed, in a territory controlled by Addicks, had appealed to their cautious instincts, and once outside the court-room they literally took to their heels and ran for a corner of the railway yard, where awaiting them was a special car and engine. They jumped aboard, yelling to the engineer: "Let her go." In the meantime eager-eyed ruffians searched the streets and hung round the hotels, looking for two men with dress-suit cases. A hundred of them were on the station platform, awaiting the departure of the regular train. Ten minutes before leaving-time one of the henchmen appeared among the gang, and passed round the word that the gents and the "stuff" had got off by a special, and it was no use waiting any longer. Later that afternoon, Addicks, to use his own words, in one of his rendezvous, "dealt out his own good money in place of that he had hoped would take care of the people's rights."

It was a fierce session of the Stock Exchange that Saturday morning. Shortly before closing time a new set of brokers were frantically grabbing for Bay State stock round 10, and Monday morning, when all the world knew that the receivership had been lifted and our company was itself again, the same crowd continued to buy fiercely. To these eager purchasers I resold all that I had previously gathered, and enough short besides, to compensate me for some of the losses I had previously suffered, for this latter I was enabled to repurchase at half price, when news came that another suit had begun against Bay State. This latter drop in price so shattered the nerves of Braman and Foster that they retired, having made up their minds that they did not know quite as much about one end of "frenzied finance" as they did about the other. As a matter of fact, nothing came of the suit in question, for it was evident when the transfer of the Boston gas companies to Rogers' control became known, that Bay State Gas receiverships had played their last successful engagement.

My readers will not object if I again call their attention to the inevitable workings of the law of compensation. The losses occasioned by the market action of Bay State stock in these four days so mixed up Braman and Foster in their financial accounts that later they were sued by their client, Buchanan, who in court stated that he in turn was so confused as to what was done in connection with this business that he really knew less after it was over than before the suits were brought. But one thing was indelibly impressed upon his mind—that his bonds had disappeared in the whirl and he had not received anything for them. I think this suit is still pending.

CHAPTER XXVIII

PEACE AT LAST

When the curtain fell on the closing scene of the performance in the Delaware court there ensued a brief interval of quiet in the affairs of Bay State Gas. Rejoicing in the temporary diversion of public attention, the chief actors proceeded to assume their former rôles, and soon affairs began to move at their old gait. Rogers took possession of all the Boston gas companies and patiently awaited the coming down the pike of some traveller with more money than brains. Having successfully corrupted the State of Delaware, Addicks was being measured for the senatorial toga, when accidentally the blind lady dropped her scales on his unprotected head, which catastrophe laid him out long enough to enable another to sneak the prize he had so long striven for. We are not at present concerned with the affairs of Delaware, and it suffices to say in passing, that after a heated contest one Richard Kenney was chosen to the senatorial seat Addicks had so long coveted, and that this man, a typical Delaware vote-rancher, after being sworn in as United States Senator, was brought back to Wilmington and tried for robbing a Delaware bank, his accomplices being some other heelers of Addicks. The disclosures made in the trial showed that the case in all characteristics conformed to the Addicks standard of indecency, for the bank officials, not satisfied with "blowing in" every dollar of deposits and capital the institution owned or controlled, had actually "lifted" in addition the building in which the bank was situated. One of the court functionaries who had heard the evidence tersely remarked: "Talk about stealing a red-hot stove: this is a case where they took the funnel with it to keep the draught going until they set it up in a new location!"

But Delaware, as my readers have doubtless gathered long ere this, is its own kind of a country, and rewards and punishments are so perversely adjusted that it seems a sort of Topsyturvydom. In this instance certain of Addicks' heelers went to State's prison and death; Kenney returned to the Senate to help make laws for the great free people of America, while the chief conspirator, with a threat to sue the blindfolded lady for damage done, began to set out the pieces on the Bay State Gas chessboard with a view to trying certain new moves that had occurred to his perpetual-motion mind.

The situation of Bay State Gas stock was fully understood by the public. While Rogers had possession of the Boston companies, he simply held them in trust, and must give them up whenever the parent corporation had coin enough to redeem them. The securities were still in the hands of the public and my friends, and my own duty to get Bay State Gas on its feet was plain. It was again a case of raising money, and to do this we had the issue of securities which we were preparing to float just before Foster and Braman swooped down on us. Addicks agreed that if I would undertake the marketing of this stock, he would issue only enough of it to redeem the properties from Rogers. His directors met and formally "resoluted" on this point, and I felt satisfied before going ahead that there was no danger of this money being put in jeopardy without actually stealing it. The company, for the nonce, had no other business but to pay office rent and clerk hire, and in spite of Addicks' financial immorality, all who knew him were aware he took no chances of ever getting himself sent to jail. So I began to sell the stock in the open market.

PART II

CHAPTER I

THE MAGIC WORLD OF FINANCE

Though this is the twentieth century and enlightenment is supposed to prevail throughout this broad land of ours, the majority of people still regard the world of finance as the world of magic. Within the fairy realm of finance the laws of nature apparently are suspended, and, overnight, wonders are worked. The ordinary mortal, wise in all other walks of life, sees the man who yesterday stood beside him at the plough or at the bench emerging from the mysterious portals bearing the fruits of the endeavors of a hundred or a thousand lives, although a moment ago he passed through them with nothing. Who can deny the magic that thus demonstrates its power, or fail to accord veneration to the magicians that work such marvels? No wonder the ordinary mortal feels that he has no license to enter the world of finance save on his knees, hat in hand, bearing tribute to the divinities enthroned within this enchanted territory.

It is my purpose to do away with this extraordinary deception and to show it up as one of the artifices with which tricksters, since the beginning of the world, have imposed upon the people. There should be nothing in finance that any man or woman of ordinary intelligence and experience cannot understand, and I purpose to explain here the machinery of the "System" so that every one will exactly understand it from headlight to rear-end lantern. Many intelligent people have no clear idea of what a certificate of stock or a bond really is, and the words "money," "stock-exchange," and "finance" are mere terms which they glibly use without knowledge of their meaning.

It is not difficult to understand the grocery or the dry-goods business. Standard articles of well-known form are sold by weight or measure over the counters for fair prices. The patrons of such businesses insist on knowing what they are buying—what they are to get in exchange for the money which is the fruit of their labor, and then, after they have been told, and they trade, they require that the goods be as described or they will know why not. The average American would consider it a huge joke should his grocer undertake to induce him to buy one hundred times more sugar than he could use, on the ground that he might find in the sugar bags when he reached home gold and diamonds. But would he not wrathfully seek the police if, after opening his sugar bag, for which he had paid $1, he found it contained only 50 cents' worth of sugar? He would tell you if you met him at this stage: "You can bet that chap on the corner cannot get away with any such trick as that—not in America. He might in Zanzibar or in the kingdom of the Sultan of Sulu, but I will show him he cannot rob Americans in these enlightened times." The grocer would be hustled to jail without a "by your leave," and thenceforward his name would be a by-word among all honest tradesmen.

And so it goes in every business but finance—finance, the most important of all, the business into which is merged all other businesses, the business of taking and preserving the results of all other businesses, of all other human endeavor. Over our land to-day are big, able Americans, long-headed and experienced, adept at a jack-knife swap or a horse trade—industrious farmers, hard-handed miners, shrewd manufacturers, each in his own line a good business man, yet these sturdy traders, whom the "gold-brick" artist or the "green-goods" practitioner would never dream of tackling, come weekly into Wall Street, or into such branch shops as exist in every community on the continent, and are done out of their savings like the veriest "come-ons." Humbly they take, in return for the gold earned with the sweat of their brows, a piece of paper of a given value which they return later and exchange for half the amount the paper cost them originally. In the space between purchase and sale fifty per cent. of their investment has disappeared—has been filched away, but yet they have no resentment. They evince none of the feelings of the man whose pocket has been picked or whose till has been robbed. On the contrary, their sentiment is of admiration for the banker, the broker, the financier through whose agency their money has been lost.

Take, for instance, the prosperous tanner who goes to his banker with $100,000, the fruit of ten years' success, and exchanges this sum for 1,000 shares of Steel Preferred. Now, if he were to examine this security with half the thought or investigation he gives to a $500 car-load of bark, he would learn that there was not 20 cents on the dollar of real value behind it. In six months the eminent tanner is again at the banker's offering for sale his thousand shares of steel. In the meantime it has declined in value and he has to part with it for $50,000. But he does not complain; indeed, he bows his way out of the palatial office of the great man and is full of sincere thanks when the banker promises to let him know the next good thing on the market. Suppose our tanner had purchased ten cars of tan bark and found that each car-load was short ten per cent. Would he not at once go to his attorney and exclaim emphatically that he would spend thousands rather than let the scoundrel who had tricked him get away with his swag?

Suppose our grocer waxing rich invests his funds in the Sugar trust. He thinks he knows all there is to be known about sugar. The business of the trust is to make the sweet commodity and sell it to the people. No mystery or magic, surely, about this simple pursuit. Yet when our grocer invests his savings, the sugar stock is many dollars more valuable than when, scared into selling by fluctuations which he cannot see any reason for, he tries to get back his investment. So many times have investors been milked of their savings by this one trust during the past twenty years that in the coffers of its creators and jugglers are hundreds of millions of money that once belonged to the people for which they have received absolutely nothing in return.

Both the tanner and the grocer must know, when they look up and down Wall Street at the great office buildings which tower into the sky on either side of the street, that these are huge hives of expensive bees who, from New Year's to New Year's, do not produce a dollar. They should realize that the hundreds of millions spent each year for the expense of running the "System's" game, and the millions which the game-makers flaunt in their faces, must have been derived from such as they—the men who produce.

It is the phenomenon of the age that millions of people throughout this great country of ours come of their own free will to the shearing pens of the "System" each year, voluntarily chloroform themselves, so that the "System" may go through their pockets, and then depart peacefully home to dig and delve for more money that they may have the debasing operation repeated on them twelve months later.

You may ask if I desire to convey the idea that the great financial institutions and trusts of this country, which have their head centre in Wall Street, are all concerned in a conspiracy to rob the people of their savings. You think, doubtless, that so sweeping a statement goes beyond the truth. I desire to go on record right here in declaring that all financial institutions which in any way are engaged in taking from the people the money that is their surplus earnings or their capital, for the ostensible purpose of safeguarding it, or putting it in use for them, or exchanging it for stocks, bonds, policies, or other paper evidences of worth, are a part of the machinery for the plundering of the people.

This is a terrible charge, I am well aware, but it is based upon a thorough knowledge of the subject and made with a full appreciation of its gravity. I do not mean to say that all the men who handle and control the different institutions I mentioned have guilty knowledge of the bearing of their actions. Many of them are of the purest minds and most honest intentions, and are quite incapable of participating voluntarily in a conspiracy to wrong any one. They do not know, however, that the relation between their own minor institution and the general financial structure constitutes the former an agency for the "System," which controls and has organized the general financial structure into an instrument for converting the money of the public to its own purposes. In fact, the "System" has cunningly possessed itself of the financial mechanism of the country and is running it, not for the object for which the machine was devised, but for the benefit and personal profit of its votaries, and so the vast correlated organization of banks, trust companies, and insurance corporations which were brought into being for the safe handling of the people's savings has become an agency for transferring these savings to the control of unscrupulous manipulators, who take liberal toll of every dollar that passes through their hands.

The duty of the American people is to unloosen the thraldom of the "System" on our financial mechanism; to pluck out of their high places the dishonest usurpers who have degraded the purposes of our financial institutions, and to restore those institutions to their legitimate functions. When the people are fully awakened to the condition I describe, surely they will arise in their wrath and sweep the money-changers from the temple.

CHAPTER II

THE "SYSTEM" AND THE LOUISIANA LOTTERY COMPARED

Years ago one of the greatest evils in this country was the Louisiana Lottery. Through that lottery millions and millions annually were taken from the people and transferred to a few unprincipled schemers, who soon found themselves in possession of enormous fortunes. Wise men called for the abatement of this awful drain on the savings of the nation, but the law-abiding, God-fearing people of the country met their plaints with "Why should we be bothered about this matter? If fools and knaves elect to gamble in such palpably fraudulent ways, let them gamble, and their losses are no affair of ours. It is none of our business." But presently these honest people had it pounded into their well-meaning heads that the principal instrument by which the swindle was conducted was their own mail service, one of the most important branches of their Government; that, in fact, in each and every city, town, village, and cross-road in all our virtuous land, Government officials were acting as distributing agents for this huge corrupter and robber.

Then the people rose in their irresistible might, and between the rising of one day's sun and its setting this powerful machine went as goes the gum-drop on the red-hot stove cover at a pop-corn soirée. It melted, leaving nothing but a faint odor and a thin stain, both of which disappeared in the next morning's scrubbing, and the Louisiana Lottery was as though it had never been. Yet during its reign its insolent votaries could prove to the absolute satisfaction of all intelligent, patriotic men that it was useless for any man or set of men to attempt the lottery's destruction, because they would be met with the accumulated resistance of the reckless spending of the vast amounts of festered dollars which had been stolen from the people. The argument of these comparatively petty thieves was: "No men nor sets of men can hope to 'stack up' against us, for their money comes hard, cents and dollars at a time; they are obliged to earn it, while we get ours in chunks by simply taking it. We can buy lawyers and can hire law-makers, and we can lease Government officials, and we can outbid any honest men, who are the only ones who object to our game. In the market for legislative or business talent you cannot get within touching distance of us." Yet the people had but to sneeze and this foul parasite was detached from their free and honest structure and was wafted away with the dead leaves and the dust to bottomless nowhere.

In the height of its prosperity the Louisiana Lottery took from the people only a paltry ten or twenty million dollars a year, while to-day there are single groups of banks, trust companies, corporations, and trusts which take from the people by might, by trick, and by theft hundreds of millions each year; and there are scores of such groups. The Sugar trust has been the instrument of gathering, in one year, a hundred millions of the people's savings, and the Steel trust alone has robbed the people of over five hundred millions of dollars in a single twelve months.

To-day the "System" and its methods are as clearly and as sharply defined in the tangibility of their relation to the people as was ever the Louisiana Lottery. On certain days the Louisiana Lottery sold its tickets, which the people bought with their savings. On a certain day the drawing took place, at which all those who had parted with their dollars expected to receive them back together with immense profits, and upon that day disappointment was spread broadcast among the many and unhealthy joy among the few. So with the "System." On certain days the public is sold their stock, bond, and insurance policy certificates. Upon other days they look for their savings and profits. On the contrary, they learn that their savings have decreased in value or have been wiped out, and that there never was any chance of profit. My critics will say that such a comparison cannot hold, for in the lottery nothing was dealt in but gambling tickets, whereas the stock or bond certificate represents an ownership in the material things of the country. This is the fallacy the "System" spends millions every year to foster and disseminate. Between the two the difference is in favor of the Louisiana Lottery, for both are gambles and the lottery game was square. Those who ran it had for their trouble a fixed percentage of the profits, an enormous percentage, it is true, but the general fund was never encroached upon by the controllers. Who is to say what percentage the votaries of the "System" take in their game? It depends on how much their victims have to lose. The public have been persuaded, too, that in purchasing stocks they do not gamble, but only invest, or, at the worst, speculate, so they are deceived as well as plundered. A few millions each year satisfied the lottery owners; the votaries of the "System," among whom the "swag" must be divided, demand millions upon millions each. The tickets of the lottery had a definite value at all times until the drawing took place. The stocks and bonds of the "System" have no rigid or unalterable value when issued or at any other time, and do not represent a fixed ownership in all the savings of the people which have been paid for them.

Morally, legally, or ethically, the Louisiana Lottery, with all its attendant curses, was a far better institution for the people to bump up against every month than is the "System" against which the whole people are now directly or indirectly dealing every working day of the year. Startling this statement may be, but not more startling than the facts. The records of the lottery company will show how many dollars it took in from the public; how many were returned in prizes and expenses; and how many went into the pockets of the owners. The records of the banks, corporations, trusts, and stock-exchanges will exhibit how many dollars were paid into the "System" by the people; how much they received back in return therefor; how much the expense of conducting the business was; and how much profit went to the votaries of the "System." Compare the two and it will be found that there is annually taken by the "System" from the people a hundred, yes, a thousand times more than the Louisiana Lottery ever obtained in the same period.

This being the fact, for how long will the people allow such a monstrous wrong to be done? How long will they suffer a few men to siphon automatically the money of the many into their own pockets?

It is only a matter of simple mathematics to ascertain the day, and that only a few years away, when ten men will be as absolutely and completely the legal owners of the entire United States and all there is of value in it, as John D. Rockefeller is the absolute legal owner of the large section of it of which he is to-day possessed.

When that day is here, the people will legally be the slaves of these ten men.

If this is so—and it is as surely so as it is that the Constitution of the United States of America guarantees to every man, woman, and child who is a part of it perpetual freedom—it is so because the legal interest alone to which the ten men will be entitled and which they must receive (or our entire structure will fall) will of itself bring to their coffers all the wealth in existence within a given time. If this is so, then why have the American people allowed themselves to reach this condition? Why are they to-day not only resting peacefully under this worse than death-bringing yoke, but assisting in the further riveting of this badge of dishonor and degradation?

The reason is simple: They have been lulled to sleep by the "System" and its cunning votaries until they have but a dull appreciation not only of existing conditions but of their coming consequences. It is almost incredible that a people as intelligent as the American people, and as alert to that individual and national honor which they have bought with so much of their blood and their peace of body and mind, can be so deceived and juggled with. When one looks about, however, and notes happenings of which one personally knows, and the degradation and dishonor to which public opinion is seemingly indifferent, nothing is incredible.

One sees a certain man openly displaying five hundred millions of dollars, a sum which represents the life earnings of 150,000 of our population, and knows that this man has secured this incredible amount during forty years of his life. One sees the second highest and most honorable office in the nation, a United States Senatorship, openly bought for a few stolen dollars by a man who up to the very day of its purchase was a watch repairer in a small country town, and who had never done a single meritorious deed or been possessed of worldly goods to the extent of $5,000. One sees a wily adventuress secure from the banks, which exist only to safeguard the people's deposited savings, hundreds of thousands of dollars on her bare story that she was the possessor of some mysterious documents. One sees a $6-a-week office-boy of one of the "System's" votaries able to borrow for the "System," on his bare note, four millions of dollars from a New York institution which only exists to safeguard the people's savings—although the law says that such institutions shall not loan to any man on any kind of collateral, even Government bonds, one-tenth that sum. One sees two men, drunk with their success, gouging and tearing at each other's hearts in Wall Street, and sees their gouging and tearing bring about a panic which takes from the people in an hour over a billion dollars and drives scores to suicide, murder, and defalcation—the two men continuing meanwhile as ornamental pillars of society instead of wearing prison stripes. One sees a great railroad corporation, in which are millions of the trust funds of widows, orphans, and charitable institutions, caught "short" (having sold something it did not own) in the stock-gambling game and held up to the tune of ten million dollars by a reckless stock gambler, who says "If you don't settle to-night it will be twenty millions to-morrow"; and the toll is paid, while the great banker who conducts the release of the hold-up charges the further tribute of twelve million dollars for his services. And then one sees this twenty-two millions of "commission" tacked on to the capital stock of the great railroad which is subsequently capitalized into a "bond" and sold to great life-insurance companies as a first-class investment for their trust funds.

When one sees these things and a hundred other as rankly fraudulent, one should not wonder at anything American connected with dollars.

Such things occur because the "System" has so far been able to keep the public in ignorance of its doings. On the surface there is nothing to suggest that a set of vampires have captured the high places of finance and are sucking away the life-blood of the nation. Our banks and trust companies all present a fair exterior and apparently are the same safe and honorable institutions they were before the canker fastened on them. Only its votaries know what the "System" is, and their way is the way of silence and darkness. A tie, stronger and more effective than the oath of the Mafia, binds them to its service, and woe be to him who dares divulge its methods. He who is bold enough to enter upon a recital of these secrets must be strong indeed to withstand the bribes to silence which would be placed in his hands. The "System" can well afford to pay any price rather than be brought face to face with its past, with an enraged people for referee. And even if the being be found who will venture an exposé of the conspiracy, he will find it strangely difficult to get his story past the traps and pitfalls which will be placed between it and the people for whose enlightenment it is intended.

CHAPTER III

THE FUNDAMENTALS OF FINANCE

Finance is easy enough to comprehend if it be explained, but so long as an explanation is deadly to the interests of the men who control it, one can be sure none will be offered. There is no term more common to-day than "trusts," and we are surrounded by "trusts," institutions whose workings during the past twenty years have awakened intense public curiosity to know what a "trust" is. Yet there is not extant a definition of a "trust" which conveys to the rank and file of the people any real idea of what a "trust" is. So vague is the general understanding of the "trust's" functions and purposes that the most intelligent and honest statesmen struggle and hopelessly flounder when they attempt to define them, and we have at the present time the able chief of our nation talking of regulating them by law, when, as a matter of fact, a "trust" is, top, sides, bottom, outsides, and insides, an absolutely illegal institution, created outside the law, existing outside the law, and having for its purpose the performance of those things and only those things which the law says cannot be performed legally. Imagine our law-makers gravely meeting to make laws for the control and regulation of the pick-pocket or burglar or counterfeiting industry, or endeavoring to prescribe legally the times, places, and amounts of national bank defalcations, or the kind of ink, paper, and pens which must be used by forgers in the pursuit of their profession—imagine it!

In entering upon an explanation of the workings of the "System," it is necessary to set forth plainly the fundamentals of finance, the few rules and inventions by and through which humanity regulates its affairs. In the beginning, of course, might was right and men supplied their wants by force, trickery, or cunning. In time the disadvantages of this became obvious, for while the stronger could overcome the weaker and satisfy desire, a combination of the weaker units acting together could always wrest the prize from the individual. To equalize things, the people got together and made for themselves rules and regulations governing the conduct of their lives and their relations with one another. This was invention No. 1: Law. Presently it developed that the physical barter of the commodities of labor was not a satisfactory basis of exchange; so to the statutes already in existence a new one was added providing an interchangeable token of value. This was invention No. 2: Money. The statute insisted that the money be of a fair and just standard, by which all the people should receive the equivalent of their labor, and no more. As conditions became more settled, there grew up a realization of the value of a man's life to those dependent on him, and of the fact that when he died his wife and his children were deprived of the livelihood his labor won for them. A new regulation was added to the code, providing that men contributing to a fund during their lifetime should be entitled at death to leave to their heirs a sum in proportion to the amount of their contribution to the fund, less the actual expense of caring therefor. This was Life Insurance—invention No. 3. But there were other calamities less distant than death to be guarded against, and a common fund, also based on the contributions of individuals, to aid and relieve in case of fire and kindred calamities, was organized. Hence invention No. 4: Fire Insurance.

And thus the fabric of civilization grew, each addition to the structure being made to cover a want which experience developed. As time went on, some of the people accumulated the fruits of labor, money, in greater quantity than was requisite for their own needs, but which less thrifty or less fortunate brethren could so profitably employ in their own affairs as to be able to pay for its use a fair proportion of what it could be made to earn. Thereupon provision was made for a common place of safety for this surplus money, a place where experts in the handling and putting to use of money could employ their talents, first, safeguarding it and, then, loaning it to others. And the law was made to say that all money put into this common place should be so guarded as to be ready for its owner when he demanded it; that its owner should receive all it earned less the necessary expense of holding it, and that the amount it earned should be only such as those who borrowed it could fairly make it earn. This was invention No. 5: The Bank.

As the years followed one another, "the bank" became one of the most important of the people's institutions and grew in number and variety. There came to be many different forms of banks. For instance, national banks, which, under the control and regulation of the Government, became depositories for the circulation of the Government's money and were privileged to lend money to individuals or corporations with or without collateral. Funds confided by the people to these national banks had always to be ready for their owners. A second form was the savings-bank, which grew out of the requirements of small depositors and was governed by the laws of its community. The savings-bank used and safeguarded money confided to it in small sums, and these amounts could be withdrawn only by their owners in person, after an agreed term of notice. The savings-bank was allowed to lend only on real estate or certain other securities, the character of which was rigidly regulated by the law. In consequence, it could use its funds for long-time loans and mortgages, so it earned larger rates of interest than the national banks. The trust company was a third variation, coming somewhere between the national and the savings-bank, and was regulated, as was the latter, by the laws of the community in which it existed. The trust company, too, received deposits from the people, but was allowed a broader latitude in employing them. It was also authorized to engage in certain other business—for example, to act as manager for a deceased person's estate and even to buy and sell securities. Because of the extra-hazardous business in which it engaged and from which the other two institutions were legally debarred, the trust company earned and paid larger rates of interest to its depositors, and the men who handled its funds were allowed to take for their own remuneration profits in excess of those derived by the custodians of national and savings-banks.

Another deficiency in the business structure growing out of the increasing prosperity of the people was next provided for. When an enterprise became so large as to necessitate several owners for its conduct, the prescribing and defining of the relation of these owners to each other and to the common property became a task of increasing difficulty. So the idea arose of welding the enterprise itself into a separate entity which could do all the things the individual might, and yet exist apart from the individual and independent of his personal dealings and comings and goings. His ownership should be an undivided interest in the whole represented by certificates of stock or bonds, which could pass from him to another without interfering with the enterprise. This was invention No. 6: The Corporation. The law then provided regulations for the creation and conduct of these corporations which compelled them to keep their affairs in such shape that all could ascertain of what each consisted.

When these six organizations had been founded, the machinery for the conduct of the business of a civilized people was almost complete. But still one other want developed: with the multiplication of the corporation tokens of property, it became necessary that there should be some place where the worth of these might be ascertained either by purchase, sale, or loan under the regulation of experts. So there was created a common market-place, to which came all those who had corporation tokens of property to sell and those who desired to purchase them; and the prices these brought were announced to the world and became the measure of the value of the institution they represented. Rules for the regulation of the business of the market-place were gradually formulated, and invention No. 7—the Stock Exchange—came into existence.

With this addition, the people's organism for safeguarding and economically handling the funds of their labor to the best advantage of all concerned and without interfering with the rights and privileges of individuals was fully equipped. Each separate institution had grown out of an actual necessity and had its own legal organic function, fully understood and defined. And there was no branch of human industry which could not be safeguarded, handled, and perpetuated through this organism, nor could evil come from the existence of any one of these seven components. The robber, the thief, and the pirate, as defences against whom they had been erected, could not seize any of them or the people's savings which they were created to safeguard, because the constitution of each provided adequate penalties for such a seizure. As long as the members of the organism performed their ordained functions the fabric of the people's fortunes was safe from plunder.

CHAPTER IV

THE MAGIC "JIMMY"

It was at this stage that the class which is now the "System"—of which the mighty robber of barbaric days was the prototype—began to cast envious eyes at the accumulated earnings of a prosperous people locked up and safeguarded against depredation, while the owners (the public) rested easy in the conviction that they had fully protected themselves against the spoilsman. The "System" reasoned: "If only a way could be devised to win control of the seven institutions so that all the benefits the people intend for themselves may revert to me and yet I be exempt from the punishment provided for those who attempt unfairly and dishonestly to secure such benefits, I can get a much easier and surer possession of the results of the labor of the people than I was wont to when I took them by might."

A need defined is half relieved. Outside the treasure-house was the robber enviously surveying its strong walls and iron doors, its locks and bolts, specially designed to defy the felonious intentions of such as he. How safely to win his way in and possess himself of the piled-up gold was his problem. And as he waited and watched, the lawyer, at his solicitation, invented for him a magic "jimmy"—an instrument with which he could not only break through the outside door, but as easily force his way past the complex locks of the chambers inside. What was still better, this magic "jimmy" was also a license to enter upon and take possession of others' properties and use them for his own benefit. It conferred on its owner a legal privilege to steal. The robber was satisfied. The "jimmy" which the lawyer had brought him was the "trust."

All this sounds very hyperbolical and far-fetched, perhaps, but it is exactly what a "trust" is. The "trust" may also be defined as a master key to the people's financial structure, which enables its owner to enter any or all of the separate institutions I have mentioned, and combine any or all of them, without affecting their respective organisms, into a new organization which possesses the potencies and the privileges of each, but is unhampered by the legal restrictions of any one of them. Like electricity, the exact nature of a "trust" does not admit of rigid definition, but it is a force which can be exerted only in conjunction with financial organisms, which it joins and yet releases, adds power to, and exempts from consequences. Let us suppose that two men are made into a "trust"—this human combine becomes at once free from the bondage of matter and the senses, sees out of the back of its head and passes in and out through solid walls. It has all the combined strength and more that the two men had and all their human privileges and possessions, but it evades nature's laws as to individuals, and the laws of man both as to individuals and other material things.

To put the description in still another way, a "trust" is an institution which endows itself with the right to use any or all of the seven institutions of the people as the people use them, but so made that its user derives from the institutions the benefits the people intended for themselves, and yet is immune from the legal consequences of appropriating such benefits. Two or more men make a "trust" by combining—acquiring the control of—an insurance company, a trust company, and a savings-bank. The new organization is all of these institutions, performs the functions of all of them, yet can legally do with their incomes, capital, and surpluses things which, from the very nature of each, none of the institutions is allowed to do—the new organization is all of these institutions until the law attempts to bring it to book; then it evades being any one of them. The trust company is empowered to lend money on speculative ventures which the insurance company and savings-bank may not do, so the "trust" lends the insurance company's vast accumulations and the savings-bank's hoard through the trust company with great profit or tremendous loss and enjoys immunity from the consequences which should follow such disobedience of the law. Moreover, when the trust company shows a profit the "trust" appropriates it, and when a tremendous loss is sustained the insurance company or the savings-bank must bear it.

An illustration: A, B, and C form a "trust." A and B are president and controller of a savings-bank and an insurance company respectively. They organize a trust company with $1,000,000 capital, of which the insurance company furnishes the majority; they then elect C president and controller of the trust company, and make him their associate or a dummy. The trust company receives $5,000,000 of the people's money on deposit. The insurance company deposits $5,000,000 of its surplus funds, and the savings-bank $5,000,000 more. The trust company now has $15,000,000 of the people's savings in its control with which by law it is allowed to do certain things; but what it does with the $5,000,000 of the savings-bank and the $5,000,000 of the insurance company the law specifically says neither one of the institutions can do itself. The "trust" then purchases for $5,000,000 the stock of an industrial corporation. It borrows the $5,000,000 and an additional $5,000,000, which represents its own first profit, from the trust company through irresponsible dummies, depositing the industrial stock as collateral. The "trust" next causes the trust company to issue bonds for $15,000,000. These bonds are based upon and secured by nothing of worth but the stock. The trust company offers these bonds for sale. The insurance company buys $7,500,000 of the bonds, and the trust company, through dummies, the other $7,500,000. By the operation so far the "trust" shows a profit of $10,000,000. After making this profit and the true worth of the bonds becoming known, these decline back to the original worth of the stock upon which they are based, $5,000,000, and there is the tremendous loss of $10,000,000 made. The trust company "busts," and there is a loss to its depositors of $10,000,000. This loss is divided as follows: $3,333,000 to the savings-bank, $3,333,000 to the insurance company, and $3,333,000 directly to the people, less the small amount which will be recovered from the stockholders. (These losses will be affected in an unimportant way by the $1,000,000 original capital.)

In this case the "trust" has done nothing for which those responsible for it can be held civilly or criminally liable. Neither has the insurance company, the savings-bank, nor the trust company, and yet, if there had been no "Trust" and any one of the three institutions had made the loss directly through its own actions, the officers of that institution would have been civilly and perhaps criminally held responsible.

The utility and convenience of the "trust" having been demonstrated, it became a popular instrument for financiers desiring to accomplish all manner of illegal purposes. Especially was it an apt tool for the "System," which in the meantime was perfecting its control of the people's institutions. The owners of railroads running through the same territory, finding cumbersome and hampering the restrictions with which the community they served had safeguarded its interests, formed "trusts." Straightway there were valuable results—the combination was emancipated from the regulations which had bound its individual members; competition was eliminated and rates were raised.

As time went on new "trust" possibilities were discovered and other institutions linked up—corporations of all kinds, insurance companies and national banks and savings-banks, were brought together for the benefit of the "System" and the detriment of the public. The end of the trustification of the institutions of the nation is not yet, but the people are to be shown a way by which the plundering process can be reversed and through which they can make their freedom complete and absolute by the complete and absolute enslavement of the "System" itself.

CHAPTER V

HOW THE "SYSTEM" DOES BUSINESS

To follow the various steps in the crimes of Amalgamated, my readers should know how the securities of a corporation are manufactured, how "put upon the market," how admitted to the Stock Exchange, how prices are made in the Stock Exchange, how fictitious and fraudulent quotations are created and disseminated, until the very shrewdest members of the Stock Exchange cannot distinguish those which are real from the fictitious in cases outside their own manufacturing. Then there is an elaborate and ingenious procedure by which public opinion is moulded, that is, by which people are made to believe that the prices at which they buy and sell the stocks and securities are bona fide; and this is a procedure as compact and as well understood by the "System's" votaries as are the methods of the bank-breaker or burglar—who sends his "pals" ahead to "pipe" the lay of the land—by felony's votaries. When I have shown these things, about which little is known to-day by the public, my readers will have no difficulty in comprehending what I shall lay before them of the actual robberies in the case of Amalgamated and other notorious enterprises.

The underlying principle of the several organisms through which the commerce of the country is conducted is the protection at once of the interests of the individuals composing them and of the public with which they do business. Provided this principle is adhered to, no harm can be wrought to either. Most of the contemporaneous swindles through which the people have been plundered were perpetrated through the agency of corporations, and this organism has become a sort of synonym for corrupt practice. Yet the original corporation invention as I have described it was devised to meet a real want of the people, and it has merely been diverted from its proper use by the lawless votaries of the "System." Consider the institution as we now understand it. Certain individuals decide to conduct their business in railroads, mines, manufactories, patents, etc., in the form of a corporation and apply to the community—the State Government—asking authorization to do so. They are compelled first to conform to the rules and regulations laid down by the State for the control of corporations, which say in one form or other:

"We create you for the purpose of doing those things that are best for the many, not the few, and if we knew you would use our authority to oppress the many in the interest of the few we would not create you." The fundamental privilege of incorporation is the legal authorization to issue paper titles of ownership to the business just incorporated. These are in the form of stocks and bonds. Whoever owns these paper titles shall possess the property and the business as the individuals did before they incorporated, and the law presumes that they shall manage and control that business, receive the benefits which come from it, and suffer any loss arising from its conduct, and that all these benefits and responsibilities shall be as laid down in the law. It follows that no harm other than that the law expressly prescribes penalties to prevent can come to any one from corporations thus created, always provided the laws are what they appear and what the people intended them to be, and that they are enforced as the people intended they should be.

It is most important to all concerned in a corporation that the paper ownership shall represent the real value of the property on which it is based, and no more. When the people exchange their savings for these authorized paper tokens, they should be able to rest confident in the State's guarantee that they are worth what they purport.

There have probably been jailed in the United States during the past twenty years thousands and thousands of American citizens whose aggregate stealings do not amount to one-tenth the total taken from the people by either the Amalgamated, the United States Steel, the American Tobacco Company, or a score of other fraudulently organized or fraudulently conducted corporations.

There are various ways of organizing corporations and issuing their stocks and bonds. Sometimes a company is organized to acquire a property; individuals and institutions set down their names to take and pay for the shares or bonds. With the money thus obtained the property is purchased. Or the individuals who own the property which is to be the basis of the corporation exchange it for all or part of the stocks and bonds. In the latter event those original owners usually sell to the public the tokens thus acquired.

Honest men in forming a corporation make publicly known the character and worth of the properties or enterprises they are organizing, what they have cost, what their profits are, and what may reasonably be expected by investors. The tricksters and the "System," with whom incorporation is generally but the first step in a conspiracy for plunder, surround the proceeding with an air of mystery and refuse information usually with: "We do our business quietly and in silence, and those who do not like our ways may keep out of this scheme." Their whole procedure is of that high and mighty order which impresses the ordinary mortal with a sense of confidence in the independence of its users and a conviction that their scheme must be so good that they do not care whether they sell or not. This is just the effect it is intended to produce.

The next step is to lead the people toward the shambles. This is done by "moulding public opinion," and for this interesting function the "System" and Wall Street have an equipment of magical potency. Public opinion is made through the daily press, through financial publications of various kinds, and through "news bureaus." Every great daily has a financial editor and a corps of experts in finance who spend their days on "the Street" cultivating the friendship of the financiers. At night they are round the clubs and hotels where the brokers and promoters congregate, debating the events of the day and organizing those of the morrow. There are also the strictly financial papers—daily, weekly, and monthly—whose corps of editors and news gatherers live on "the Street," and know and care for nothing but finance. And lastly, there are the news bureaus, with runners out everywhere to gather in items of news affecting stocks, Wall Street or finance. These are printed on small square sheets of paper, and delivered by an army of boys at brief intervals while the Stock Exchange is open at the offices of the bankers, brokers, insurance companies, and hotels; or the same matter is disseminated by means of an automatic printing machine called a news-ticker. For this service the offices pay the bureaus from $1 to $2 a day. News bureaus form an important cog in the machinery for making stock-markets, as it is through the news they furnish to the Stock Exchange and to the offices where investors and speculators gather together that the big operators affect the market. A decision to buy, sell, or "stand pat" is often based on the on dits of these printed slips.

The first step toward "moulding public opinion" is taken when the "System's" votaries send for the dishonest chief of a news bureau, a man usually up in every trick of the trade. I will later describe one of them, a scoundrel so able and experienced that, to use the vernacular of the gutter of "the Street," he can give cards and spades to the frenziedest of frenzied financiers. To this man the "System's" votary will say something like this: "We are going to work off blank millions of blank stock; it costs us thus and so, and we want to sell for so and so many millions." Nothing is kept back from this head panderer and procurer, for it would be useless to attempt to deceive him, and, to quote his always picturesque language: "Never send a sucker to fish for suckers or he'll lose your bait, so spread out your bricks and I'll get the 'gang' to polish up their gildings." After the quality and amount the "System" intends to work off in exchange for the people's savings are explained, that part of the plunder which is to come to the head news-bureau man is settled upon. The amount varies with the size and quality of the robbery to be perpetrated. In some cases as high as a million dollars in cash or stock or their equivalent has been paid to a "moulder of opinion" for simply so shaping up a game that the people might be deceived into thinking one dollar of worth was four, six, or eight dollars.

The head of the news bureau, having taken the contract to lay out and carry through the deceptive part of the scheme by which the people are to be buncoed, now begins operations. First, bargains are made with conscienceless financial editors of the daily and weekly newspapers, whereby for so much stock or for "puts" or "calls" or both, they agree to insert in their paper's financial column whatever yarns are fed them by the bureau man, regardless of their truth or falsehood. To justify the attention paid the subject by each editor, a certain amount of money is spent in advertising, in the newspaper that employs him, the merits of the enterprise. The financial journals are dealt with about on the same basis. In return for straight advertising or for "puts" or "calls" they agree to insert the manufactured news. The news-bureau man then puts his entire staff to work inventing fairy tales of one kind or another to excite the interest and attention of the people, and these tales must be so concocted that the public is drawn into believing that the statements disseminated represent actual conditions. I shall, later, give real instances of the working of this nefarious game of "moulding public opinion," and present it in the lime-light necessary for its appreciation. To show the extent to which this "moulding" process is carried, I know in one instance of a high-priced financial scribe being sent to live in St. Petersburg for no other purpose than to send certain "news items" to a confederate located in Germany, who would get these items to a reputable English banking-house through whom they were given out in London as news: the whole object of this complicated system being that the news items might be sent back to New York without Wall Street suspecting they were bogus.

I must not be understood as meaning to say that all financial editors, news gatherers, or news bureaus are engaged in this, one of the lowest forms of swindling, for such is not the case. On the contrary, there are many of them whom no amount of money or influence could make waver in their allegiance to the truth and to honest dealings. With some of the others I hope to deal specifically later, and I shall not hesitate to set forth in detail certain transactions in which they have been engaged.

CHAPTER VI

HOW WALL STREET'S MANIPULATIONS AFFECT THE COUNTRY

What is the connection between the "System" and the minor financial institutions throughout the country which are owned and controlled by groups of sturdy men who know not Wall Street and its frenzied votaries, and who are ignorant of "made dollars"? Let us see. We will take five national banks in different parts of the country, each having a capital of $200,000 and deposits of $2,000,000. One is in the farming district of Kansas; another is in Louisiana in a cotton district; a third is in the orange groves of California; in the mining district of Montana is a fourth; the fifth in the logging and lumber country of Maine. These $10,000,000 of deposits represent savings earned by the type of men who have made America what it is, and who laugh when they read in their local papers: "Panic in Wall Street; stocks shrink a billion dollars in a day." "Fools and their money are easily parted," they say, "but Wall Street gets none of our honestly earned money." Now the officers of these five banks are honest men and they know nothing of the "System," yet the day of the panic they each telegraph to their Illinois correspondent, the big Chicago bank, "Loan our balance, $200,000, at best rate." That day the Chicago bank with similar telegrams from forty-five other correspondents in various parts of the country, wires its New York correspondent, the big Wall Street bank, "Loan our balance, $2,000,000, at best rates."

Thereupon the great New York bank sends its brokers out upon "the Street" to loan on inflated securities of one kind or another which its officers, the votaries of the "System," have purchased in immense quantities at slaughter prices the millions belonging to the Chicago bank and to other correspondents of its own in Cincinnati and Omaha and St. Louis and other big cities. The decline is stayed, and then the world learns that the panic is over and that the stocks, of which the people have been "shaken out" to the extent of a billion dollars, have recovered in a day $500,000,000 of it, and that probably in a few days more will recover the other $500,000,000. Who has recovered this vast sum? The people who had been "shaken out"? No, indeed! The votaries of the "System" have made it—they and the frenzied financiers whose haunt is Wall Street, and whose harvest is in such wreckage.

The part that the five little banks innocently played in this terrific robbery was unimportant. What is important is that it was the funds of their depositors and others like them which the "System" used to turn the Stock Market and make an immense profit out of the recovery of values. It is true the banks received but two and one-half or three per cent. for the use of their balances, and their officers would scorn the suggestion that they had put any of their money in jeopardy in a Wall Street gamble. But what I have outlined happened, and has happened many a time before and since, and goes to prove my assertion that every financial institution which is taking the money of the people for the ostensible purpose of safeguarding it or putting it to use for them, is a part of the machinery for the plundering of the people.

Sooner or later, every dollar taken by the "System" through Wall Street's manipulation of stocks directly affects every man, woman, and child in the United States. Let us, for example, see how a stock slump in New York affects the owner of a small life-insurance policy in Wyoming. The shares of the American and English ocean steamship companies were bought up by the "System" at double their worth and converted into a "trust." New stocks and bonds to a number of times their value were issued and sold to the public. The great insurance companies bought many millions worth of these securities, using for the purpose the money they had collected from the policy-holders, a dollar at a time. This "investment," at the moment it was made, actually represented a loss to the purchasing insurance companies of millions of money, for millions more than the property was worth or could possibly be made worth had gone to the people who formerly owned the steamship properties, and many millions more to the "System" as its share of the swag. And it should be remembered that the men who organized the steamship trust were the men who invested the insurance company's money in its securities.

The policy-holder in Wyoming knows about the steamship trust and about the terrible loss sustained by those who invested in its securities. He does not realize, however, that his insurance company has been buying such poor stuff, for he is persuaded it is a great and noble institution, and far above Wall Street and its rash gamblers. Even when he and his kind find their yearly dividends on their policies growing less and less and their premiums rising "because of the tremendous increase in the expense of doing business," they do not dream of connecting these misfortunes with the "System's" trustifications of inflated securities; nor do they associate them with the glowing accounts of the half-million-dollar seaside palace built by the insurance company's officer who entered the employ of the institution a few years before, with his salary for his fortune, and who is now pointed to as an example of thrift, being worth from ten to fifteen millions.

CHAPTER VII

ECONOMICS OF COPPER

A thorough familiarity with the facts and conditions set forth in the preceding chapters will help my readers to an understanding of the series of complicated transactions through which the snaky course of Amalgamated must be pursued. Its flotation was the most tremendous and public ever even attempted, much less successfully carried out, and in its market career the full resources of stock jugglery were exercised on its behalf. The crimes of Amalgamated are to the delinquencies of Bay State Gas as the screaming of eagles to the chirping of crickets. From its birth this great enterprise went hand-in-hand with fraud and financial dishonor, and the facts I shall proceed to reveal are so formidable in their indictment as to startle even those calloused to the trickery of modern stock deals.

An armistice followed that last desperate battle of the gas fight in the Delaware court-house, and gave me time to turn my whole attention to the plans I had long been maturing in my mind in connection with quite another project—"Coppers."

For sixty years past Boston had been the home of the copper industry. From it great fortunes had been derived, and there was in course of development a copper aristocracy which threatened the supremacy of the East India aristocracy that had so long lorded it in Boston society. Indeed, so far had the rival contingents progressed that there was a serious searching of the pretensions of any new-comer whose origin had to do with other enterprises. "Coppers" were respectable, were genteel, and, above all, were not "trade," for the average old-time Bostonian affects the Anglo-Saxon contempt for the traffickings of retail commerce.

For the benefit of those in the outer darkness, to whom the ways of Boston are strange, it may be explained that the East India trade goes elsewhere under other less euphonious names, and consisted in the swapping of New England rum, made from molasses, water, and other things, for human cotton-pickers. It was a most profitable industry, with a spice of adventure to it, and in which at the time it flourished a gentleman might honorably engage. It may be said that with the paradoxical conscientiousness characteristic of the Puritan mind, the first outcry against the personal ownership of human chattels was voiced by New England, and her leading citizens generously devoted the incomes of the fortunes their forefathers had amassed in the slave traffic to releasing their colored fellow-creatures from bondage. That, however, is still another story.

To return to "Coppers." In my young days in "the Street" in the early '70s, the first task I remember performing was making deliveries of copper stocks traded in by "the house" which was entitled to my twelve-year-old services in return for the three large dollars which I received each Saturday with far more honest pride than any three millions I have since handled. As I grew up I watched Calumet and Hecla advance from a dollar to 450 (it afterward sold at 900) because of its real worth, and imbibed the conviction, which all true Bostonians entertain, that money acquired through copper is at least 33 per cent. better than money from any other source. I sympathized with the State Street code which declares, or should: "Gold can be found in a day by any one with eyes, silver in a week by any one with hands, and money in a year by any one with sense enough to save it, but no man gets into copper without capital, fortitude, patience, and brains." As a matter of fact, it requires, even to-day, with all of to-day's facilities and rush, $5,000,000 in money and five years of spending it after a copper deposit has been found before it can be made to yield returns. Is it surprising that a project requiring so much money for so long a time should appeal to Boston's regard for endurance, expensiveness, and exclusiveness? Could there be found an enterprise better calculated to discourage the upstart?

My daily round of errands led me from broker to broker and from bank to bank, and always I heard talk of copper. It is not remarkable that my youthful mind became impressed with the profound importance of the metal and all pertaining to it. I picked up a great deal of information on the subject, which I fortified later with a careful study of copper the metal, copper the mine, and copper the investment. As I mulled over the immense returns obtained from their ventures by the men I knew had their money in copper, it struck me as extraordinary that this industry should be so much more profitable than others. Here was a great staple, a necessity of the people, which had been in use since men began to sit up, and would be needed until Father Time smashed his glass, that returned 100 per cent. gross profit on the business done in it, while the business done in any other staple did not return, gross, over ten to eighteen per cent.; which gross profit gave to the capital invested in copper a net profit of sixteen to twenty-five per cent., while that invested in the other staples returned a net profit of only three and three-fourths to four and one-fourth per cent. The value of money had decreased with the world's development; the cost of the great commodities of life had all come down with the decline in interest—all but copper, which kept its old places throughout all the changes that had occurred in the relations of capital to labor and business. I realized that copper, in that year, would afford a gross profit of 100 cents on each $2 worth produced; that this great gross profit was legitimate, was not brought about through unfair restrictions or forced combination, or evasion of the country's laws, but was wholly natural, being founded on the fact that the supply was so limited that the demand prevented the price dropping below a certain figure, and that this under ordinary circumstances represented at least 100 per cent. of gross profit to the producer after he had paid for labor and material the highest ruling prices.

No better illustration of the main facts about copper can be found than the condition of the industry to-day, in 1905. The metal is now fifteen and a half cents per pound, and the consumption so great that the price still advances, yet if through an agreement among the producing mines this sales-rate should be dropped twenty-five per cent., it would so increase consumption as to force back the price to a point that would again discourage consumption; and yet in the old mines the cost of producing the metal sold at fifteen and a half is but six to seven and a half cents, in some even lower.

Compare these conditions with those existing in the steel industry. Therein unlawful combinations and unnatural restrictions are essential if those engaged would show a gross profit of even fifteen per cent. on their gross output. If more than fair or going returns are earned, then new capital flows into competition and the surplus again shrinks to an uninviting point. The same is true in wheat, corn, and cotton—big prices invite fresh investments and the planting of broader acreage. Hence the sorry spectacle of the cotton planter who, in 1905, will receive no more for his twenty per cent. increased crop, coming from over two millions increased acreage planted last year, than for his smaller one of the year before.

That my readers may quickly, and once for all, grasp the point I wish to make, I will illustrate:

The Steel trust in 1904 did a gross business of $432,000,000, upon which they made a profit of $71,400,000, and yet this vast amount was only five per cent. upon the trust's inflated capital of $1,400,000,000 odd; and as the "System," in regulating the capitalization, arranged that the preferred stock (and bonds), which represented the "System's" profit, should receive seven per cent., there was not a dollar in dividends for the $520,000,000 of common stock which had been sold to the people for, in round figures, $300,000,000.

At the same time the Calumet & Hecla Copper Company produced and sold over $10,000,000 worth of copper, upon which it earned, net, over $5,000,000, which enabled it to pay to the people who had invested in its 100,000 shares of stock (par value, $25), 160 per cent., or a total of

$4,000,000, and, at the same time, carry an enormous amount to its surplus.

In the commercial world copper occupies an impregnable position. To compete, it is first necessary to find a copper deposit; then to lock up a vast sum of money for a long term of years before returns begin to accrue. And new copper deposits are as rare and few and far between as Lincolns and Roosevelts in politics or Grants and Lees in war. In the last eight years, or since the metal has been prominently before the world of capital, but two great producers of copper have been created—the Copper Range at Lake Superior, Michigan, and the Greene Consolidated in Mexico—and these two mines have only, at the end of six years, after an immense expenditure of millions (Copper Range, with a capital of $38,500,000, 385,000 shares, par $100, which sold in the open market a few years ago at $6, now selling at $75, and Greene Consolidated, with a capital of $8,650,000, 865,000 shares, par $10, now selling in the open market at $25), reached the point of profitable production. Their combined output, while reaching the (for young mines) unprecedented amount of one hundred and odd million pounds of metal per annum, constitutes but a fraction of that which Mother Earth has given up during the period of their development, namely, 2,500,000,000 pounds, all of which has been disposed of and cannot again be used to satisfy a ravenous consumption.

It seemed to me, then, a curious anomaly that, while capital was chasing investments which promised but four per cent., it eschewed copper which yielded from sixteen to twenty-five per cent., and my investigations told me that a producing copper-mine is the surest business venture a man engages in, for, by the time it begins to produce profitably, it must be so far developed that its owners are certain of ore to work on for decades ahead. A good copper-mine is really a safe-deposit vault of stored-up dividends, which cannot be stolen nor destroyed by fire, flood, or famine. Calumet & Hecla, for instance, though it cost its first owners but a dollar a share, has paid out $87,000,000, or $870 per share, or 3,480 per cent. on its par value of $25, and while it has been paying dividends over thirty-five years, it paid last year $40 per share, and has more in sight than it has yet paid. And Copper Range, though but six years old, will be producing soon as much as Calumet & Hecla, and has now in sight ore to keep it going fifty or sixty years.

Having pieced together all the facts and circumstances in this connection, I was sure that I had grasped a principle of great commercial value, and I set about finding a cause why the world of capital should for so long have overlooked the tremendous potentialities of this industry. I found the cause in Boston herself, in the characteristics of the city, which was headquarters for copper, and which had grown in financial power with the revenues her mines earned for her investors. Boston controlled and managed the copper industry, and had since the days when copper-mining was a hazardous pursuit, in which only bold and speculative souls dared engage. In the early days the canny Bostonian demanded for the honorable dollar his parent had earned—exchanging five-cent rum for human beings worth $1,000 apiece—at least twenty per cent. interest, and having acquired this habit, it became a principle, and such principles as these are clung to in Boston with the zeal of a miser for his hoard or of a martyr to his faith. Looking back over the years, I still recall with chagrin the quiescent hilarity of the scion of a Back Bay family whose good father had been one of the most successful and most brutal of all the "East India traders," when I suggested to him that he was fortunate in obtaining twenty per cent. on some copper ventures about which he was grumbling. (My readers must not confuse a Boston grumble with the ordinary ejaculations of discontent indulged in by the inhabitants of other portions of the world remote from the Hub of the Universe. A Boston grumble consists of an upward movement of the eyebrow, a slight twitch of the mustache and a murmur cross-bred from "Deuce take it!" and "Scoundrelly!") "Young man," he said, "my father said that such a hazardous venture as copper should return at least thirty per cent. to be safe, and I feel if I receive but twenty per cent. that something is radically and unpardonably wrong with the management of the mine." I did not pursue the argument, for I knew he inherited with his fortune a line of Boston reasoning, and I remembered once having watched a country boy put his tongue on a frosty iron doorknob. I knew better than to invoke again that wintry Boston smile, which in a Western or Southern community would be used to frappé mint-juleps or cold-storage hogs with.

No better illustration of the attitude of the shrewd New York investor to "Copper" can possibly be given than to detail my first interview with H. H. Rogers and William Rockefeller on the subject. To-day Mr. Rogers is known throughout the world as the leading figure of the copper world—the copper Czar, so to speak; yet it was only nine years ago when I said to him at the end of a gas-talk:

"Mr. Rogers, would Mr. Rockefeller and yourself look into Copper?"

"Copper?" said he in an amused way, "copper? What kind of copper?"

"Why, copper such as we know in Boston—copper the metal, copper the industry, copper stocks."

He burst into one of his jolly laughs. "Look into it? Why, I don't know a thing about copper other than that we had old copper kettles when I was a boy which were used to fry doughnuts in, but I suppose my plumbers would look at anything you wanted, for I remember I get big bills for copper tanks at the house."

CHAPTER VIII

MY PLAN FOR "COPPERS"

The plan I had so carefully formulated in connection with "Coppers" was simple in application yet vast in scope. It was to buy up all the good producing mines at their market price, or double if necessary, to organize them into a new corporation and offer its stock to the public at a capitalization of double the original cost. By advertising the exceptional merits of the copper industry and the financial power of the men who were backing it, the public would become educated to a knowledge of the values of "Coppers." Under this education the world of capital would invest in copper shares until the price had advanced, because of so much capital seeking this form of investment, to a point where the net return was brought down to the going rate of, say, four per cent. This would mean that the old going prices of good producing Boston copper-mines would advance 100 to 200 per cent., which in turn meant that those who risked their money in the first venture (which I figured would require $100,000,000) would make $100,000,000 to $200,000,000, while at the same time the public would make $200,000,000 to $400,000,000. This seems like an "Aladdin-lamp" story when it is told, but, as a matter of fact, prices afterward did advance in this ratio, and 100 and 200 per cent. beyond, and many of them, notwithstanding the tremendous drops that have taken place since, still show from 200 to 300 per cent. advance over the prices then in vogue. Never in all the history of business was there afforded capitalists so fair an opportunity to make honestly and legitimately so vast a sum of money and at the same time to do so much for the people. Nor was there a more honorable undertaking nor one which a man could be more justly proud of carrying to success.

As time went on, this big enterprise was more and more in my thoughts, and I tested it in every way I knew, going over in my mind and trying out each successive step and link until I was certain the whole structure was unassailable. Then it became my purpose in life to launch the venture. The difficulties of the task were never for a moment overlooked, for I well knew that much money would be required, but with strong backing success was sure, and such a success was tremendously worth attaining. Next to putting in force my financial invention which would remedy the evils of the "System," this great copper project seemed the thing—the dollar thing—best worth doing in all the world. It was to execute this project that I allied myself with the "Standard Oil" party, for with their money and backing I knew I could carry through my plans on the lines I had so carefully mapped out.

The chief indictment my critics brought against me when my series of articles appeared in Everybody's Magazine was that I had turned "State's evidence." Having been "in with" "Standard Oil" in their robberies of the public, it was not until we disagreed and "split" that I thought of taking the public into my confidence. The truth is, my relation with "Standard Oil" was different from that any other man ever had with that mysterious and reticent institution, and throughout the copper crusade I insistently blurted out our plans and purposes through every channel of publicity I could command. At no time was there the slightest secrecy. From the very first day of the campaign I told the story as I tell it here, and I told it from the housetops by newspaper interviews and advertisements, market letters and circulars frankly and freely explaining what I was about. The absolute truth of the foregoing is easily proved through existing records, for the press of the country contains an almost continuous story, beginning in 1896 and running up to date, wherein I have openly and fairly told what I knew about "Coppers" and detailed the progress of our plans. Time and again, during this period, financial writers commented on my frankness, quoting brokers and bankers to the effect that "Lawson will surely have his head dropped into the 'Standard Oil' basket if he keeps telling people all he knows in this fashion." For the complete realization of my project the public's interest was essential. The creation of the vast business structure that I had designed required the participation of the great mass of the people, and I was determined that no subservience to the selfish ends of my associates should swerve me from my plan. I saw the enterprise whole; saw that there was great profit for all concerned, for "Standard Oil," for myself, and for the public; but if the public were not taken care of or were discouraged from participation, then my institution would surely be only another combination of capitalists and I should fail in my ambition.

This is why I so persistently kept in the open throughout my "Copper" campaign. I fully realized how anomalous my position was and how far I had departed from "Standard Oil" precedents; but my thought was to protect the integrity of my enterprise, and the best way to do this was to have the people partners in its conception and development. To be perfectly frank, the prospect of millions of profit counted for less in my calculations than the honor and prestige I foresaw in the success of my copper structure. As proof of this, witness how I voluntarily gave back the millions I had secured, to make good. To create a great institution, to erect a new and absolutely staple investment, and in doing so to make millions for one's partners, one's self, and the public, would be to live not in vain. The knowledge of my attitude will perhaps help my readers to comprehend the enthusiasm with which I entered into my "Copper" crusade; help them to understand how strongly I resisted, and how deeply resented, the perversion of my fair structure into a pitfall for those I had expected to benefit. My indignation against the "System" is that which any honest man would feel against ruffians who had used his best ideas and his most generous feelings to lure innocent and unoffending people into some den of vice and infamy. If I have not troubled to correct the misstatements of detractors who, in an attempt to discredit my facts, have tried to pillory me as a traitor, it is because I knew that when my complete story reached the public it would make plain how and what I had been doing. The succeeding chapters of this narrative will yield unimpeachable evidence that all my dealing in "Coppers" as an associate of "Standard Oil" were open and as much in the interests of the people as it was possible to have them.

CHAPTER IX

BIRTH OF "COPPERS"

Active upon the Boston market during my Bay State Gas operations were two copper-mining companies—the Butte & Boston and the Boston & Montana. Their properties were in Montana and both were large producers of the metal, that is, they were old and equipped mines. These two organizations form to-day the most valuable part of the Amalgamated Copper Company—in fact, more than three-quarters of all the real worth owned by that corporation.

Butte & Boston and Boston & Montana were essentially Boston institutions, and were both officered and directed by the same set of men. It had come to my knowledge, in the course of my stock business, that there had been bought for the Butte & Boston, with its money, some very valuable mines; instead of transferring these to that corporation, however, its directors at the last minute had turned the titles over to the Boston & Montana. It is only fair to these men to say that up to the present this alleged fact has not been proven, although set forth in cases still pending in the courts. This curious proceeding was part of a plot the subsequent steps in which would be to run Butte & Boston through the bankruptcy mill, and, by placing it in the hands of a receiver, to drop the stock to a nominal figure, at which it might all be gathered in from the public. I verified my information sufficiently to decide to act, and swung the red danger-signal in a public statement telling the stockholders and people in general of the coming move. At once there arose a chorus of denials and recriminations from the management, and the cry, "He's short of the stock and is working a fake to scare us into throwing over our holdings that he may buy them," from the Stock Exchange, stockholders, and the hireling moulders of opinions, the "News Bureaus."

The rôle of Cassandra is not more popular to-day than it was in ancient Troy. The swinger of the red danger-signal is seldom heeded, and is invariably suspected of interested motives by the human moths circling round the flickering flames of frenzied finance. When I gave my warning, Butte & Boston was selling between 25 and 30. In accordance with their plan the insiders began to sell, and soon the price began to slide downward, for the great majority of the stock was held by the people. There was a halt when the denials of the management were heard, but only for a moment. The decline continued, growing swifter as it got lower until the stock struck $2 per share. At this stage, while the stock was on the way to $2, just as I had predicted, the property was cleverly slid into a receiver's hands by the very men who had so indignantly denied my statement that such would be their action. An assessment of $10 per share was next levied, and those who held on, hoping against hope, began to throw over their holdings for what they would bring—which was around a dollar.

So far the scheme had slipped smoothly along the single-rail track constructed for it by those in the deal, and just as my information had led me to expect. At this juncture, however, the train struck an open switch, and with a painful jolt for the conductor and the engineers it slid out on a siding—it was my siding. From the time the stock struck $2 a mysterious purchaser took in all that was offered, and when it struck bottom he was still buying. Suddenly the schemers "tumbled" that the plums they were shaking off the tree were dropping into some other bag than their own, and they started into competition for the coveted fruit.

Next day, and for several days afterward, there were strenuous doings in Butte & Boston on the Boston Stock Exchange. The trading was heavy and the price pushed up from the bottom to 6-1/2. Soon, however, it was slammed to 2-3/4, then back to 6 again, down to 3-1/4, back to 5-3/4, and so on, until the middle of the fourth day, when the rival NewsBureau to the "System's" favorite opinion-moulder sprang the following notice set forth on a double-leaded sheet:

"We have just solved the Butte & Boston conundrum. The enormous blocks of stock purchased during the past few days have come in for transfer, and the management now know who owns the bag into which all the stock they have for months been planning to acquire dropped. We have unmistakable evidence that the bag belonged to Lawson, and that he now is in control of the Butte & Boston Company. A hasty investigation amongst the leading floor brokers which we have just made brings out a consensus of opinion that there will now be music in Coppers."

The announcement was calculated to interest a good many persons, and I was the target of a thousand inquiries. In answer to the innumerable calls for a denial or confirmation of the statement, I issued the following:

'Tis true. 'Tis my bag, and there are 46,000 shares in it.

It was not until the following morning that I realized what a rarely presumptuous thing I had done. I had invaded a valuable preserve. I had coarsely "butted into" a private copper domain without a by-your-leave to the natives who thought it belonged to them. I was an interloper, an intruder, an upstart. The prevailing opinion seemed to be that it now devolved on me to present what I had purchased to those who had been a bit late in getting to the bargain-counter, or that I should, at least, turn it over to the conscience fund of the Stock Exchange. The copper market reflected the indignation of the baffled schemers. It entered for once into an open competition with Donnybrook Fair, and to judge by the action and feeling developed in both individual and corporation classes, the Hub had Donnybrook jigged to a wind-up. In my various contests with the "System" I had accumulated a certain hardihood which now stood me in good stead. I had learned before this that breaking into a secluded treasure-trove is about as pleasant as taking the lining out of a steel furnace with the metal sizzling and the blower on.

I stood to my guns for the time being and then charged into the ranks of the enemy. I issued the following statement:

TO MY FELLOW-BROKERS AND THE PUBLIC

I have stumbled on the fact that the stock—capital 200,000 shares—of the Butte & Boston Copper Mining Company is a nugget. I bought about 46,000 shares of it at an average of something over 2-1/4, or, with the assessment paid, 12-1/4 per share. I am going to hold it until I get over 50 for it. Barring accidents, I shall get it.

I advise—strongly and unqualifiedly advise—all my friends and the public to load up with it at anything under that price. My friends and the public know whether or not I mean a thing when I say it. I pledge them that I not only mean this but that I shall fight it out, and shall not sell until there is an active and legitimate market for not only my stock, but for what they buy, at over $50 per share. All intending purchasers must bear in mind this is not a sure thing, for the men who are opposing, and will oppose me, are not conducting their operations from a graveyard, but are as lively and aggressive as Bengal tigers at raw-meat time; but they may rest easy in the knowledge that barring tripping over stumps or into bogs, I'll give whoever buy a run for their investments.

Buy and watch Butte all the time, and, above all, pay no attention to what the fake "News Bureau" says.

This was the formal declaration of war. State and Wall streets, familiar with my style of fighting, at once lined up and took sides. The papers entered the controversy. According to what one read, Butte & Boston was either the greatest mine in the world or a hole in the ground. Feeling intensified; Geneva and Queensberry conventions were forgotten; it became a go-as-you-please scramble; mud batteries filled the air with liquid dirt, and both sides used Gatling guns to fire off their libels. It was altogether a lusty and vociferous contest, which meant destruction and death for the lame, the halt, and the slow-footed who got between the fighting lines. I was naturally the chief mark for the enemy, and was deluged with vilification. In the Bay State campaign I had learned the personal cost of antagonizing the "System"; the copper magnates showed me that they had terrors at command which might make even "Standard Oil" jealous. In those days I don't believe my bank account varied thirty-five cents without the news being passed around before the ink on the bank-book was dry, and my family, down to my ten-year-old, received daily or weekly through the mails pictorial representations of their parent being hustled along to the realms where sulphur is the standard of all values. Here is a sample of my usual breakfast-table reading:

C. W. Barron, the proprietor of the "Boston News Bureau," feels it his duty to inform his readers, the banks and bankers and brokers and representative investors of New England, that that faking ass of State Street, that knave of knaves, Tom Lawson, is braying again, and such braying!—"Butte is to sell at 50, and going to be worth 50." It would be such a joke that this conservative paper would be only too happy to circulate this scoundrel's vaporings, if it were not for the sad part of such schemer's work—if it were not that the poor and ignorant unfortunates who are unacquainted with this knave, may buy Butte because of his advertised lies at $14 or $15 a share and thereby be robbed of what they can ill afford to lose. There is no more chance of Butte & Boston stock selling at $50, or even $25, than there is of Tom Lawson telling the truth; and this paper does not hesitate to say that if Butte stock ever does sell at 50, we will upon that day close up our office and forever leave Boston and our lucrative business of guarding investors against such knaves as this lying thief; for any man who would do what he is doing to fleece investors is a thief and should wear stripes, and it is surprising to us he has so long escaped.

It was not so long after the above appeared that Butte & Boston stock was selling at $130 per share, and that the same Mr. Barron was using his own and his "News Bureau's" best efforts to induce the people whose Butte showed them over $115 a share profit to exchange it for Amalgamated. At this latter time he was acting for "Standard Oil."

It may be added that this same Butte & Boston stock, which I was such a knave to advise the people to buy at twelve and fifteen, sells to-day in the form of a share of Amalgamated, for which it was exchanged at seventy-five to eighty-dollars, not cents.

My chief weapon in this Butte & Boston fight was publicity. Every morning while the battle waxed hottest I had huge, striking advertisements in the papers urging the public to buy and to hold on to what they had bought.

My opponents responded in kind, and being intrenched in the management, told such alarming stories of the mine that it was often as much as I could do to prevent my followers from being scared into throwing over their holdings. The tremendous expense of this mode of warfare, together with the immense sums my market operations required, kept me hustling, and there were times when things looked distinctly blue. However, the value of victory is measured by the fierceness of the tussle, and far be it from me to complain of my opponents' energy. There was good fighting over Butte & Boston.

The more deeply I became interested in this struggle and the more familiar I grew with "Coppers," the more advantageous and profitable seemed the prospects of such a consolidation of copper properties as I had in mind. The large holdings of Butte & Boston I had accumulated in the battle gave me a practical basis for my structure, for I could now afford to do all my own part of the work of organization for what I would eventually make when the consolidation was brought about, and I could get for my shares what I knew they were worth. It was at this stage I broached the subject of "Coppers" to Mr. Rogers, and discovered to my surprise that he knew nothing about it or its possibilities, notwithstanding that "Standard Oil" has a department for the sole purpose of keeping the "System" posted about what the world is doing in various directions. Indeed, both he and Mr. Rockefeller laughed when I informed them that we had been trading in copper stocks in Boston long before the Standard Oil Company received its birth certificate.

Before I could get down to business on the subject I had to take advantage of five gas-talks, offering at each a few interesting and striking facts about the metal. One day Mr. Rogers said to me, laughing pleasantly: "Lawson, we're beginning to look for all your talks to taper off with, 'I wish I could get you to listen to Coppers!'"

"Why don't you then?" I said. "It's the biggest opportunity in the world to-day."

"I'll tell you what I'll do," replied Mr. Rogers. "If you will put through for us right away thus and so" (naming quite a difficult little bit of work in connection with the Brooklyn Gas Company), "and do it in good shape, I'll ask John Moore to run up to Boston next week and listen to your story. If he says it looks anything like good, I'll go over it with you to a finish."

The Brooklyn job was done on time, and I began on John Moore in my office at my hotel in Boston just after breakfast one bleak, rainy morning the week following. I talked for five straight-away hours, and he listened. He was a good listener. On all stock things he was admirably posted, and it was not necessary to waste words. I wasted none. I knew my subject from the letter-head to "Yours truly," and I was playing for a stake that looked as big to me as the sun does to a solitary-confinement life prisoner. At the end of the five uninterrupted hours I agreed with Moore that I had nothing more to produce, and I looked for my verdict. Before starting I had felt sure of winning him; when I was half through I knew nothing could stand against my arguments, and when I had said the last word I felt satisfied that, being human and intelligent, he must be convinced. It took him only ten minutes to show me that I had been talking against ten-inch armor-plate, and that he meant it absolutely when he said, "Lawson, I want to see it your way, but I can't."

It was John Moore's turn then, and he showed me the good thing in an industrial scheme he was floating at that time, and as he wound up he said pleasantly:

"Lawson, we must do something to show for our long talk, so I'll put you down for $50,000 underwriting." And he did.

If John Moore had seen "Coppers" as I tried to show them to him that wet morning he could not have made for himself less than three to five millions, for in the operation which hung on his decision I had expected to buy stocks that soon after doubled and trebled in value. Calumet & Hecla then sold at 256, and later as high as 900, while Boston & Montana, then 50, mounted to 520. On the other hand, the stock of which he had sold me $50,000 worth returned at the end of the year but a mere fraction of that amount, and was one of the worst failures of the industrial boom period. It cost John Moore not only an enormous amount of money, but also prestige, and its miscarriage was one of the few bad disappointments of his brilliant career. Afterward, when "Coppers" were the rage and all Wall Street was green with envy at our success and his enterprise was trying to hide itself behind the garbage barrels, John Moore said to me:

"Lawson, we all think we are the masters of our own fortunes, but we are not. We are only working on a schedule laid out by some One who does not take our desires into consideration."

And it is so. The ablest Wall Street man is only like the burglar who, after working for weeks to loot a second story, is astounded to find, while lugging his swag by the police station, that the bag he thought full of dead sealskins contains a live parrot with a lusty vocabulary, "Police! Robbers!"

CHAPTER X

ROGERS GRASPS "COPPERS"

The next day our gas business brought me to New York, and after Mr. Rogers and myself had threshed out the matter I had come about, he said with a smile:

"Well, I've heard from John Moore. Are you satisfied now? Will you drop that copper will-o'-the-wisp?"

"Far from it," I replied. "I'm surer than ever of my position. In going over the ground with Moore I got the whole business in perspective, and now I know I'm right. All his argument amounted to anyway was that it was impossible for so gigantic a thing to have lain out in the travelled highways all these years."

I ran on vigorously for a few moments, in a way I felt might pique his curiosity, if it did not gain my point. Finally he said:

"Well, Lawson, what more can I do?"

"This," I answered: "go over the matter fully with me yourself. I will surely carry it through one way or another; if not with you, with others, and I cannot drop it with you until I have your personal judgment."

Instantly came one of those flash decisions for which H. H. Rogers is noted among his business associates, the oft-proved correctness of which goes far toward making him the pre-eminent American financier of the day.

"Lawson," he said, "be in New York next Sunday, and I will listen until you have run the subject out."

That decision changed the face of the copper world.

Sunday is Mr. Rogers' pick of days for a lengthy hearing, and returning from church, he came directly to the "stowaway" rooms at the Murray Hill Hotel, at which we frequently met while the Wall Street world was trying to trace and keep track of our movements. I had been there for some time awaiting him and was keyed for the struggle.

Of my ability to land John Moore I had felt confident, yet I had failed; but this time in advance I knew success was mine. Experience has taught me that in all dollar matters the man to "talk up to" is the actual owner of the dollars you are after, who when he hears your story and weighs your goods can deal out the yes or no which means business. I had discovered some years before that few bull's-eyes are scored shooting at a target by mail or messenger. One's finest word-pictures sound better than they read, and if you would have the next man see them in as vivid colors as they appear on your mind's canvas, you must paint them before his eyes. The enthusiasm of the artist, his love of the subject, the deep or high tones of his voice, the very movements of his hands, are all factors in aiding the other man's vision. When he sees what you do, you have won. Nowadays when I have things to sell, I engage the eyes as well as the ears of my purchaser. When the other fellow would make me his customer, he must first sell his goods to my secretary, who may, if he can, sell them to me. Thus I am always able to dispose of the only merchandise I keep in stock, honest goods, and I seldom buy chromos for oils.

As I waited the coming of my most powerful customer, I could not keep my mind off the momentousness of the interview before me. I knew I was at a fork of the road, at one of those departure points from which coming events must date, and I thought of a dream I had had years before in which I found myself drifting with the grim ferryman across the brimming flood, the far bank of which is eternity. In my hand was a long staff with strange and irregular notches on it. And these represented the actions of my life. Some were shallow, others deep and wide, and as I ran my fingers up and down, I seemed to remember what each nick commemorated—the good things and the bad things, here a death, there a disappointment, this a victory, that an error. I wondered, as the circumstances of the dream came to my mind, what kind of marking this day's events would make on my life staff, and I felt a conviction that it would be both deep and wide.

Then, as I heard Mr. Rogers' footstep outside my door, I forgot all about dreams and notches and plunged into my argument.

"Mr. Rogers," I began, "you and your associates have unlimited money. You have not always had it. You have obtained it through business projects and you are using it in business projects to get more. There are two ways of adding new dollars to those in your possession: by taking them from others so they are losers and you the gainer, whereby you win at the cost of their happiness; or by expanding the world's wealth so that others gain when you do. You, I know, prefer the latter, that others should make money when you do, rather than that they should lose and suffer when you are benefited."

I did not then know "Standard Oil's" and the "System's" religion as I do now. I had yet to learn the cruelly cynical principles that guide this financial Juggernaut in its relation with men and things. I imputed to it the generosity and freedom which seemed to characterize Henry H. Rogers' personality, ignorant that the man and the machine he served might stand for different things. The "System's" Big Book says: "A dollar honestly made makes another for some one else; but a dollar taken is two dollars, because it increases our power and diminishes the people's. Between the 'System' and the people must be eternal war, and it is the price of the 'System's' existence that all opportunities of weakening the people are sternly utilized."

"Mr. Rogers," I continued, "I have discovered in 'Coppers' an opportunity whereby you and your associates can, by the investment of a hundred millions of dollars, obtain these results: First, your money will be as safe as in anything you now have it invested in. Second, by indorsing this form of investment with the seal of your business success, you will make it known to all who have money and there will at once arise a tremendous demand for its securities. This demand will drive prices up until dividend returns are in normal proportion to the legitimate value of the security, namely, four to six per cent., which is, as I can prove to you, a little more than can be got from anything else but 'Copper' with the same elements of safety. Third, when the advance I foresee occurs, your one hundred millions have doubled, and all those who have joined us in the venture or have held on to their stock will gain in the same proportion. As I estimate that we will have but a third interest in all the good American 'Coppers,' there should be something like $200,000,000 for the people, while we will have made $100,000,000. To bring this about I have planned a campaign which will make what you have done known from one end of the world to the other, and will persuade the people at large to look at 'Standard Oil' in a more favorable light than they do now. And, what is more, all this money can be made and all these benefits rendered without taxing any one a single additional dollar, for there will not be a penny a ton added to the price of copper the metal, nor a reduction of a mill a year taken from the wages of those who mine it or work it."

Here I halted. I had made a beginning, and I was familiar with Mr. Rogers' system of diagnosis and treatment. Propositions placed on his operating-table are invariably dissected in parts—this is the winner's method; so if, under the probe of his keen mind, one section or limb is found stiff, dead, or unhitchable to that to which it belongs, he at once stops operating and the corpse is removed.

"How is it the situation is as you outline it?"

I drew the picture of copper Boston as I have given it in the early part of this chapter. It astonished him.

"How do you prove that safety in this class of investment is more assured than in others?"

I reeled off the facts: A copper-mine, from the very nature of the business, must be developed years and years ahead before it entered the ranks as a regular producer. The price of the metal being practically fixed within certain limits, the mine's value, present and future, could always be told to a certainty.

He saw it. He put me through a thorough examination about my second claim that the price would advance 100 per cent. I again astonished him by showing him what a market there was and had been for many years for copper stocks, and that it was simply a question of educating investors at large to their merits to advance them to the price my plans called for.

When he came to the question of the amount to be invested and the aggregate amount of profit, he did not attempt to disguise his surprise when I showed him there were 150,000 shares of Boston & Montana which had been selling at 20-odd and were now 50-odd, and could surely be bought between 50 and 100; and 200,000 shares of Butte & Boston, 100,000 outside of what I and those who had bought with me owned that could be had at an average of 20 or 25; that there were 100,000 shares of Calumet & Hecla, selling at 250, large quantities of which could be gathered in between that price and 400, and so on through the list. Mine after mine I enumerated to him, all as sure dividend earners in the future as they had been in the past, to an aggregate, without touching any of the uncertain ones, which it would surely take one hundred millions to purchase, and as I called them off, he listened patiently while I gave him a full history of each.

Then I outlined my sensational but never before attempted plan of campaign for educating the public, he vigorously questioning me as to details and particulars the while.

It does not take Henry H. Rogers months, weeks, nor even days to grasp any plan, however vast, nor many minutes to come to a decision after he has grasped it. I believe he would, if the world were going to be auctioned off next week, be the first man on earth to decide upon a limit price that he would take it at, and three minutes after it was knocked down to him he would be selling stock in it at 150 per cent. profit.

Just before lunch-time I saw that the effect of my arguments on Mr. Rogers was the exact opposite to that they had made on John Moore. When I had come to a finish, Mr. Rogers simply said: "It's curious, Lawson, why I have not listened to you before. I'll talk with William Rockefeller to-morrow. No—I'll make it this afternoon if I can get at him."

And his eyes snapped a bit when, as I was helping him on with his coat, he said, "We must not lose a minute in getting to work."

As he left the hotel and before I crossed the street to the Grand Central to take my train back to Boston—I suppose I should not say it, but I shook my own hand in self-congratulation. How many times since I have thought that had old Dame Fate but hung out a danger-signal for this faithful servitor of her behests, or had but given him a glimpse ahead through the years 1899, 1900, 1901, 1902, 1903, and 1904, instead of using his hands in cordial self-clasping he would have employed his feet in the more fitting task of kicking himself.

If Henry H. Rogers had been slow at getting started on "Coppers," once in he made up for his early tardiness. After our Sunday interview things moved swiftly forward. Before noon next day he called me up on the telephone to say that both he and William Rockefeller were impatient to have my facts and figures verified, and would I at once send my data to start his experts on? I mailed him a bale of "pointers," and from that hour until the flotation of Amalgamated Mr. Rogers' enthusiasm on "Coppers" constantly grew until there actually came a time when it went beyond my own. It took him months to complete that rounding-up of the situation which is the absolutely necessary preliminary to the making of final decisions on any far-reaching and important project to which the magic name of "Standard Oil" is to be permanently attached.

This period of waiting I duly improved by continuing my fight on Butte & Boston, and by way of intensifying the campaign I included Boston & Montana in the tussle, and led a fierce attack into the stronghold of my opponents. While this war was at its bitter height I received word from 26 Broadway that at last reports were all in, and that they were ready to talk business. Next day I was in New York.

"Lawson," said Mr. Rogers, "our experts have examined your plans step by step and have verified your conclusions. It is an exceptional situation, and one we are equipped to handle."

Then and there we had a "to-a-finish-sit-down," and while I had in my time gone pretty thoroughly into the general subject of "Coppers," and thought myself well informed thereon, I was surprised at the completeness and detail of the reports that had been prepared for the "System's" master. In beautiful shape, concise, clear, comprehensive, the entire copper industry of the world was spread out before me. Every mine had its place and its history—not merely the mines of America, but those of Europe as well; and fully set forth were the extent and cost of the product of each, the profit it made, the men who owned it, and—miraculous "Standard Oil"—the standing, financial and otherwise, of the men who might have to be dealt with in our prospective trades.

Rogers smiled watching my growing surprise as I ran over the extraordinary budget of facts he had collected. I said to him:

"This is wonderful. You have here all there's to be known about the subject, and I marvel how you got hold of so much inside information."

"'Standard Oil' has its own way of doing things," he replied. "You told us your copper plans would mean an investment of $100,000,000 of our money, and now's the time, not after we have parted with it, to find just what we are to get for it."

The world has never yet heard of "Standard Oil" locking its barn door after some one has stolen its mule; for that matter, it is not of record that any one ever locked the gate after his barn had been visited by "Standard Oil." The reason is that, with the thoroughness characteristic of this great reaping-machine, it never fails to take the barn with the mule.

At this meeting it was agreed that Henry H. Rogers, William Rockefeller, and myself should become partners in my plan of "Coppers," they to furnish the capital and to have three-quarters of the profit, I to have the remaining quarter. The campaign for the execution of the enterprise I agreed to work out and submit as soon as possible, and we parted.

As I bade them good-by Mr. Rogers said to me:

"Your baby is born, Lawson, and if you put the same kind of work on raising it you have in bringing it into the world, it will be a giant."

From that day it was understood that we were together, and that all my dealings in "Coppers" outside Butte & Boston were for the joint account—that is, they were to have the right to come into all my operations. Those they did not care to join in I had the right to put through alone. On the other hand, I must not undertake anything on their behalf without a specific understanding with them.

Thus began Amalgamated, that extraordinary dollar-thing which shot up in a night and grew as grows the whirlwind, until even its creators wondered at its mightiness. It waxed greater and stronger while the world watched and waited, until finally there came that tremendous and unprecedented culmination when lines of investors fought round the portals of the greatest money mart in America, the National City Bank, for a chance to obtain the $100 shares of this $75,000,000 institution. And the world wondered indeed when it was announced that Amalgamated had been oversubscribed over $300,000,000.

Thus began Amalgamated. It might have brought to all the world good-will and happiness, and to the men who made it much glory and the great regard of their fellows. Instead, it has wrought havoc and desolation, and its Apache-like trail is strewn with the scalped and mutilated corpses of its victims. The very name Amalgamated conjures up visions of hatred and betrayal, of ambush, pitfalls, and assassination. It stands forth the Judas of corporations, a monument to greed and a warning to rapacity. May the story that I am to tell so set forth its infamies and horrors that never again shall such a monster be suffered to violate and defile our civilization.

www.ingramcontent.com/pod-product-compliance
Lightning Source LLC
Chambersburg PA
CBHW081156020426
42333CB00020B/2524